INTRODUCTION TO CHRISTIANITY

JOSEPH CARDINAL RATZINGER

INTRODUCTION TO CHRISTIANITY

Translated by J. R. Foster and Michael J. Miller

With a New Preface

COMMUNIO BOOKS

IGNATIUS PRESS   SAN FRANCISCO

Title of the German original:
Einführung in das Christentum
© 1968 by Kösel-Verlag GmbH, Munich
English translation © 1969 by Burns and Oates, Ltd.
New with ecclesiastical approval
German edition, published with a new preface, 2000

Diptych: *Adoration of the Magi* and *The Crucifixion*.
Museo Nazionale del Bargello, Florence, Italy
Scala/Art Resource, N.Y.

Cover design by Riz Boncan Marsella

Revisions to the English edition and Preface
© 1990 © 2004 Ignatius Press, San Francisco
ISBN 978-1-58617-029-5 (PB)
ISBN 978-1-68149-268-1 (eBook)
Library of Congress Control Number 2004103523
Printed in the United States of America

CONTENTS

INTRODUCTION: "I BELIEVE—AMEN"

PART ONE: GOD

PART TWO: JESUS CHRIST

PREFACE TO THE NEW EDITION

"Introduction to Christianity"

Yesterday, Today, Tomorrow

Since this work was first published, more than thirty years have passed, in which world history has moved along at a brisk pace. In retrospect, two years seem to be particularly important milestones in the final decades of the millennium that has just come to an end: 1968 and 1989. The year 1968 marked the rebellion of a new generation, which not only considered postwar reconstruction in Europe as inadequate, full of injustice, full of selfishness and greed, but also viewed the entire course of history since the triumph of Christianity as a mistake and a failure. These young people wanted to improve things at last, to bring about freedom, equality, and justice, and they were convinced that they had found the way to this better world in the mainstream of Marxist thought. The year 1989 brought the surprising collapse of the socialist regimes in Europe, which left behind a sorry legacy of ruined land and ruined souls. Anyone who expected that the hour had come again for the Christian message was disappointed. Although the number of believing Christians throughout the world is not small, Christianity failed at that historical moment to make itself heard as an epoch-making alternative. Basically, the Marxist doctrine of salvation (in several differently orchestrated variations, of course) had taken a stand as the sole ethically motivated guide to the future that was at the same time consistent with a scientific world view. Therefore, even after the shock of 1989, it did not simply abdicate. We need only to recall how little was said about the horrors of the Communist gulag, how isolated Solzhenitsyn's voice remained: No one speaks about any of that. A sort of shame forbids it; even Pol Pot's murderous regime is mentioned only occasionally in passing. But there was still disappointment and a deep-seated perplexity. People no longer trust grand moral promises, and after all, that is what Marxism had understood itself to be. It was about justice for all, about peace, about doing away with unfair master-servant relationships, and so on. They believed that they had to dispense with ethical principles for the time being and that they were allowed to use terror as a beneficial means to these noble ends. Once the resulting human devastation became visible, even for a moment, the former ideologues preferred to retreat to a pragmatic position or else declared quite openly their contempt for ethics. We can observe a tragic example of this in Colombia, where a campaign was started, under the Marxist banner at first, to liberate small farmers who had been downtrodden by wealthy financiers. Today, instead, a rebel republic has developed, beyond governmental control, which quite openly depends on drug trafficking and no longer seeks any moral justification for it, especially since it thereby satisfies a demand in wealthy nations and at the same time gives bread to people who would otherwise not be able to expect much of anything from the world economy. In such a perplexing situation, should not Christianity try very seriously to rediscover its voice, so as to "introduce" the new millennium to its message and to make it comprehensible as a general guide for the future?

Anyway, where was the voice of the Christian faith at that time? In 1967, when the book was being written, the fermentation of the early postconciliar period was in full swing. This is precisely what the Second Vatican Council had intended: to endow Christianity once more with the power to shape history. The nineteenth century had seen the formulation of the opinion that religion belonged to the subjective, private realm and should have its place there. But precisely because it was to be categorized as something subjective, it could not be a determining factor in the overall course of history and in the epochal decisions that had to be made as part of it. Now, following the Council, it was supposed to become evident again that the faith of Christians embraces all of life, that it stands in the midst of history and in time and has relevance beyond the realm of subjective notions. Christianity—at least from the viewpoint of the Catholic Church—was trying to emerge again from the ghetto to which it had been relegated since the nineteenth century and to become involved once more in the world at large. We do not need to discuss here the intra-ecclesiastical disputes and frictions that arose over the interpretation and assimilation of the Council. The main thing affecting the status of Christianity in that period was the idea of a new relationship between the Church and the world. Although Romano Guardini in the 1930s had coined the expression *Unterscheidung des Christlichen* [distinguishing what is Christian]—something that was extremely necessary then—such distinctions now no longer seemed to be important; on the contrary, the spirit of the age called for crossing boundaries, reaching out to the world and becoming involved in it. It was demonstrated already upon the Parisian barricades in 1968 how quickly these ideas could emerge from the academic discussions of churchmen and find a very practical application: a revolutionary Eucharist was celebrated there, thus putting into practice a new fusion of the Church and the world under the banner of the revolution that was supposed to bring, at last, the dawn of a better age. The leading role played by Catholic and Protestant student groups in the revolutionary upheavals at universities, both in Europe and beyond, confirmed this trend.

This new translation of ideas into practice, this new fusion of the Christian impulse with secular and political action, was like a lightning bolt; the real fires that it set, however, were in Latin America. The theology of liberation seemed for more than a decade to point the way by which the faith might again shape the world, because it was making common cause with the findings and worldly wisdom of the hour. No one could dispute the fact that there was in Latin America, to a horrifying extent, oppression, unjust rule, the concentration of property and power in the hands of a few, and the exploitation of the poor, and there was no disputing either that something had to be done. And since it was a question of countries with a Catholic majority, there could be no doubt that the Church bore the responsibility here and that the faith had to prove itself as a force for justice. But how? Now Marx appeared to be the great guidebook. He was said to be playing now the role that had fallen to Aristotle in the thirteenth century; the latter's pre-Christian (that is, "pagan") philosophy had to be baptized, in order to bring faith and reason into the proper relation to each other. But anyone who accepts Marx (in whatever neo-Marxist variation he may choose) as the representative of worldly reason not only accepts a philosophy, a vision of the origin and meaning of existence, but also and especially adopts a practical program. For this "philosophy" is essentially a "praxis", which does not presuppose a "truth" but rather creates one. Anyone who makes Marx the philosopher of theology adopts the primacy of politics and economics, which now become the real powers that can bring about salvation (and, if misused, can wreak havoc). The redemption of mankind, to this way of thinking, occurs through politics and economics, in which the form of the future is determined. This primacy of praxis and politics meant, above all, that God could not be categorized as something "practical". The "reality" in which one had to get involved now was solely the material reality of given historical circumstances, which were to be viewed critically and reformed, redirected to the right goals by using the appropriate means, among which violence was indispensable. From this perspective, speaking about God belongs neither to the realm of the practical nor to that of reality. If it was to be indulged in at all, it would have to be postponed until the most important work had been done. What remained was the figure of Jesus, who of course appeared now, no longer as the Christ, but rather as the embodiment of all the suffering and oppressed and as their spokesman, who calls us to rise up, to change society. What was new in all this was that the program of changing the world, which in Marx was intended to be not only atheistic but also antireligious, was now filled with religious passion and was based on religious principles: a new reading of the Bible (especially of the Old Testament) and a liturgy that was celebrated as a symbolic fulfillment of the revolution and as a preparation for it.

It must be admitted: by means of this remarkable synthesis, Christianity had stepped once more onto the world stage and had become an "epoch-making" message. It is no surprise that the socialist states took a stand in favor of this movement. More noteworthy is the fact that, even in the "capitalist" countries, liberation theology was the darling of public opinion; to contradict it was viewed positively as a sin against humanity and mankind, even though no one, naturally, wanted to see the practical measures applied in his own situation, because he, of course, had already arrived at a just social order. Now it cannot be denied that in the various liberation theologies there really were some worthwhile insights as well. All of these plans for an epoch-making synthesis of Christianity and the world had to step aside, however, the moment that that faith in politics as a salvific force collapsed. Man is, indeed, as Aristotle says, a "political being", but he cannot be reduced to politics and economics. I see the real and most profound problem with the liberation theologies in their effective omission of the idea of God, which, of course, also changed the figure of Christ fundamentally (as we have indicated). Not as though God had been denied—not on your life! He simply was not needed in regard to the "reality" that mankind had to deal with. God had nothing to do.

One is struck by this point and suddenly wonders: Was that the case only in liberation theology? Or was this theory able to arrive at such an assessment of the question about God—that the question was not a practical one for the long-overdue business of changing the world—only because the Christian world thought much the same thing, or, rather, lived in much the same way, without reflecting on it or noticing it? Has not Christian consciousness acquiesced to a great extent—without being aware of it—in the attitude that faith in God is something subjective, which belongs in the private realm and not in the common activities of public life where, in order to be able to get along, we all have to behave now *etsi Deus non daretur* (as if there were no God). Was it not necessary to find a way that would be valid in case it turned out that God did not exist? And so actually it happened automatically, when the faith stepped out of the inner sanctum of ecclesiastical matters into the general public, that it had nothing for God to do and left him where he was: in the private realm, in the intimate sphere that does not concern anyone else. It did not take any particular negligence, and certainly not a deliberate denial, to leave God as a God with nothing to do, especially since his name had been misused so often. But the faith would really have come out of the ghetto only if it had brought its most distinctive feature with it into the public arena: the God who judges and suffers, the God who sets limits and standards for us; the God from whom we come and to whom we are going. But as it was, it really remained in the ghetto, having by now absolutely nothing to do.

Yet God is "practical" and not just some theoretical conclusion of a consoling world view that one may adhere to or simply disregard. We see that today in every place where the deliberate denial of him has become a matter of principle and where his absence is no longer mitigated at all. For at first, when God is left out of the picture, everything apparently goes on as before. Mature decisions and the basic structures of life remain in place, even though they have lost their foundations. But, as Nietzsche describes it, once the news really reaches people that "God is dead" and they take it to heart, then everything changes. This is demonstrated today, on the one hand, in the way that science treats human life: man is becoming a technological object while vanishing to an ever greater degree as a human subject, and he has only himself to blame. When human embryos are artificially "cultivated" so as to have "research material" and to obtain a supply of organs, which then are supposed to benefit other human beings, there is scarcely an outcry, because so few are horrified any more. Progress demands all this, and they really are noble goals: improving the quality of life—at least for those who can afford to have recourse to such services. But if man, in his origin and at his very roots, is only an object to himself, if he is "produced" and comes off the production line with selected features and accessories, what on earth is man then supposed to think of man? How should he act toward him? What will be man's attitude toward man when he can no longer find anything of the divine mystery in the other, but only his own know-how? What is happening in the "high-tech" areas of science is reflected wherever the culture, broadly speaking, has managed to tear God out of men's hearts. Today there are places where trafficking in human beings goes on quite openly: a cynical consumption of humanity while society looks on helplessly. For example, organized crime constantly brings women out of Albania on various pretexts and delivers them to the mainland across the sea as prostitutes, and because there are enough cynics there waiting for such "wares", organized crime becomes more powerful, and those who try to put a stop to it discover that the Hydra of evil keeps growing new heads, no matter how many they may cut off. And do we not see everywhere around us, in seemingly orderly neighborhoods, an increase in violence, which is taken more and more for granted and is becoming more and more reckless? I do not want to extend this horror-scenario any farther. But we ought to wonder whether God might not in fact be the genuine reality, the basic prerequisite for any "realism", so that, without him, nothing is safe.

Let us return to the course of historical developments since 1967. The year 1989, as I was saying, brought with it no new answers; rather it deepened the general perplexity and nourished scepticism about great ideals. But something did happen. Religion became modern again. Its disappearance is no longer anticipated; on the contrary, various new forms of it are growing luxuriantly. In the leaden loneliness of a God-forsaken world, in its interior boredom, the search for mysticism, for any sort of contact with the divine, has sprung up anew. Everywhere there is talk about visions and messages from the other world, and wherever there is a report of an apparition, thousands travel there, in order to discover, perhaps, a crack in the world through which heaven might look down on them and send them consolation. Some complain that this new search for religion, to a great extent, is passing the traditional Christian churches by. An institution is inconvenient, and dogma is bothersome. They are looking for experience, an encounter with the entirely Other. I cannot say that I am in unqualified agreement with this complaint. At the World Youth Days, such as the one recently in Paris, faith becomes experience and provides the joy of fellowship. Something of an ecstasy, in the good sense, is communicated. The dismal and destructive ecstasy of drugs, of hammering rhythms, noise, and drunkenness is confronted with a bright ecstasy of light, of joyful encounter in God's sunshine. Let it not be said that this is only a momentary thing. Often it is so, no doubt. But it can also be a moment that brings about a lasting change and begins a journey. Similar things happen in the many lay movements that have sprung up in the last few decades. Here, too, faith becomes a form of lived experience, the joy of setting out on a journey and of participating in the mystery of the leaven that permeates the whole mass from within and renews it. Eventually, provided that the root is sound, even apparition sites can be incentives to go again in search of God in a sober way. Anyone who expected that Christianity would now become a mass movement was, of course, disappointed. But mass movements are not the ones that bear the promise of the future within them. The future is made wherever people find their way to one another in life-shaping convictions. And a good future grows wherever these convictions come from the truth and lead to it.

The rediscovery of religion, however, has another side to it. We have already seen that this trend looks for religion as an experience, that the "mystical" aspect of religion is an important part of it: religion that offers me contact with the entirely Other. In our historical situation, this means that the mystical religions of Asia (parts of Hinduism and of Buddhism), with their renunciation of dogma and their minimal degree of institutionalization, appear to be more suitable for enlightened humanity than dogmatically determined and institutionally structured Christianity. In general, however, the result is that individual religions are relativized; for all the differences and, yes, the contradictions among these various sorts of belief, the only thing that matters, ultimately, is the inside of all these different forms, the contact with the ineffable, with the hidden mystery. And to a great extent people agree that this mystery is not completely manifested in any one form of revelation, that it is always glimpsed in random and fragmentary ways and yet is always sought as one and the same thing. That we cannot know God himself, that everything that can be stated and described can only be a symbol: this is nothing short of a fundamental certainty of modern man, which he also understands somehow as his humility in the presence of the infinite. Associated with this relativizing is the notion of a great peace among religions, which recognize each other as different ways of reflecting the one Eternal Being and should leave up to the individual which path he will grope along to find the One who nevertheless unites them all. Through such a relativizing process, the Christian faith is radically changed, especially at two fundamental places in its essential message:

1. The figure of Christ is interpreted in a completely new way, not only in reference to dogma, but also and precisely with regard to the Gospels. The belief that Christ *is* the only Son of God, that God really dwells among us as man in him, and that the man Jesus is eternally in God, is God himself, and therefore is, not a figure in which God appears, but rather the sole and irreplaceable God—this belief is thereby excluded. Instead of being the man who *is* God, Christ becomes the one who has *experienced* God in a special way. He is an enlightened one and therein is no longer fundamentally different from other enlightened individuals, for instance, Buddha. But in such an interpretation the figure of Jesus loses its inner logic. It is torn out of the historical setting in which it is anchored and forced into a scheme of things that is alien to it. Buddha—and in this he is comparable to Socrates—directs the attention of his disciples away from himself: his own person does not matter, but only the path he has pointed out. Someone who finds the way can forget Buddha. But with Jesus, what matters is precisely his Person, Christ himself. When he says, "I am he", we hear the tones of the "I AM" on Mount Horeb. The way consists precisely in following him, for "*I* am the way, and the truth, and the life" (Jn 14:6). He himself is the way, and there is no way that is independent of him, on which he would no longer matter. Since the real message that he brings is not a doctrine but his very person, we must of course add that this "I" of Jesus refers absolutely to the "Thou" of the Father and is not self-sufficient; rather, it is indeed truly a "way". "My teaching is not mine" (Jn 7:16). "I seek not my own will but the will of him who sent me" (Jn 5:30). The "I" is important, because it draws us completely into the dynamic of mission, because it leads to the surpassing of self and to union with him for whom we have been created. If the figure of Jesus is taken

out of this inevitably scandalous dimension, if it is separated from his Godhead, then it becomes self-contradictory. All that is left are shreds that leave us perplexed or else become excuses for self-affirmation.

2. The concept of God is fundamentally changed. The question of whether God should be thought of as a person or impersonally now seems to be of secondary importance; no longer can an essential difference be noted between theistic and nontheistic forms of religion. This view is spreading with astonishing rapidity. Even believing and theologically trained Catholics, who want to share in the responsibilities of the Church's life, will ask the question (as though the answer were self-evident): "Can it really be that important whether someone understands God as a person or impersonally?" After all, we should be broad-minded—so goes the opinion—since the mystery of God is in any case beyond all concepts and images. But such concessions strike at the heart of the biblical faith. The *shema*, the "Hear, O Israel" from Deuteronomy 6:4–9, was and still is the real core of the believer's identity, not only for Israel, but also for Christianity. The believing Jew dies reciting this profession; the Jewish martyrs breathed their last declaring it and gave their lives for it: "Hear, O Israel. He is our God. He is one." The fact that this God now shows us his face in Jesus Christ (Jn 14:9)—a face that Moses was not allowed to see (Ex 33:20)—does not alter this profession in the least and changes nothing essential in this identity. Of course, the fact that God is personal is not mentioned in the Bible using that term, but it is apparent nevertheless, inasmuch as there is a name of God. A name implies the ability to be called on, to speak, to hear, to answer. This is essential for the biblical God, and if this is taken away, the faith of the Bible has been abandoned. It cannot be disputed that there have been and there are false,

superficial ways of understanding God as personal. Precisely when we apply the concept of person to God, the difference between our idea of person and the reality of God—as the Fourth Lateran Council says about all speech concerning God—is always infinitely greater than what they have in common. False applications of the concept of person are sure to be present whenever God is monopolized for one's own human interests and thus his name is sullied. It is not by chance that the Second Commandment, which is supposed to protect the name of God, follows directly after the First, which teaches us to adore him. In this respect we can always learn something new from the way in which the "mystical" religions, with their purely negative theology, speak about God, and in this respect there are avenues for dialogue. But with the disappearance of what is meant by "the name of God", that is, God's personal nature, his name is, no longer protected and honored, but abandoned outright instead.

But what is actually meant, then, by God's name, by his being personal? Precisely this: Not only can we experience him, beyond all [earthly] experience, but also he can express and communicate himself. When God is understood in a completely impersonal way, for instance in Buddhism, as sheer negation with respect to everything that appears real to us, then there is no positive relationship between "God" and the world. Then the world has to be overcome as a source of suffering, but it no longer can be shaped. Religion then points out ways to overcome the world, to free people from the burden of its semblance, but it offers no standards by which we can live in the world, no forms of societal responsibility within it. The situation is somewhat different in Hinduism. The essential thing is the experience of identity: At bottom I am one with the hidden ground of reality itself—the famous *tat tvam asi* of the Upanishads. Salvation consists of liberation from individuality, from being a person, in overcoming the differentiation from all other beings that is rooted in being a person: the deception of the self concerning itself must be put aside. The problem with this view of being has come very much to the fore in Neo-Hinduism. Where there is no uniqueness of persons, the inviolable dignity of each individual person has no foundation, either. In order to bring about the reforms that are now under way (the abolition of caste laws and of immolating widows, and so on) it was specifically necessary to break with this fundamental understanding and to introduce into the overall system of Indian thought the concept of person, as it has developed in the Christian faith out of the encounter with the personal God. The search for the correct "praxis", for right action, in this case has begun to correct the "theory": We can see to some extent how "practical" the Christian belief in God is and how unfair it is to brush these disputed but important distinctions aside as being ultimately irrelevant.

With these considerations we have reached the point from which an "introduction to Christianity" must set out today. Before I attempt to extend a bit farther the line of argument that I have suggested, another reference to the present status of faith in God and in Christ is called for. There is a fear of Christian "imperialism", a nostalgia for the beautiful multiplicity of religions and their supposedly primordial cheerfulness and freedom. Colonialism is said to be essentially bound up with historical Christianity, which was unwilling to accept the other in his otherness and tried to bring everything under its own protection. Thus, according to this view, the religions and cultures of South America were downtrodden and stamped out, and violence was done to the soul of the native peoples, who could not find themselves in the new order and were forcibly deprived of the old. Now there are milder and harsher variants of this opinion. The milder version says that we should finally grant to these lost cultures the right of domicile within the Christian faith and allow them to devise for themselves an aboriginal form of Christianity. The more radical view regards Christianity in its entirety as a sort of alienation, from which the native peoples must be liberated. The demand for an aboriginal Christianity, properly understood, should be taken as an extremely important task. All great cultures are open to one another and to the truth. They all have something to contribute to the Bride's "many-colored robes" mentioned in Psalms 45:14, which patristic writers applied to the Church. To be sure, many opportunities have been missed, and new ones present themselves. Let us not forget, however, that those native peoples, to a notable extent, have already found their own expression of the Christian faith in popular devotions. That the suffering God and the kindly Mother in particular have become for them the central images of the faith, which have given them access to the God of the Bible, has something to say to us, too, today. But of course, much still remains to be done.

Let us return to the question about God and about Christ as the centerpiece of an introduction to the Christian faith. One thing has already become evident: The mystical dimension of the concept of God, which the Asian religions bring with them as a challenge to us, must clearly be decisive for our thinking, too, and for our faith. God has become quite concrete in Christ, but in this way his mystery has also become still greater. God is always infinitely greater than all our concepts and all our images and names. The fact that we now acknowledge him to be triune does not mean that we have meanwhile learned everything about him. On the contrary, he is only showing us how little we know about him and how little we can comprehend him or even begin to take his measure. Today, after the horrors of totalitarian regimes (I remind the reader of the memorial at Auschwitz), the problem of theodicy urgently and mightily [*mit brennender Gewalt*] demands the attention of us all; this is just one more indication of how little we are capable of defining God, much less fathoming him. After all, God's answer to Job explains nothing; rather, it sets boundaries to our mania for judging everything and being able to say the final word on a subject, and it reminds us of our limitations. It admonishes us to trust the mystery of God in its incomprehensibility.

Having said this, we must still emphasize the brightness of God, too, along with the darkness. Ever since the Prologue to the Gospel of John, the concept of *logos* has been at the very center of our Christian faith in God. *Logos* signifies reason, meaning, or even "word"—a meaning, therefore, that is Word, that is relationship, that is creative. The God who is *logos* guarantees the intelligibility of the world, the intelligibility of our existence, the aptitude of reason to know God [*die Gottgemässheit der Vernunft*] and the reasonableness of God [*die Vernunftgemässheit Gottes*], even though his understanding infinitely surpasses ours and to us may so often appear to be darkness. The world comes from reason, and this reason is a Person, is Love—this is what our biblical faith tells us about God. Reason can speak about God; it must speak about God, or else it cuts itself short. Included in this is the concept of creation. The world is not just *maya*, appearance, which we must ultimately leave behind. It is not merely the endless wheel of sufferings, from which we must try to escape. It is something positive. It is good, despite all the evil in it and despite all the sorrow, and it is good to live in it. God, who is the Creator and declares himself in his creation, also gives direction and measure to human action. We are living today in a crisis of moral values [*Ethos*], which by now is, no longer merely an academic question about the ultimate foundations of ethical theories, but rather an entirely practical matter. The news is getting around that moral values cannot be grounded in something else, and the consequences of this view are working themselves out. The published works on the theme of moral values are stacked high and almost toppling over, which, on the one hand, indicates the urgency of the question but, on the other hand, also suggests the prevailing perplexity. Kolakowski, in his line of thinking, has very emphatically pointed out that deleting faith in God, however one may try to spin or turn it, ultimately deprives moral values of their grounding. If the world and man do not come from a creative intelligence, which stores within itself their measures and plots the path of human existence, then all that is left are traffic rules for human behavior, which can be discarded or maintained according to their usefulness. All that remains is the calculus of consequence—what is called teleological ethics or proportionalism. But who can really make a judgment beyond the consequences of the present moment? Will not a new ruling class, then, take hold of the keys to human existence and become the managers of mankind? When dealing with a calculus of consequences, the inviolability of human dignity no longer exists, because nothing is good or bad in itself any more. The problem of moral values is on the order of the day in our time, and it is an item of great urgency. Faith in the Logos, the Word in the beginning, understands moral values as *responsibility*, as a response to the Word, and thus gives them their intelligibility as well as their essential orientation. Connected with this also is the task of searching for a common understanding of responsibility, together with all honest, rational inquiry and with the great religious traditions. In this endeavor there is, not only the intrinsic proximity of the three great monotheistic religions, but also significant lines of convergence with another strand of Asian religiosity, as we encounter it in Confucianism and Taoism.

If it is true that the term *logos*—the Word in the beginning, creative reason and love—is decisive for the Christian image of God, and if the concept of *logos* simultaneously forms the core of Christology, of faith in Christ, then the indivisibility of faith in God and faith in his incarnate Son Jesus Christ is only confirmed once more. We will not understand Jesus any better or come any closer to him if we bracket off faith in his divinity. The fear that belief in his divinity might alienate him from us is widespread today. It is not only for the sake of the other religions that some would like to deemphasize this faith as much as possible. It is first and foremost a question of our own Western fears. All of this seems incompatible with our modern world view. It must just be a question of mythological interpretations, which were then transformed by the Greek mentality into metaphysics. But when we separate Christ and God, behind this effort there is also a doubt as to whether God is at all capable of being so close to us, whether he is allowed to bow down so low. The fact that we do not want this appears to be humility. But Romano Guardini correctly pointed out that the higher form of humility consists in allowing God to do precisely what appears to us to be unfitting and to bow down to what he does, not to what we contrive about him and for him. A notion of God's remoteness from the world is behind our apparently humble realism, and therefore a loss of God's presence is also connected with it. If God is not in Christ, then he retreats into an immeasurable distance, and if God is no longer a God-with-us, then he is plainly an absent God and thus no God at all: A god who cannot work is not God. As for the fear that Jesus moves us too far away if we believe in his divine Sonship, precisely the opposite is true: If he was only a man, then he has retreated irrevocably into the past, and then only a distant recollection can perceive him more or less clearly. But if God has truly assumed manhood and thus is at the same time true man and true God in Jesus, then he participates, as man, in the presence of God, which embraces all ages. Then, and only then, is he, not just something that happened yesterday, but is present among us, our contemporary in our today. That is why I am firmly convinced that a renewal of Christology must have the courage to see Christ in all of his greatness, as he is presented by the four Gospels together in the many tensions of their unity.

If I had this *Introduction to Christianity* to write over again today, all of the experiences of the last thirty years would have to go into the text, which would then have to include also the context of interreligious discussions to a much greater degree than seemed fitting then. But I believe that I was not mistaken as to the fundamental approach, in that I put the question of God and the question about Christic in the very center, which then leads to a "narrative Christology" and demonstrates that the place for faith is in the Church. This basic orientation, I think, was correct. That is why I venture to place this book once more in the hands of the reader today.

Rome, April 2000   *Joseph Cardinal Ratzinger*

PREFACE TO THE 1968 EDITION

The question of the real content and meaning of the Christian faith is enveloped today in a greater fog of uncertainty than at almost any earlier period in history. Anyone who has watched the theological movement of the last decade and who is not one of those thoughtless people who always uncritically accept what is new as necessarily better might well feel reminded of the old story of "Clever Hans". The lump of gold that was too heavy and troublesome for him he exchanged successively, so as to be more comfortable, for a horse, a cow, a pig, a goose, and a whetstone, which he finally threw into the water, still without losing much; on the contrary, what he now gained in exchange, so he thought, was the precious gift of complete freedom. How long his intoxication lasted, how somber the moment of awakening from the illusion of his supposed liberation, is left by the story, as we know, to the imagination of the reader. The worried Christian of today is often bothered by questions like these: Has our theology in the last few years not taken in many ways a similar path? Has it not gradually watered down the demands of faith, which had been found all too demanding, always only so little that nothing important seemed to be lost, yet always so much that it was soon possible to venture on the next step? And will poor Jack, the Christian who trustingly let himself be led from exchange to exchange, from interpretation to interpretation, not really soon hold in his hand, instead of the gold with which he began, only a whetstone that he can safely be advised to throw away?

To be sure, such questions are unfair if they are posed in too general terms. It is simply not correct to assert that "modern theology" as a whole has taken a path of this sort. But it is just as undeniable that there is widespread support for a trend that does indeed lead from gold to whetstone. This trend cannot be countered, it is true, by merely sticking to the precious metal of the fixed formulas of days gone by, for then it remains just a lump of metal, a burden instead of something offering by virtue of its value the possibility of true freedom. This is where the present book comes in: its aim is to help understand faith afresh as something that makes possible true humanity in the world of today, to expound faith without changing it into the small coin of empty talk painfully laboring to hide a complete spiritual vacuum.

The book arose out of lectures I gave at Tübingen in the summer term of 1967 for students from all faculties. It is an attempt to repeat, in the changed circumstances of our generation, what Karl Adam accomplished almost half a century ago at the same university in such a masterly fashion with his *Spirit of Catholicism*. The language has been modified to suit publication in book form, but the structure and scope of the lectures have not been altered, and notes on sources have only been added insofar as it was desirable to name the tools that served directly in the preparation of the lectures.

The dedication of the book to those who heard my lectures at the various stages of my academic career is intended to express my gratitude for their questions and intellectual cooperation, which were certainly among the factors from which the enterprise grew. I should also like to thank in particular the publisher Dr. Heinrich Wild, but for whose patient yet unyielding insistence I would scarcely have plucked up the courage to venture on such a bold undertaking as any book of this sort is bound to be. Finally, I must thank all those who have taken so much trouble to help bring the work into existence.

Tübingen, Summer 1968   JOSEPH RATZINGER

PREFACE TO THE 1969 EDITION

When this book was first published a year ago, I had no idea what an extraordinary reception it would find. The fact that it has been helpful to many people, on both sides of the boundary between East and West, as well as across denominational lines, fills me with gratitude and great joy. Certain technical questions were raised by the reviews that have appeared meanwhile, and in response I expressed my opinions in the periodical *Hochland* [vol. 61 (1969): 533], since it did not seem right to me to burden the book with such a discussion. The book itself is being reprinted with the text unaltered; just a few minor errors have been corrected. I thank especially the Reverend Pastor Strohl Freudenstadt and Pastor Hans-Joachim Schmidt (Goslar) for their kind comments, and I thank the latter also for graciously compiling the index of Bible passages that has been added to this edition of the book. I accept this assistance with particular gratitude as a sign of the bonds that unite Catholic and Protestant Christians in the apostolic faith, which this *Introduction* attempts to serve.

Tübingen, September 1969   *Joseph Ratzinger*

INTRODUCTION

"I BELIEVE—AMEN"

Chapter I

BELIEF IN THE WORLD OF TODAY

1. DOUBT AND BELIEF—MAN'S SITUATION BEFORE THE QUESTION OF GOD

Anyone who tries today to talk about the question of Christian faith in the presence of people who are not thoroughly at home with ecclesiastical language and thought (whether by vocation or by convention) soon comes to sense the alien— and alienating—nature of such an enterprise. He will probably soon have the feeling that his position is only too well summed up in Kierkegaard's famous story of the clown and the burning village, an allegory taken up again recently by Harvey Cox in his book *The Secular City*.[1] According to this story, a traveling circus in Denmark caught fire. The manager thereupon sent the clown, who was already dressed and made up for the performance, into the neighboring village to fetch help, especially as there was a danger that the fire would spread across the fields of dry stubble and engulf the village itself. The clown hurried into the village and requested the inhabitants to come as quickly as possible to the blazing circus and help to put the fire out. But the villagers took the clown's shouts simply for an excellent piece of advertising, meant to attract as many people as possible to the performance; they applauded the clown and laughed till they cried.

[1] H. Cox, *The Secular City*, 2nd ed. (London: Pelican Books, 1968), p. 256.

The clown felt more like weeping than laughing; he tried in vain to get people to be serious, to make it clear to them that this was no stunt, that he was not pretending but was in bitter earnest, that there really was a fire. His supplications only increased the laughter; people thought he was playing his part splendidly—until finally the fire did engulf the village; it was too late for help, and both circus and village were burned to the ground.

Cox cites this story as an analogy of the theologian's position today and sees the theologian as the clown who cannot make people really listen to his message. In his medieval, or at any rate old-fashioned, clown's costume, he is simply not taken seriously. Whatever he says, he is ticketed and classified, so to speak, by his role. Whatever he does in his attempts to demonstrate the seriousness of the position, people always know in advance that he is in fact just—a clown. They are already familiar with what he is talking about and know that he is just giving a performance that has little or nothing to do with reality. So they can listen to him quite happily without having to be seriously concerned about what he is saying. This picture indubitably contains an element of truth in it; it reflects the oppressive reality in which theology and theological discussion are imprisoned today and their frustrating inability to break through accepted patterns of thought and speech and make people recognize the subject matter of theology as a serious aspect of human life.

But perhaps our examination of conscience should go still deeper. Perhaps we should admit that this disturbing analogy, for all the thought-provoking truth contained in it, is still a simplification. For after all it makes it seem as if the clown, or in other words the theologian, is a man possessed of full knowledge who arrives with a perfectly clear message. The villagers to whom he hastens, in other words, those outside the faith, are conversely the completely ignorant, who only have to be told something of which they are completely unaware; the clown then need only take off his costume and his makeup, and everything will be all right. But is it really quite such a simple matter as that? Need we only call on the *aggiornamento*, take off our makeup, and don the mufti of a secular vocabulary or a demythologized Christianity in order to make everything all right? Is a change of intellectual costume sufficient to make people run cheerfully up and help to put out the fire that according to theology exists and is a danger to all of us? I may say that in fact the plain and unadorned theology in modern dress appearing in many places today makes this hope look rather naïve. It is certainly true that anyone who tries to preach the faith amid people involved in modern life and thought can really feel like a clown, or rather perhaps like someone who, rising from an ancient sarcophagus, walks into the midst of the world of today dressed and thinking in the ancient fashion and can neither understand nor be understood by this world of ours. Nevertheless, if he who seeks to preach the faith is sufficiently self-critical, he will soon notice that it is not only a question of form, of the kind of dress in which theology enters upon the scene. In the strangeness of theology's aims to the men of our time, he who takes his calling seriously will clearly recognize not only the difficulty of the task of interpretation but also the insecurity of his own faith, the oppressive power of unbelief in the midst of his own will to believe. Thus anyone today who makes an honest effort to give an account of the Christian faith to himself and to others must learn to see that he is not just someone in fancy dress who need only change his clothes in order to be able to impart his teaching successfully. Rather will he have to understand that his own situation is by no means so different from that of others as he may have thought at the start. He will become aware that on both sides the same forces are at work, albeit in different ways.

First of all, the believer is always threatened with an uncertainty that in moments of temptation can suddenly and unexpectedly cast a piercing light on the fragility of the whole that usually seems so self-evident to him. A few examples will help to make this clear. That lovable Saint Thérèse of Lisieux, who looks so naïve and unproblematical, grew up in an atmosphere of complete religious security; her whole existence from beginning to end, and down to the smallest detail, was so completely molded by the faith of the Church that the invisible world became, not just a part of her everyday life, but that life itself. It seemed to be an almost tangible reality that could not be removed by any amount of thinking. To her, "religion" really was a self-evident presupposition of her daily existence; she dealt with it as we deal with the concrete details of our lives. Yet this very saint, a person apparently cocooned in complete security, left behind her, from the last weeks of her passion, shattering admissions that her horrified sisters toned down in her literary remains and that have only now come to light in the new verbatim editions. She says, for example, "I am assailed by the worst temptations of atheism". Her mind is beset by every possible argument against the faith; the sense of believing seems to have vanished; she feels that she is now "in sinners' shoes." [2]

---

[2] Cf. the informative survey provided by *Herder Korrespondenz* 7, no. 3 (1962): 561–65, under the title, "The Genuine Texts of St. Thérèse of Lisieux" (the quotations cited here occur there on p. 564). This survey is based mainly on the article by M. Morée, "La Table des pécheurs", *Dieu vivant* 24:13–104. Morée refers particularly to the studies and editions of A. Combes; cf. especially *Le Problème de l' "Histoire d'une âme" et des œuvres complètes de Ste. Thérèse de Lisieux* (Paris, 1950). Further literature: A. Combes, "Theresia von Lisieux", in *Lexikon für Theologie und Kirche* (LThK), 10:102–4.

In other words, in what is apparently a flawlessly interlocking world someone here suddenly catches a glimpse of the abyss lurking—even for her—under the firm structure of the supporting conventions. In a situation like this, what is in question is not the sort of thing that one perhaps quarrels about otherwise—the dogma of the Assumption, the proper use of confession—all this becomes absolutely secondary. What is at stake is the whole structure; it is a question of all or nothing. That is the only remaining alternative; nowhere does there seem anything to cling to in this sudden fall. Wherever one looks, only the bottomless abyss of nothingness can be seen.

Paul Claudel has depicted this situation in a most convincing way in the great opening scene of the *Soulier de Satin*. A Jesuit missionary, brother of Rodrigue, the hero of the play (a worldling and adventurer veering uncertainly between God and the world), is shown as the survivor of a shipwreck. His ship has been sunk by pirates; he himself has been lashed to a mast from the sunken ship, and he is now drifting on this piece of wood through the raging waters of the ocean.[3] The play opens with his last monologue:

Lord, I thank thee for bending me down like this. It sometimes happened that I found thy commands laborious and my will at a loss and jibbing at thy dispensation. But now I could not be bound to thee more closely than I am, and however violently my limbs move they cannot get one inch away from thee. So I really am fastened to the cross, but the

---

[3] This recalls in a striking way the text from Wisdom 10:4 that has become so important for early Christian theology of the Cross: "Wisdom saved the drowning world, steering on a paltry raft one innocent man to safety." For the interpretation of this text in the theology of the Fathers, see H. Rahner, *Symbole der Kirche* (Salzburg, 1964), pp. 504–47.

cross on which I hang is not fastened to anything else. It drifts on the sea.[4]

Fastened to the cross—with the cross fastened to nothing, drifting over the abyss. The situation of the contemporary believer could hardly be more accurately and impressively described. Only a loose plank bobbing over the void seems to hold him up, and it looks as if he must eventually sink. Only a loose plank connects him to God, though certainly it connects him inescapably, and in the last analysis he knows that this wood is stronger than the void that seethes beneath him and that remains nevertheless the really threatening force in his day-to-day life.

This picture contains in addition yet another dimension, which indeed seems to me the really important thing about it. This shipwrecked Jesuit is not alone; he foreshadows, as it were, the fate of his brother; the destiny of his brother is present in him, that brother who considers himself a nonbeliever, who has turned his back on God because he sees his business, not as waiting, but as "possessing the attainable . . . , as though he could be anywhere else than where Thou art".

We do not need here to follow the intricacies of Claudel's conception, as he uses the interweaving lines of these two apparently antithetical destinies as guiding threads, up to the point when finally Rodrigue's fate touches that of his brother, in that the conqueror of the world ends up as a slave on a ship, a slave who must be glad when a ragged old nun with a rusty frying pan takes him with her, too, as worthless chattel. Instead, we can return without any more imagery to our own situation and say: If, on the one hand, the believer can perfect his faith only on the ocean of nihilism, temptation, and doubt, if he has been

---

[4] *Le Soulier de Satin*, act I, scene I.

assigned the ocean of uncertainty as the only possible site for his faith, on the other, the unbeliever is not to be understood undialectically as a mere man without faith. Just as we have already recognized that the believer does not live immune to doubt but is always threatened by the plunge into the void, so now we can discern the entangled nature of human destinies and say that the nonbeliever does not lead a sealed-off, self-sufficient life, either. However vigorously he may assert that he is a pure positivist, who has long left behind him super-natural temptations and weaknesses and now accepts only what is immediately certain, he will never be free of the secret uncertainty about whether positivism really has the last word. Just as the believer is choked by the salt water of doubt constantly washed into his mouth by the ocean of uncertainty, so the nonbeliever is troubled by doubts about his unbelief, about the real totality of the world he has made up his mind to explain as a self-contained whole. He can never be absolutely certain of the autonomy of what he has seen and interpreted as a whole; he remains threatened by the question of whether belief is not after all the reality it claims to be. Just as the believer knows himself to be constantly threatened by unbelief, which he must experience as a continual temptation, so for the unbeliever faith remains a temptation and a threat to his apparently perma-nently closed world. In short, there is no escape from the dilemma of being a man. Anyone who makes up his mind to evade the uncertainty of belief will have to experience the uncertainty of unbelief, which can never finally eliminate for certain the possibility that belief may after all be the truth. It is not until belief is rejected that its unrejectability becomes evident.

It may be appropriate at this point to cite a Jewish story told by Martin Buber; it presents in concrete form the above-mentioned dilemma of being a man.

An adherent of the Enlightenment [writes Buber], a very
learned man, who had heard of the Rabbi of Berditchev,
paid a visit to him in order to argue, as was his custom, with
him, too, and to shatter his old-fashioned proofs of the truth
of his faith. When he entered the Rabbi's room, he found
him walking up and down with a book in his hand, rapt in
thought. The Rabbi paid no attention to the new arrival.
Suddenly he stopped, looked at him fleetingly, and said, "But
perhaps it is true after all." The scholar tried in vain to collect himself—his knees trembled, so terrible was the Rabbi
to behold and so terrible his simple utterance to hear. But
Rabbi Levi Yitschak now turned to face him and spoke quite
calmly: "My son, the great scholars of the Torah with whom
you have argued wasted their words on you; as you departed
you laughed at them. They were unable to lay God and his
Kingdom on the table before you, and neither can I. But
think, my son, perhaps it is true." The exponent of the
Enlightenment opposed him with all his strength; but this
terrible "perhaps" that echoed back at him time after time
broke his resistance.[5]

Here we have, I believe—in however strange a guise—a
very precise description of the situation of man confronted
with the question of God. No one can lay God and his
Kingdom on the table before another man; even the believer
cannot do it for himself. But however strongly unbelief may
feel justified thereby, it cannot forget the eerie feeling induced
by the words "Yet perhaps it is true." That "perhaps" is the
unavoidable temptation it cannot elude, the temptation in
which it, too, in the very act of rejection, has to experience the unrejectability of belief. In other words, both the
believer and the unbeliever share, each in his own way, doubt
and belief, if they do not hide from themselves and from

[5] M. Buber, *Werke*, vol. 3 (Munich and Heidelberg, 1963), p. 348.

the truth of their being. Neither can quite escape either doubt or belief; for the one, faith is present *against* doubt; for the other, *through* doubt and in the *form* of doubt. It is the basic pattern of man's destiny only to be allowed to find the finality of his existence in this unceasing rivalry between doubt and belief, temptation and certainty. Perhaps in precisely this way doubt, which saves both sides from being shut up in their own worlds, could become the avenue of communication. It prevents both from enjoying complete self-satisfaction; it opens up the believer to the doubter and the doubter to the believer; for one, it is his share in the fate of the unbeliever; for the other, the form in which belief remains nevertheless a challenge to him.

2. THE ORIGIN OF BELIEF—PROVISIONAL ATTEMPT AT A DEFINITION OF BELIEF

Even though what has been said has shown that the image of the incomprehensible clown and the unsuspecting villagers is inadequate to represent the interplay of belief and unbelief in the world of today, it cannot be denied that it does express one specific aspect of the problem of belief today. For the basic question in an introduction to Christianity, which must try to elucidate what it means when a person says "I believe", poses itself to us in a quite definite temporal context. In view of our historical consciousness, which has become a part of our self-consciousness, of our basic understanding of the human situation, it can only be posed in the form, "What is the meaning and significance of the Christian profession 'I believe' *today*, in the context of our present existence and our present attitude to reality as a whole?"

And this brings us immediately to an analysis of the text that will provide the guiding thread of our whole investigation, namely, the Apostles' Creed, which in origin is intended to be an "introduction to Christianity" and a summary of its essential contents. This text begins characteristically with the words "I believe". We shall not attempt at this point to expound this phrase by reference to its content, nor shall we ask what is signified by the fact that this basic assertion, "I believe", occurs in a set formula, in connection with a clearly defined content and conditioned by a ritual context. It is true, of course, that both kinds of context, that of the ritual form and that of the particular contents, help to mold the meaning of this little word *credo*, just as, vice versa, the word *credo* supports and molds everything that follows and also the ritual framework. Nevertheless, for the moment we must put aside both considerations in order to ask a more radical question and to ponder quite deeply what kind of attitude is implied if Christian existence expresses itself first and foremost in the word *credo*, thus determining—what is by no means self-evident—that the kernel of Christianity shall be that it is a "belief". We generally assume rather unthinkingly that "religion" and "belief" are always the same thing and that every religion can therefore just as well be described as a "belief". But this is true only to a limited extent; many of the other religions have other names for themselves and thus establish different centers of gravity. The Old Testament as a whole classified itself, not as "belief", but as "law". It is primarily a way of life, in which, to be sure, the act of belief acquires by degrees more and more importance. Again, by *religio* Roman religious feeling understood in practice mainly the observance of certain ritual forms and customs. It was not crucial that there should be an act of faith in the supernatural; even the complete absence of such faith did not imply any disloyalty to this religion. As it was essentially a system of rites, the crucial factor was the careful observance of these. We could go on like this through the whole history of religions, but enough has been said to make clear that it is by no means self-evident that the central expression of Christianity should be the word *credo*, that the Christian should describe this attitude to reality as being that of "belief". But this only makes our question all the more urgent: What attitude is really signified by this word? And, further, how is it that it is becoming so difficult for our individual, personal "I" to enter into this "I believe"? How is it that, again and again, it seems almost impossible for us to identify our present-day egos— each of them inalterably separate from everyone else's—with that "I" of the "I believe", which has been predetermined and shaped by past generations?

Let us have no illusions; entering into that "I" of the creed formula, transforming that schematic "I" of the formula into the flesh and blood of the personal "I", was always an unsettling and seemingly almost impossible affair; often, instead of the schema's being filled with flesh and blood, the "I" itself was transformed into a schema. And when today as believers in our age we hear it said, a little enviously perhaps, that in the Middle Ages everyone without exception in our lands was a believer, it is a good thing to cast a glance behind the scenes, as we can today, thanks to historical research. This will tell us that even in those days there was the great mass of nominal believers and a relatively small number of people who had really entered into the inner movement of belief. It will show us that for many belief was only a ready-made mode of life, by which for them the exciting adventure really signified by the word *credo* was at least as much concealed as disclosed. This is simply because there is an infinite gulf between God and man; because man is fashioned in such a way that his eyes are only capable of seeing what is not God, and thus for man God is and always will be the essentially invisible, something lying outside his field of vision. God is essentially invisible—this fundamental assertion of biblical faith in God in its opposition to the visibility of the gods (in the plural) is at the same time, indeed primarily, an assertion about man: Man is a seeing creature, whose living area seems to be marked off by the range of what he can see and grasp. But in this area of things that can be seen and grasped, the area that determines the living space of man, God does not occur and will never occur, however much the area may be extended. I believe it is important that in principle the Old Testament contains this assertion: God is not just he who at present lies in fact outside the field of vision but could be seen if it were possible to go farther; no, he is the being who stands *essentially* outside it, however far our field of vision may be extended.

We now begin to discern a first vague outline of the attitude signified by the word *credo*. It means that man does not regard seeing, hearing, and touching as the totality of what concerns him, that he does not view the area of his world as marked off by what he can see and touch but seeks a second mode of access to reality, a mode he calls in fact belief, and in such a way that he finds in it the decisive enlargement of his whole view of the world. If this is so, then the little word *credo* contains a basic option vis-à-vis reality as such; it signifies, not the observation of this or that fact, but a fundamental mode of behavior toward being, toward existence, toward one's own sector of reality, and toward reality as a whole. It signifies the deliberate view that what cannot be seen, what can in no wise move into the field of vision, is not unreal; that, on the contrary, what cannot be seen in fact represents true reality, the element that supports and makes possible all the rest of reality. And it signifies the view that this element that makes reality as a whole possible is also what grants man a truly human existence, what makes him possible as a human being existing in a human way. In other words, belief signifies the decision that at the very core of human existence there is a point that cannot be nourished and supported on the visible and tangible, that encounters and comes into contact with what cannot be seen and finds that it is a necessity for its own existence.

Such an attitude is certainly to be attained only by what the language of the Bible calls "turning back", "con-version". Man's natural inclination draws him to the visible, to what he can take in his hand and hold as his own. He has to turn around inwardly in order to see how badly he is neglecting his own interests by letting himself be drawn along in this way by his natural inclination. He must turn around to recognize how blind he is if he trusts only what he sees with his eyes. Without this change of direction, without this resistance to the natural inclination, there can be no belief. Indeed belief *is* the conversion in which man discovers that he is following an illusion if he devotes himself only to the tangible. This is at the same time the fundamental reason why belief is not demonstrable: it is an about-turn; only he who turns about is receptive to it; and because our inclination does not cease to point us in another direction, it remains a turn that is new every day; only in a lifelong conversion can we become aware of what it means to say "I believe".

From this we can see that it is not just today, in the specific conditions of our modern situation, that belief or faith is problematical, indeed almost something that seems impossible, but that it has always meant a leap, a somewhat less obvious and less easily recognizable one perhaps, across an infinite gulf, a leap, namely, out of the tangible world that

presses on man from every side. Belief has always had something of an adventurous break or leap about it, because in
every age it represents the risky enterprise of accepting what
plainly cannot be seen as the truly real and fundamental. Belief
was never simply the attitude automatically corresponding
to the whole slant of human life; it has always been a decision calling on the depths of existence, a decision that in
every age demanded a turnabout by man that can only be
achieved by an effort of will.

3. THE DILEMMA OF BELIEF IN THE WORLD OF TODAY

Once one has perceived the adventure essentially implicit in
the whole attitude of belief, it is impossible to avoid a second consideration, namely, that of the particularly acute difficulty in believing that affects us today. On top of the gulf
between "visible" and "invisible" there comes, to make things
harder for us, the gulf between "then" and "now". The basic
paradox already present in belief as such is rendered even
more profound by the fact that belief appears on the scene in
the garb of days gone by and, indeed, seems itself to be something old-fashioned, the mode of life and existence current
a long time ago. All attempts at modernization, whether intellectual, academic "demythologization", or ecclesiastical, pragmatic *aggiornamento*, do not alter this fact; on the contrary,
they strengthen the suspicion that a convulsive effort is being
made to proclaim as contemporary something that is, after
all, really a relic of days gone by. It is these attempts at modernization that first make us fully aware just how old-
fashioned what we are being offered really is. Belief appears
no longer as the bold but challenging leap out of the apparent all of our visible world and into the apparent void of the

invisible and intangible; it looks much more like a demand to bind oneself to yesterday and to affirm it as eternally valid. And who wants to do that in an age when the idea of "tradition" has been replaced by the idea of "progress"?

We touch here on a specific element in our present situation that is of some importance to our question. For intellectual circles in the past, the concept of "tradition" embraced a firm program; it appeared to be something protective on which man could rely; he could think himself safe and on the right lines if he could appeal to tradition. Today precisely the opposite feeling prevails: tradition appears to be what has been laid aside, the merely out-of-date, whereas progress is regarded as the real promise of life, so that man feels at home, not in the realm of tradition, of the past, but in the realm of progress and the future.[6] From this point of view, too, a belief that comes to him under the label "tradition" must appear to be something already superseded, which cannot disclose the proper sphere of his existence to a man who has recognized the future as his real obligation and opportunity. All this means that the primary stumbling block to belief, the distance between the visible and the invisible, between God and Not-God, is concealed and blocked by the secondary stumbling block of Then and Now, by the

[6] A newspaper advertisement that I read recently seems to me to typify this attitude: "You do not want to buy tradition but rational progress." In this connection it is worth drawing attention to the curious fact that in its reflections on the concept of tradition, Catholic theology has been quietly tending more and more strongly for about a century to equate tradition with progress and to reinterpret the idea of tradition into the idea of progress, by understanding tradition, not as the firmly fixed legacy of the earliest days, but as the forward-striving force of the sense of faith. Cf. J. Ratzinger, "Tradition", in LthK, 2nd ed., 10:293–99; Ratzinger, "Kommentar zur Offenbarungskonstitution", in LThK, supplementary 2:498ff. and 515–28.

antithesis between tradition and progress, by the loyalty to
yesterday that belief seems to include.

That neither the subtle intellectualism of demythologization nor the pragmatism of the *aggiornamento* can supply a convincing solution certainly makes it clear that this distortion of
the basic scandal of Christian belief is itself a very far-reaching
affair that cannot be easily settled either by theories or by action.
Indeed, in one sense it is only here that the peculiarity of the
specifically *Christian* scandal becomes visible; I refer to what
might be termed Christian positivism, the ineradicable positivity of Christianity. What I mean is this: Christian belief is
not merely concerned, as one might at first suspect from all the
talk of belief or faith, with the eternal, which as the "entirely
Other" would remain completely outside the human world and
time; on the contrary, it is much more concerned with God
in history, with God as man. By thus seeming to bridge the gulf
between eternal and temporal, between visible and invisible,
by making us meet God as a man, the eternal as the temporal,
as one of us, it understands itself as revelation. Its claim to be
revelation is indeed based on the fact that it has, so to speak,
introduced the eternal into our world: "No one has ever seen
God; the only-begotten Son, who is in the bosom of the Father,
he has made him known" (Jn 1:18)—one could almost say, in
reference to the Greek text, that it has become the "exegesis"
of God for us.[7] But let us stick to the English word; the original empowers us to take it quite literally: Jesus has really made
God known, drawn him out of himself or, as the First Epistle
of St. John puts it even more drastically, made him manifest for
us to look upon and touch, so that he whom no one has ever
seen now stands open to our historical touch.[8]

---

[7] Θεὸν οὐδεὶς ἑώρακεν πώποτε· μονογενὴς θεὸς ... ἐξηγήσατο.
[8] 1 Jn 1:1–3.

At first glance this really seems to be the maximum degree of revelation, of the disclosure of God. The leap that previously led into the infinite seems to have been reduced to something on a human scale, in that we now need only take the few steps, as it were, to that person in Galilee in whom God himself comes to meet us. But things are curiously double-sided: what at first seems to be the most radical revelation and to a certain degree does indeed always remain revelation, *the* revelation, is at the same moment the cause of the most extreme obscurity and concealment. The very thing that at first seems to bring God quite close to us, so that we can touch him as a fellow man, follow his footsteps and measure them precisely, also becomes in a very profound sense the precondition for the "death of God", which henceforth puts an ineradicable stamp on the course of history and the human relationship with God. God has come so near to us that we can kill him and that he thereby, so it seems, ceases to be God for us. Thus today we stand somewhat baffled before this Christian "revelation" and wonder, especially when we compare it with the religiosity of Asia, whether it would not have been much simpler to believe in the Mysterious Eternal, entrusting ourselves to it in longing thought; whether God would not have done better, so to speak, to leave us at an infinite distance; whether it would not really be easier to ascend out of the world and hear the eternally unfathomable secret in quiet contemplation than to give oneself up to the positivism of belief in one single figure and to set the salvation of man and of the world on the pinpoint, so to speak, of this one chance moment in history. Surely a God thus narrowed down to one point is bound to die definitively in a view of the world that remorselessly reduces man and his history to a tiny grain of dust in the cosmos, that can see itself as the center of the universe only in the naïve years of its childhood and now, grown out of childhood, ought finally to have the courage to awake from sleep, rub its eyes, shake off that beautiful but foolish dream, and take its place unquestioningly in the huge context in which our tiny lives have their proper function, lives that should find new meaning precisely by accepting their diminutiveness?

It is only by putting the question in a pointed form like this and so coming to see that behind the apparently secondary stumbling block of "then" and "now" lies the much deeper difficulty of Christian "positivism", the "limitation" of God to one point in history, that we can plumb the full depths of the question of Christian belief as it must be answered today. Can we still believe at all? Or rather—for the question must be posed in a more radical fashion—is it still permissible to believe? Have we not a duty to break with the dream and to face reality? The Christian of today must ask himself this question; he is not at liberty to remain satisfied with finding out that by all kinds of twists and turns an interpretation of Christianity can still be found that no longer offends anybody. When some theologian explains that "the resurrection of the dead" simply means that one must cheerfully set about the work of the future afresh every day, offense is certainly avoided. But are we then really still being honest? Is there not serious dishonesty in seeking to maintain Christianity as a viable proposition by such artifices of interpretation? Have we not much rather the duty, when we feel forced to take refuge in solutions of this sort, to admit that we have reached the end of the road? Are we not then bound to emerge from the fog and to face straightforwardly the abiding reality? Let us be quite plain about it: An "interpreted" Christianity of this kind that has lost all contact with reality implies a lack of sincerity in dealing with the questions of the non-Christian, whose "perhaps not" should worry us as seriously as we want the Christian "perhaps" to worry him.

If we try like this to accept the interrogation of the other side as the everlasting self-questioning of our own being, which cannot be reduced to a treatise and afterward laid aside, then, on the other hand, we shall have the right to observe that here a counterquestion arises. We are inclined today as a matter of course to suppose that only what is palpably present, what is "demonstrable", is truly real. But is it really permissible to do this? Should we not ask rather more carefully what "the real" actually is? Is it only the ascertained and ascertainable, or is ascertaining perhaps only one particular method of making contact with reality, one that can by no means comprehend the whole of reality and that even leads to falsification of the truth and of human existence if we assume that it is the only definitive method? By asking this question we are brought back once again to the dilemma of "then" and "now" and at any rate confronted with the specific problem of our "now". Let us try to discern its essential elements somewhat more clearly.

4. THE BOUNDARY OF THE MODERN UNDERSTANDING OF REALITY AND THE PLACE OF BELIEF

If by means of the historical knowledge we enjoy today we survey the road taken by the human spirit so far as it is visible to us, we shall observe that in the various periods of this spirit's development there are various basic attitudes toward reality—the magical, the metaphysical, and finally today the scientific ("scientific" here being used in the sense in which we speak of the natural sciences). Each of these basic human orientations has to do in its own way with belief, and each

of them is also in its own way an obstacle to it. None of
them is equivalent to it, but none of them is simply neutral
toward it, either; each of them can help it, and each of them
can hinder it. Characteristic of our contemporary scientific
attitude, which molds, whether we like it or not, every single individual's feeling for life and shows us our place in reality, is the limitation to "phenomena", to what is evident and
can be grasped. We have given up seeking the hidden "in-
itselfness" of things and sounding the nature of being itself;
such activities seem to us to be a fruitless enterprise; we have
come to regard the depths of being as, in the last analysis,
unfathomable. We have limited ourselves to our own perspective, to the visible in the widest sense, to what can be
seized in our measuring grasp. The methodology of natural
science is based on this restriction to phenomena. It suffices
us. We can deal with it and thus create for ourselves a world
in which we can live as men. As a result, a new concept of
truth and reality has gradually developed in modern thinking and living, a concept that holds sway, for the most part
unconsciously, as the assumption on which we think and speak
and that can only be overcome if it, too, is exposed to the
test of consciousness. At this point the function of nonsci-
entific thinking becomes perceptible, that of considering the
unconsidered and bringing the human problems it raises before
the gaze of consciousness.

a. The first stage: The birth of the historical approach

If we try to understand how the attitude just described arose,
we shall be able to distinguish, unless I am mistaken, two
stages in the intellectual revolution. The first, for which the
way was prepared by Descartes, attained its full development
in Kant and, even before that, in a somewhat different

intellectual context, in the Italian philosopher Giambattista Vico (1668–1744), who was almost certainly the first to formulate a completely new idea of truth and knowledge and who, in a piece of bold anticipation, coined the typical formula of the modern spirit when it comes to dealing with the question of truth and reality. Against the Scholastic equation *verum est ens* (being is truth) he advances his own formula, *verum quia factum*. That is to say, all that we can truly know is what we have made ourselves. It seems to me that this formula denotes the real end of the old metaphysics and the beginning of the specifically modern attitude of mind. The revolutionary character of modern thinking in comparison with all that preceded it is here expressed with absolutely inimitable precision. For the ancient world and the Middle Ages, being itself is true, in other words, apprehensible, because God, pure intellect, made it, and he made it by thinking it. To the creative original spirit, the *Creator Spiritus*, thinking and making are one and the same thing. His thinking is a creative process. Things are, because they are thought. In the ancient and medieval view, all being is, therefore, what has been thought, the thought of the absolute spirit. Conversely, this means that since all being is thought, all being is meaningful, *logos*, truth.[9] It follows from this traditional view that human thinking is the rethinking of being itself, rethinking of the thought that is being itself. Man can rethink the *logos*, the meaning of being, because his own *logos*, his own reason, is *logos* of the one *logos*, thought of the original thought, of the creative spirit that permeates and governs his being.

[9] This statement is of course only fully true of Christian thinking, which with the idea of the *creatio ex nihilo* attributes to God the material, too; for the ancient world, this remained the a-logical element, the universal matter alien to the divine, thus also marking the limit to which reality could be comprehended.

In contrast to this, from the point of view of the ancient world and the Middle Ages, the work of man seems contingent and transitory. Being is thought and therefore thinkable, the object of thought and of the science that strives after wisdom. The work of man, on the other hand, is a mixture of *logos* and the a-logical, something, moreover, that with the passage of time sinks away into the past. It does not admit of full comprehension, for it is lacking in presence, the prerequisite for being looked at, and it is lacking in *logos*, in thoroughgoing meaningfulness. For this reason ancient and medieval philosophy took the view that knowledge of human things could only be *techne*, manual skill, but never real cognition and, hence, never real science. Therefore in the medieval university the *artes*, the arts, remained only the first step to real science, which reflects on being itself. This standpoint is still clearly evident at the beginning of the modern era in Descartes, who expressly disputes history's claim to be science. The historian, he says, who claims to be familiar with Roman history knows in the last analysis less about it than a cook in Rome did, and to understand Latin means no more than possessing the same ability as Cicero's maid. About a hundred years later, Vico was to turn the Middle Ages' criterion of truth, redefined once again here in Descartes, on its head, thus giving expression to the fundamental revolution that marks the arrival of the modern spirit. This was the start of the attitude that introduces the "scientific" age, in which we are still living.[10]

Let us try to think about this a little further, since it is fundamental to our question. To Descartes the only thing

[10] For the historical background, see the survey in K. Löwith, *Weltgeschichte und Heilsgeschehen*, 3rd ed. (Stuttgart, 1953), pp. 109–28, and also N. Schiffer's book *Anfragen der Physik an die Theologie* (Düsseldorf, 1968).

that seems an absolute certainty is the purely formal intellectual certainty purged of the uncertainties of the factual. Nevertheless there are signs of the approach of the modern period in the fact that he models this intellectual certainty on mathematical certainty and elevates mathematics to the position of prototype of all rational thinking.[11] But whereas here the facts still have to be bracketed off if one desires certainty, Vico advances the diametrically opposite thesis. Following formally in Aristotle's footsteps, he asserts that real knowledge is the knowledge of causes. I am familiar with a thing if I know the cause of it; I understand something that has been proved if I know the proof. But from this old thought something completely new is deduced: If part of real knowledge is the knowledge of causes, then we can truly know only what we have made ourselves, for it is only ourselves that we are familiar with. This means that the old equation of truth and being is replaced by the new one of truth and factuality; all that can be known is the *factum*, that which we have made ourselves. It is not the task of the human mind— nor is it within its capacity—to think about being; rather, it is to think about the *factum*, what has been made, man's own particular world, for this is all we can truly understand. Man did not produce the cosmos, and its bottommost depths remain opaque to him. Complete, demonstrable knowledge is attainable only within the bounds of mathematics and in the field of history, which is the realm of man's own activities and can therefore be known by him. In the midst of the sea of doubt that threatened to engulf man at the beginning of the modern period after the collapse of the old metaphysics, the *factum* was here discovered as the dry land on which man could try to build a new existence for himself. The

[11] Schiffers, *Anfragen.*

dominance of the fact began, that is, man's complete devotion to his own work as the only certainty.

With this is connected that revaluation of all values that
made subsequent history really a "new" age as compared
with the old one. History, previously despised and regarded
as unscientific, now remained, alongside mathematics, the
only true science left. That which alone had hitherto seemed
worthy of the free mind, thinking about the meaning of
being, now seemed an idle and aimless enterprise offering
no hope of attaining genuine knowledge. Thus mathematics and history now became the dominant disciplines; indeed,
history devoured, so to speak, the whole world of learning
and transformed it all fundamentally. Through Hegel, and
in a different way through Comte, philosophy became a
historical question, in which being itself is to be understood as a historical process. With F. C. Baur, theology turned
into history, and its path became that of rigorous historical
research, which asks what happened in the past and thereby
hopes to reach the bottom of the matter. With Marx, economics was given a historical slant. Indeed, even the natural sciences were affected by this general tendency toward
history: with Darwin, the classification of living beings was
understood as a history of life; the constancy of what stays
as it was created was replaced by a line of descent in which
all things came from one another and could be traced back
to one another.[12] Thus the world finally appeared no longer as the firm housing of being but as a process whose
continual expansion is the movement of being itself. This
meant that henceforth the world was only knowable insofar

---

[12] K. Löwith, *Weltgeschichte*, p. 38. On the complete change in the middle
of the nineteenth century, see also the informative investigation by J. Dör-
mann, "War J. J. Bachofen Evolutionist?" *Anthropos* 60 (1965): 1–48.

as it was something made by man. In the last analysis man was no longer in a position to look beyond himself except on the level of the fact, where he had to recognize himself as the chance product of age-old developments. This now produced a very curious situation. At the very moment when radical anthropocentrism set in and man could know only his own work, he had to learn to accept himself as merely a chance occurrence, just another "fact". Here, too, the heaven from which he seemed to come was torn down, so to speak, and he was left with just the earth and its facts in his hands—the earth in which he now sought with the spade to decipher the laborious history of his development.

b. The second stage: The turn toward technical thinking

Verum quia factum: this program that directs man to history as the receptacle of truth could not suffice, it is true, in itself. It only became fully effective when it was allied to a second principle, which, again a good hundred years later, Karl Marx formulated in his classical statement: "So far philosophers have merely interpreted the world in various ways; it is necessary to change it." With this the task of philosophy was once again fundamentally redefined. Translated into the language of the philosophical tradition, this maxim meant that *verum quia factum*—what is knowable, tending toward truth, is what man has made and what he can now contemplate—was replaced by the new program *verum quia faciendum*—the truth with which we are now concerned is feasibility. To put it again in another way: The truth with which man is concerned is neither the truth of being, nor even in the last resort that of his accomplished deeds, but the truth of changing the world, molding the world—a truth centered on future and action.

Verum quia faciendum—this means that the dominance of the fact since the middle of the nineteenth century is being succeeded to an increasing degree by the dominance of the *faciendum*, of what can and must be done, and that consequently the dominance of history is being supplanted by that of *techne*. For the farther man advances along the new way of concentrating on the fact and seeking certainty in it, the more he also has to recognize that even the fact, his own work, largely eludes him. The verifiability for which the historian strives, and which appeared at first in the nineteenth century to be the great triumph of history as opposed to speculation, always retains something disputable about it, an element of reconstruction, of interpretation and ambiguity, so that, as early as the beginning of the twentieth century, history reached a crisis and the historical approach with its proud claim to knowledge became open to question. It grew clearer and clearer that there is no such thing as the pure fact and its unshakable certainty, that even the fact is subject to interpretation and the ambiguity this implies. It became less and less possible for people not to admit to themselves that once again they did not hold in their hands the certainty they had at first promised themselves when they turned away from speculation to investigation of the facts.

So the conviction was bound to spread more and more that in the final analysis all that man could really know was what was repeatable, what he could put before his eyes at any time in an experiment. Everything that he can see only at secondhand remains the past and, whatever proofs may be adduced, is not completely knowable. Thus the scientific method, which consists of a combination of mathematics (Descartes!) and devotion to the facts in the form of the repeatable experiment, appears to be the one real vehicle of reliable certainty. The combination of mathematical thinking and factual thinking has produced the science-orientated intellectual standpoint of modern man, which signifies devotion to reality insofar as it is capable of being shaped.[13] The fact has set free the *faciendum*, the "made" has set free the "makable", the repeatable, the provable, and only exists for the sake of the latter. It comes to the primacy of the "makable" over the "made", for in fact what can man do with what has merely existed in the past? He cannot find his real purpose in making himself into the museum attendant of his own past if he wants to master his own contemporary situation.

Like history before it, *techne* now ceases to be a subordinate, preliminary stage in the intellectual development of man, even if to a decidedly arts-oriented mentality it still retains a certain hint of barbarity. The structure of the general intellectual situation has been fundamentally altered: *techne* is no longer banished to the "House of Commons" of learning, or, to be more accurate, here, too, the House of Commons has become the decisive element in the constitution; in comparison with it the "House of Lords" now seems only a collection of aristocratic pensioners. *Techne* has become the real potential and obligation of man. What was previously at the bottom is now on top. Simultaneously the perspective is changing once again: at first, in ancient and medieval times, man had concentrated on the eternal, then, during the short-lived predominance of the historical approach, on the past; but now the *faciendum*, the "makable" aspect of things, directs his attention to the future of what he himself can create. If before, perhaps through the conclusions implicit in the doctrine of the origin of species, he might have resignedly noted

[13] Cf. H. Freyer, *Theorie des gegenwärtigen Zeitalters* (Stuttgart, 1958), especially pp. 15–78.

that so far as his past was concerned he was just earth, a mere chance development, if he was disillusioned by such knowledge and felt degraded, he does not need to be disturbed by this any longer, for now, wherever he comes from, he can look his future in the eye with the determination to make himself into whatever he wishes; he does not need to regard it as impossible to make himself into the God who now stands at the end as *faciendum*, as something makable, not at the beginning, as *logos*, meaning. This is already working itself out concretely today in the form of the anthropological approach. What already seems more important than the theory of evolution, which for practical purposes already lies behind us as something self-evident, is cybernetics, the "planability" of the newly to be created man, so that theologically, too, the manipulation of man by his own planning is beginning to represent a more important problem than the question of man's past—although the two questions cannot be separated from each other and in their general tendency largely govern each other reciprocally: the reduction of man to a "fact" is the precondition for understanding him as a *faciendum*, which is to be led out of its own resources into a new future.

c. The question of the place of belief

When the modern mind took this second step, when it turned to the idea of "makability", it simultaneously wrecked theology's first attempt to come to terms with the new situation. For theology had sought to meet the problem of the historical approach, its reduction of truth to facts, by presenting belief itself as history. At first sight it could be perfectly content with this turn of events. After all, so far as its content is concerned, Christian belief is essentially centered on history; the statements of the Bible are not metaphysical but factual in character. So on the face of it, when the hour of metaphysics was succeeded by that of history, theology could only agree; for this seemed to mean at the same time that its own hour had at last struck. Perhaps, indeed, it might even be permissible to put down this whole new development as a product of its own point of departure.

The progressive dethronement of history by *techne* has swiftly killed these hopes again. Instead another idea is now in the air—people feel tempted to shift belief away from the plane of the fact onto that of the *faciendum* and to expound it by means of a "political theology" as a medium for changing the world.[14] I think myself that this is only doing again in the present situation what "history of salvation" thinking attempted one-sidedly to do in the situation created by the historical approach. People see that the world of today is governed by the notion of the "makable" and respond by transposing belief itself to this plane. Now I should not want to dismiss these two attempts as senseless. That would certainly not be just to them. On the contrary, both bring to light essential factors that in other contexts had been more or less overlooked. Christian belief really is concerned with the *factum;* it lives in a specific way on the plane of history, and it is no accident that history and the historical approach grew up precisely in the atmosphere of Christian belief. And indubitably belief also has something

[14] Characteristic of this attitude is the book by H. Cox mentioned in footnote 1, and also the "theology of revolution" that has been coming into fashion recently; cf. T. Rendtorff and H. E. Tödt, *Theologie der Revolution, Analysen und Materialen* (Frankfurt, 1968). There is also a tendency in this direction in J. Moltmann, *Theologie der Hoffnung*, 5th ed. (Munich, 1966), and in J. B. Metz, *Zur Theologie der Welt* (Mainz and Munich, 1968).

to do with changing the world, with shaping the world, with the protest against the lethargy of human institutions and of those who profit from them. Again, it is hardly an accident that the comprehension of the world as something to be "made" grew up in the atmosphere of the Christian-Jewish tradition and was conceived and formulated precisely in Marx out of the inspiration provided by it, albeit as an antithesis to it. To this extent it is indisputable that both approaches brought to light aspects of the real meaning of Christian belief that had previously remained only too well hidden. Christian belief has a decisive connection with the motivational forces of the modern age. It is in fact the great opportunity of our historical moment that we can gain from it a completely new understanding of the position of faith between fact and *faciendum;* it is the task of theology to accept this challenge, to make use of this possibility, and to find and fill the blind spots of past periods.

But it is just as wrong here to jump to conclusions as it is to pass swift judgment. When either of the two approaches described above is adopted exclusively and belief is consigned wholly to the plane of the fact or of "makability", in the end this only conceals what it really means when a man says "*Credo*"—"I believe". For when he says this, he is not primarily enunciating a program for changing the world or simply attaching himself to a chain of historical events. By way of an attempt to shed some light on what really is involved I should like to suggest that the act of believing does not belong to the relationship "know-make", which is typical of the intellectual context of "makability" thinking, but is much better expressed in the quite different relationship "stand-understand". It seems to me that here we can discern two general conceptions and possibilities of human existence that, though not unconnected

with each other, must nevertheless be distinguished from
each other.

5. FAITH AS STANDING FIRM AND UNDERSTANDING

In contrasting the two pairs of concepts stand–understand
and know–make, I am alluding to a basic biblical statement
about belief that is ultimately untranslatable. Luther tried to
capture the profundity of this statement's play on words when
he coined the formula, "If you do not believe, then you do
not abide." A more literal translation would be, "If you do
not believe [if you do not *hold* firm to Yahweh], then you
will have no *foothold*" (Is 7:9). The *one* root word *'mn* (amen)
embraces a variety of meanings whose interplay and differentiation go to make up the subtle grandeur of this sentence.
It includes the meanings truth, firmness, firm ground, ground,
and furthermore the meanings loyalty, to trust, entrust oneself, take one's stand on something, believe in something;
thus faith in God appears as a holding on to God through
which man gains a firm foothold for his life. Faith is thereby
defined as taking up a position, as taking a stand trustfully on
the ground of the word of God. The Greek translation of
the Old Testament (the so-called Septuagint) transferred the
above-mentioned sentence onto Greek soil not only linguistically but also conceptually by formulating it as "If you do
not believe, then you do not understand, either." It has often
been said that this translation is in itself a typical example of
the process of Hellenization, of the way in which the Septuagint is less "biblical" than the Hebrew text. Belief, so it is
said, became intellectualized; instead of expressing the notion
of standing on the firm ground of the reliable word of God,
it is now linked with understanding and reason and thus

removed to a quite different and completely inappropriate plane. There may be some truth in this. Nevertheless, I think that on the whole the essential meaning is preserved, even if the imagery is different. Standing, as presented in the Hebrew as the content of belief, certainly has something to do with understanding. We shall have to think further about this in a moment. For the time being we can simply take up the thread of our earlier reflections and say that belief operates on a completely different plane from that of making and "makability". Essentially, it is entrusting oneself to that which has not been made by oneself and never could be made and which precisely in this way supports and makes possible all our making. But this also means that on the plane of practical knowledge, on the plane of *verum quia factum seu faciendum*, it neither occurs nor ever could occur and be discovered and that any attempt to "lay it on the table", to demonstrate it as one would a piece of practical knowledge, is doomed to failure. It is not to be met in the context of this kind of knowledge, and anyone who nevertheless "lays it on the table" has laid something false on the table. The penetrating "perhaps" that belief whispers in man's ear in every place and in every age does not point to any uncertainty *within* the realm of practical knowledge; it simply queries the absoluteness of this realm and relativizes it, reminding man that it is only *one* plane of human existence and of existence in general, a plane that can only have the character of something less than final. In other words, we have now reached a point in our reflections where it becomes evident that there are *two* basic forms of human attitude or reaction to reality, neither of which can be traced back to the other because they operate on completely different planes.

It is perhaps permissible here to draw attention to a distinction made by Martin Heidegger, who speaks of the duality of calculating and reflective thought. Both modes of thought are legitimate and necessary, but for this very reason neither can be absorbed in the other. There must therefore be both: calculating thought, which is concerned with "makability", and reflective thought, which is concerned with meaning. And one cannot deny that the Freiburg philosopher has a good deal of justification for expressing the fear that in an age in which calculating thought is celebrating the most amazing triumphs man is nevertheless threatened, perhaps more than ever before, by thoughtlessness, by the flight from thought. By thinking only of the practicable, of what can be made, he is in danger of forgetting to reflect on himself and on the meaning of his existence. Of course, this temptation is present in every age. Thus in the thirteenth century the great Franciscan theologian Bonaventure felt obliged to reproach his colleagues of the philosophical faculty at Paris with having learned how to measure the world but having forgotten how to measure themselves. Let us repeat the same thing once again in another form: Belief in the sense intended by the Creed is not an incomplete kind of knowledge, an opinion that subsequently can or should be converted into practical knowledge. It is much rather an essentially different kind of intellectual attitude, which stands alongside practical knowledge as something independent and particular and cannot be traced back to it or deduced from it. Belief is ordered, not to the realm of what can be or has been made, although it is concerned with both, but to the realm of basic decisions that man cannot avoid making, in *one* form. This form we call belief. It seems to me indispensable that this should be seen quite clearly: every man must adopt some kind of attitude toward the realm of basic decisions, decisions that, by their very nature, can only be made by entertaining belief. There is a realm that allows no other response but that of entertaining a belief, and no man can completely avoid this realm. Every man is bound to have some kind of "belief".

The most impressive attempt so far to incorporate the attitude of "belief" into the attitude of practical knowledge is to be found in Marxism. For here the *faciendum*, the future that we ourselves are to create, simultaneously represents the purpose or meaning of man, so that the bestowal of meaning, which in itself is accomplished or assumed in belief, seems to be transposed onto the plane of what can be made. Thereby the logical outcome of modern thinking is unquestionably reached: it looks as if a successful effort has been made to absorb the meaning of man completely into the practicable, to equate one with the other. However, if one looks more closely, it becomes clear that not even Marxism has succeeded in squaring the circle. For not even Marxism can turn the idea of the "makable" as the purpose of life into something that can be known; it can only promise that such is the case and leave the decision to belief. What makes this Marxist belief seem so attractive today and so immediately accessible is the impression it evokes of harmony with practical knowledge.

Let us return after this little detour to ask once again and more comprehensively: What is belief really? We can now reply like this: It is a human way of taking up a stand in the totality of reality, a way that cannot be reduced to knowledge and is incommensurable with knowledge; it is the bestowal of meaning without which the totality of man would remain homeless, on which man's calculations and actions are based, and without which in the last resort he could not calculate and act, because he can only do this in the context of a meaning that bears him up. For in fact man does not live on the bread of practicability alone; he lives as *man* and, precisely in the intrinsically human part of his being, on the word, on love, on meaning. Meaning is the bread on which man, in the intrinsically human part of his being, subsists. Without the word, without meaning, without love he falls into the situation of no longer being able to live, even when earthly comfort is present in abundance. Everyone knows how sharply this situation of "not being able to go on any more" can arise in the midst of outward abundance. But meaning is not derived from knowledge. To try to manufacture it in this way, that is, out of the provable knowledge of what can be made, would resemble Baron Munchhausen's absurd attempt to pull himself up out of the bog by his own hair. I believe that the absurdity of this story mirrors very accurately the basic situation of man. No one can pull himself up out of the bog of uncertainty, of not being able to live, by his own exertions; nor can we pull ourselves up, as Descartes still thought we could, by a *cogito ergo sum*, by a series of intellectual deductions. Meaning that is self-made is in the last analysis no meaning. Meaning, that is, the ground on which our existence as a totality can stand and live, cannot be made but only received.

Thus, starting from a quite general analysis of the basic attitude of "belief", we have arrived directly at the Christian mode of belief. For to believe as a Christian means in fact entrusting oneself to the meaning that upholds me and the world; taking it as the firm ground on which I can stand fearlessly. Using rather more traditional language, we could say that to believe as a Christian means understanding our existence as a response to the word, the *logos*, that upholds and maintains all things. It means affirming that the meaning we do not make but can only receive is already granted to us, so that we have only to take it and entrust ourselves to it. Correspondingly, Christian belief is the option for the view that the receiving precedes the making—though this does not mean that making is reduced in value or proclaimed to be superfluous. It is only because we have received that we can also "make". And further: Christian belief—as we have already said—means opting for the view that what cannot be seen is more real than what can be seen. It is an avowal of the primacy of the invisible as the truly real, which upholds us and hence enables us to face the visible with calm composure—knowing that we are responsible before the invisible as the true ground of all things. To that extent it is undeniable that Christian belief is a double affront to the attitude that the present world situation seems to force us to adopt. In the shape of positivism and phenomenalism it invites us to confine ourselves to the "visible", the "apparent", in the widest sense of the terms; to extend the basic methodology to which natural science is indebted for its successes to the totality of our relationship with reality. Again, in the shape of *techne* it calls upon us to rely on the "makable" and to expect to find in this the ground that upholds us. The primacy of the invisible over the visible and that of receiving over making run directly counter to this basic situation. No doubt that is why it is so difficult for us today to make the leap of entrusting ourselves to what cannot be seen. Yet the freedom of making, like that of enlisting the visible in our service by means of methodical investigation, is in the last analysis only made possible by the provisional character that Christian belief assigns to both and by the superiority it has thus revealed.

6. THE RATIONALITY OF FAITH

If one ponders all this, one will note how closely the first and last words of the Creed—"I believe" and "Amen"—chime in with one another, encircling the totality of individual assertions and thus providing the inner space for all that lies between. In the harmony of "*Credo*" and "Amen" the meaning of the whole becomes visible, the intellectual movement that it is all about. We noted earlier that the word "Amen" belongs in Hebrew to the root from which the word "belief" is also derived. Thus "Amen" simply says once again in its own way what belief means: the trustful placing of myself on a ground that upholds me, not because I have made it and checked it by my own calculations but, rather, precisely because I have not made it and cannot check it. It expresses the abandonment of oneself to what we can neither make nor need to make, to the ground of the world as meaning, which first of all discloses to me the freedom to make.

Yet what happens here is not a blind surrender to the irrational. On the contrary, it is a movement toward the *logos*, the *ratio*, toward meaning and so toward truth itself, for in the final analysis the ground on which man takes his stand cannot possibly be anything else but the truth revealing itself. At this point, where we might least expect it, we stumble yet again on one last antithesis between practical knowledge and belief. Practical knowledge must—as we have already seen—by its own intrinsic aim be positivistic; it must be confined to what is given and can be measured. But the consequence of this is that it no longer inquires after truth. It achieves its successes precisely by renouncing the quest for truth itself and by directing its attention to the "rightness", the "soundness" of the system whose hypothetical design must prove itself in the functioning of the experiment. In other words, practical knowledge does not inquire what things are like on their own and *in themselves*, but only whether they will function *for us*. The turn toward practical knowledge was accomplished precisely by contemplating, no longer being in itself, but only how it functioned with regard to our own work. This means that, in the separation of the question of truth from being and in its shifting to the fact and the *faciendum*, the very concept of truth was itself fundamentally altered. The notion of the truth of being in itself has been replaced by that of the utility of things for us, which is confirmed by the rightness of the results. What is pertinent and irrevocable about this is that only this rightness is vouchsafed to us as something that can be calculated; the truth of being itself eludes knowledge of the calculating variety.

The Christian attitude of belief is expressed in the little word "Amen", in which the meanings trust, entrust, fidelity, firmness, firm ground, stand, truth all interpenetrate each other; this means that the thing on which man can finally take his stand and that can give him meaning can only be truth itself. Truth is the only ground suitable for man to stand upon. Thus the Christian act of faith intrinsically includes the conviction that the meaningful ground, the *logos*, on which we take our stand, precisely because it is meaning, is also truth.[15] Meaning or sense that was not truth would be nonsense. The indivisibility of meaning, ground, and truth that is expressed both in the Hebrew word "Amen" and in the Greek *logos* at the same time intimates a whole view of the world. The way—for us inimitable—in which words such as these embrace the indivisibility of meaning, ground, and truth throws into relief the whole network of coordinates by which Christian faith surveys the world and takes up its position in relation to it. But this also means that in its original nature belief or faith is no blind collection of incomprehensible paradoxes. It means, furthermore, that it is nonsense to

[15] The Greek word *logos* displays in its range of meanings a certain correspondence with the Hebrew root *'mn* ("Amen"): word, meaning, rationality, truth are all included in its semantic range.

plead the "mystery", as people certainly do only too often, by way of an excuse for the failure of reason. If theology arrives at all kinds of absurdities and tries, not only to excuse them, but even where possible to canonize them by pointing to the mystery, then we are confronted with a misuse of the true idea of "mystery", the purpose of which is not to destroy reason but rather to render belief possible *as* understanding. In other words, it is certainly true that belief or faith is not knowledge in the sense of practical knowledge and its particular kind of calculability. It can never become that, and in the last analysis it can only make itself ridiculous if it tries to establish itself in those forms. But the reverse is also true: calculable practical knowledge is limited by its very nature to the apparent, to what functions, and does not represent the way in which to find truth itself, which by its very method it has renounced. The tool with which man is equipped to deal with the truth of being is not *knowledge* but *understanding:* understanding of the meaning to which he has entrusted himself. And we must certainly add that "understanding" only reveals itself in "standing", not apart from it. One cannot occur without the other, for understanding means seizing and grasping as *meaning* the meaning that man has received as *ground*. I think this is the precise significance of what we mean by understanding: that we learn to grasp the ground on which we have taken our stand as meaning and truth; that we learn to perceive that *ground* represents *meaning*.

If this is so, understanding not only implies no contradiction with belief but represents its most intrinsic property. For knowledge of the functional aspect of the world, as procured for us so splendidly by present-day technical and scientific thinking, brings with it no understanding of the world and of being. Understanding grows only out of belief. That is why theology as the understanding, *logos-like* (= rational,

understanding through reason) discussion of God is a fundamental task of Christian faith. This context is also the basis
of the inalienable right of Greek thought to a place in Christianity. I am convinced that at bottom it was no mere accident that the Christian message, in the period when it was
taking shape, first entered the Greek world and there merged
with the inquiry into understanding, into truth.[16] Believing
and understanding belong together no less than believing
and "standing", simply because standing and understanding
are inseparable. To this extent the Greek translation of the
sentence in Isaiah about believing and abiding reveals a dimension that is implicit in the biblical attitude itself if it is not to
be degraded into fanaticism, sectarianism.

To be sure, it is a characteristic of understanding that it
continually goes beyond our mere ability to *apprehend* and
attains the awareness of the fact that we are comprehended.
But if understanding is the apprehension of the fact that
we are comprehended, then that means that we cannot yet
comprehend that fact once again [in a second moment of
understanding]; it furnishes us with meaning precisely because
it comprehends *us*. In *this* sense we can rightly speak of
mystery as the ground that precedes us and always and ever
goes beyond us, which can never be caught up or overtaken.
But precisely in being comprehended by that which is not
apprehended a second time, understanding's responsibility is

---

[16] In this connection one can point to the significant passage in Acts (16:6–
10) in which the Holy Spirit forbids Paul "to speak the word in Asia" and the
Spirit of Jesus does not allow him to go into Bithynia; and there is the vision
with the Macedonian saying, "Come over to Macedonia and help us." This
mysterious text might well represent something like a first attempt at a "theology of history", intended to underline the crossing of the gospel to Europe,
"to the Greeks", as a divinely arranged necessity. Cf. also on this E. Peterson,
"Die Kirche", in *Theologische Traktate* (Munich, 1951), pp. 409–29.

fulfilled, a responsibility without which belief would be undig-
nified and bound in the end to destroy itself.

7. "I BELIEVE IN YOU"

In all that has been said so far the most fundamental feature
of Christian faith or belief has still not been specified; namely,
its personal character. Christian faith is more than the option
in favor of a spiritual ground to the world; its central formula is not "I believe in something", but "I believe in you." [17]
It is the encounter with the man Jesus, and in this encounter
it experiences the meaning of the world as a person. In Jesus'
life from the Father, in the immediacy and intensity of his
converse with him in prayer and, indeed, face to face, he is
God's witness, through whom the intangible has become tangible, the distant has drawn near. And further: he is not simply the witness whose evidence we trust when he tells us
what he has seen in an existence that had really made the
complete about-turn from a false contentment with the foreground of life to the depths of the whole truth; he is the
presence of the eternal itself in this world. In his life, in the
unconditional devotion of himself to men, the meaning of
the world is present before us; it vouchsafes itself to us as
love that loves even me and makes life worth living by this
incomprehensible gift of a love free from any threat of fading
away or any tinge of egoism. The meaning of the world is
the "you", though only the one that is not itself an open

[17] Cf. H. Fries, *Glauben-Wissen* (Berlin, 1960), especially pp. 84–95; J. Mour-
oux, *Ich glaube an dich* (Einsiedeln, 1951); C. Cirne-Lima, *Der personale Glaube*
(Innsbruck, 1959).

question but rather the ground of all, which needs no other ground.

Thus faith is the finding of a "you" that upholds me and amid all the unfulfilled—and in the last resort unfulfillable—hope of human encounters gives me the promise of an indestructible love that not only longs for eternity but also guarantees it. Christian faith lives on the discovery that not only is there such a thing as objective meaning but that this meaning knows me and loves me, that I can entrust myself to it like the child who knows that everything he may be wondering about is safe in the "you" of his mother. Thus in the last analysis believing, trusting, and loving are one, and all the theses around which belief revolves are only concrete expressions of the all-embracing about-turn, of the assertion "I believe in you"—of the discovery of God in the countenance of the man Jesus of Nazareth.

Of course, this does not do away with the need for reflection, as we have already seen earlier. "Are you really he?" This question was asked anxiously in a dark hour even by John the Baptist, the prophet who had directed his own disciples to the rabbi from Nazareth and recognized him as the greater, for whom he could only prepare the way. Are you really he? The believer will repeatedly experience the darkness in which the contradiction of unbelief surrounds him like a gloomy prison from which there is no escape, and the indifference of the world, which goes its way unchanged as if nothing had happened, seems only to mock his hope. We have to pose the question, "Are you really he?", not only out of intellectual honesty and because of reason's responsibility, but also in accordance with the interior law of love, which wants to know more and more him to whom it has given its Yes, so as to be able to love him more. Are you really he? Ultimately, all the reflections contained in this book are subordinate to this question and thus revolve around the basic form of the confession: "I believe in you, Jesus of Nazareth, as the meaning (*logos*) of the world and of my life."

Chapter 2

THE ECCLESIASTICAL FORM OF FAITH

1. INTRODUCTORY REMARKS ON THE HISTORY
AND STRUCTURE OF THE APOSTLES' CREED[1]

All that we have said so far has done no more than attempt to answer the formal question of what belief as such is and where in the world of modern thought it can find a starting point and a function to perform. The more far-reaching problems relating to its content thus necessarily remained open— with the whole subject perhaps looking only too pale and ill-defined. The answers can only be found by looking at the concrete shape of Christian belief, and this we now mean to consider, using the so-called Apostles' Creed as a guiding thread. It may be useful to preface the discussion with a few facts about the origin and structure of the Creed; these will at the same time throw some light on the legitimacy of the procedure. The basic form of our profession of faith took

[1] The standard work on this subject remains F. Kattenbusch, *Das Apostolische Symbol* (vol. 1, 1894; vol. 2, 1900; unchanged reprint, Darmstadt, 1962); henceforth referred to as Kattenbusch. Other important books are: J. de Ghellinck, *Patristique et Moyen-âge*, 2nd ed., vol. 1 (Paris, 1949); the survey by J. N. D. Kelly, *Early Christian Creeds* (London, 1950); and W. Trillhaas, *Das apostolische Glaubensbekenntnis: Geschichte, Text, Auslegung* (Witten, 1953). A short summary and further literature are to be found in the patrologies; for example, B. Altaner and A. Stuiber, *Patrologie*, 7th ed. (Freiburg, 1966), pp. 85ff.; J. Quasten, *Patrology*, vol. 1 (Utrecht, 1962), pp. 23–29; see also J. N. D. Kelly, "Apostolisches Glaubensbekenntnis", in LthK, 2nd ed., 1:760ff.

shape during the course of the second and third centuries in connection with the ceremony of baptism. So far as its place of origin is concerned, the text comes from the city of Rome; but its internal origin lies in worship; more precisely, in the conferring of baptism. This again was fundamentally based on the words of the risen Christ recorded in Matthew 28:19: "Go therefore and make disciples of all nations, baptizing them in the name of the Father and of the Son and of the Holy Spirit." In accordance with this injunction, three questions are put to the person to be baptized: "Do you believe in God the Father Almighty? Do you believe in Jesus Christ, the Son of God . . . ? Do you believe in the Holy Spirit . . . ?"[2] The person being baptized replies to each of these three questions with the word "*Credo*"—I believe—and is then each time immersed in the water. Thus the oldest form of the confession of faith takes the shape of a tripartite dialogue, of question and answer, and is, moreover, embedded in the ceremony of baptism.

Probably in the course of the second century, and even more in the third, the originally quite simple tripartite formula, which simply uses the written text of Matthew 28, was expanded in the middle section, that is, the question about belief in Christ. Here, after all, the decisively Christian element was involved, and it was felt necessary to give within the framework of this question a brief summary of what Christ means for the Christian; similarly, the third question, the profession of faith in the Holy Spirit, was further clarified and developed as a confession of faith in the present and future of the Christian attitude. Then in the fourth

[2] Cf., for example, the text of the *Sacramentarium Gelasianum*, ed. Wilson, p. 86, cited in Kattenbusch 2:485, and especially the text in the *Traditio apostolica* of St. Hippolytus, ed. Botte, 2nd ed. (Münster, 1963), pp. 48ff.

century we meet a continuous text detached from the question-and-answer format; that it is still in Greek makes it probable that it dates originally from the third century, since by the fourth the final change to Latin even in the liturgy had been made in Rome. A Latin translation also appears very soon afterward in the fourth century. Because of the special position belonging to the Church of Rome in relation to the whole of the West, the Roman baptismal profession (known as the *symbolum*, symbol) was quickly able to gain currency in the whole Latin-speaking area. It is true that in the process it underwent a series of minor textual alterations, until finally Charlemagne secured the recognition of one form of the text throughout his empire, a form that—based on the old Roman text—had received its final shape in Gaul. This unified text was adopted in the city of Rome in the ninth century. From about the fifth century, possibly as early as the fourth, we come across the legend of the apostolic origin of this text. Very soon (probably still in the fifth century) this legend crystallized into the assumption that each of the twelve articles into which the whole was now divided had been contributed by one of the twelve apostles.

In the East this Roman symbol or creed remained unknown; it came as no small surprise to the Roman representatives at the ecumenical Council of Florence in the fifteenth century when they learned from the Greeks that the *symbolum* presumed to stem from the apostles was not employed by them. The East had never developed a unified symbol of this sort because no individual Church there occupied a position comparable with that of Rome in the West—as the one "apostolic see" in the Western world. The East was always characterized by the variety of its symbols, which also deviate somewhat in theological type from the Roman symbol.

The Roman creed (and with it the Western creed in general) is more concerned with the history of salvation and with Christology. It lingers, so to speak, on the positivistic side of the Christian story; it simply accepts the fact that to save us God became man; it does not seek to penetrate beyond this story to its causes and to its connection with the totality of being. The East, on the other hand, has always sought to see the Christian faith in a cosmic and metaphysical perspective, which is mirrored in professions of faith above all by the fact that Christology and belief in creation are related to each other, and thus the uniqueness of the Christian story and the everlasting, all-embracing nature of the creation come into close association. We shall return later to discuss how today this enlarged perspective is at last beginning to gain currency in the Western consciousness as well, especially as a result of stimuli from the work of Teilhard de Chardin.

2. LIMITS AND MEANING OF THE TEXT

The rough sketch of the history of the Creed I have just attempted possibly suggests a brief supplementary reflection. For this swift glance at the growth of the text is sufficient to show that this process of growth mirrors the whole tension of the first millennium of the Church's history, with all its splendor and misery. It seems to me that this, too, is a statement that has something to do with the question of Christian belief itself and makes its intellectual physiognomy perceptible. First, the Creed cuts right across all cleavages and tensions and expresses the common ground of belief in the triune God. It is an answer to the challenge that went out from Jesus of Nazareth: "Make disciples of all nations and baptize them." It is a profession of faith in him as the nearness of God, in him as the true future of man. But it also expresses already the beginning of the fateful split between East and West. The special position that belonged to Rome in the West as the administrative center of apostolic tradition and the tension that consequently arose for the Church as a whole become visible in its history. And finally in its present shape this text also expresses the politically inspired uniformity impressed on the Church in the West and thus the political alienation of belief, its utilization as a means to imperial unity. In using this text, which was promoted as the "Roman" one and, in the process, forced on Rome in this shape from outside, we find present in it the necessity for belief to break through the prison bars of political aims and to assert its own independence. Thus the fate of this text demonstrates how the answer to the call from Galilee mingles, at the moment of its entry into history, with all the human circumstances of man: with the special interests of one region, with the estrangement of those called to unity among themselves, with the tricks of the powers of this world. I think it is important to see this, for this, too, is a part of the worldly reality of believing, namely, that the bold leap into the infinite signified by it can only take place on the petty scale of everything human; that here, too, where man makes his greatest venture, so to speak, the leap over his own shadow to the meaning that bears him up, his action is not pure, noble greatness, but instead it shows him up as a divided being pitiful in his greatness, yet still great while he is pitiful. Something absolutely central becomes visible here, namely, that faith has to do, and must have to do, with forgiving; that it aims at leading man to recognize that he is a being that can only find himself in the reception and transmission of forgiveness, a being that needs forgiveness even in his best and purest moments.

When one follows up in this way the traces left behind in the text of the Creed by man and his human attributes, the doubt may well arise whether it is right to use this text as a peg on which to hang the sort of introduction to the basic content of the Christian faith aimed at in this book. Is it not to be feared that by doing so we are already moving on dubious terrain? The question must be posed, but anyone who follows it up will nevertheless be able to confirm that, in spite of its checkered history, this Creed does represent at all decisive points an accurate echo of the ancient Church's faith, which for its part is, in its kernel, the true echo of the New Testament message. The differences between East and West of which we spoke just now are in fact differences of theological emphasis, not differences of creed. It remains true, of course, that in our attempt at understanding the Creed we must take care to keep referring the whole to the New Testament and to read and interpret it in the light of the aims of the latter.

3. CREED AND DOGMA

Yet another point must also be made. When we concern ourselves here with a text whose original setting was the ceremony of baptism, we meet at the same time the original meaning of "doctrine" and "creed" in Christianity, and with them also the meaning of what was later to be called "dogma". We saw earlier that the Creed is pronounced within the framework of baptism as the triple answer to the triple question, "Do you believe in God—in Christ—in the Holy Spirit?" We can now add that it thereby represents the positive corollary to the triple renunciation that precedes it: "I renounce the devil, his service, and his works." [3]

This means that faith is located in the act of conversion, in the turn of one's being from worship of the visible and practicable to trust in the invisible. The phrase "I believe" could here be literally translated by "I hand myself over to", "I assent to". [4] In the sense of the Creed, and by origin, faith is not a recitation of doctrines, an acceptance of theories about things of which in themselves one knows nothing and therefore asserts something all the louder; it signifies an all-encompassing movement of human existence; to use Heidegger's language, one could say that it signifies an "about-turn" by the whole person that from then on constantly structures one's existence. In the procedure of the threefold renunciation and the threefold assent, linked as it is with the thrice-repeated death symbol of drowning and the thrice-repeated symbolization of resurrection to new life, the true nature of faith or belief is clearly illustrated: it is a conversion, an about-turn, a shift of being.

In this process of turning about, as which faith must consequently be understood, the I and the We, the I and the You interact in a way that expresses a whole image of man. On the one side, we have a highly personal process, whose inalienable individuality finds clear expression both in the triple "*I* believe" and in the triple "*I* renounce" that precedes it: it is *my* existence that must turn here, that is to trans-form itself. But together with this extremely personal element we also find here that the decision of the I is made

---

[3] Hippolytus, *Traditio apostolica* 46: "Renuntio tibi, Satana, et omni servitio tuo et omnibus operibus tuis."

[4] Kattenbusch 2:503.

in answer to a question, in the interplay of "Do you believe?" and "I do believe!" This original form of the symbol, which consisted at first only of the two-in-oneness of question and answer, seems to me to be a very much more accurate expression of the structure of faith than the later simplified, collective "I"-form. If we wish to feel our way toward the fundamental nature of Christian faith, it will be right to go back beyond the later, purely dogmatic texts and to regard this its first dialogue form as the most appropriate one ever created. This form is also more suited to its purpose than the We-type of creed, which (unlike our I-creed) was developed in Christian Africa and then at the big Eastern Councils.[5] The latter kind represents a new type of creed, no longer rooted in the sacramental context of the ecclesiastical ceremony of conversion, in the execution of the about-turn, and thus in the real birthplace of faith, but proceeding from the striving of the bishops assembled at the Council for the right doctrine and thus clearly becoming the first step toward the future form of dogma. All the same, it is important that these councils did not get to the point of formulating doctrinal statements; their striving for the right doctrine still takes the form of striving for a perfect ecclesiastical profession of faith and, thus, of striving for the true mode of that conversion, that about-turn, which being a Christian implies.

This could be clearly demonstrated from the dramatic struggle over the question, "Who is, who was Christ?" which shook the Church in the fourth and fifth centuries. This striving was not concerned with metaphysical speculations; such things could not have shaken those two centuries down

---

[5] Cf. A. Hahn, *Bibliothek der Symbole und Glaubensregeln der Alten Kirche*, 3rd ed. (1897; repr., Hildesheim, 1962); G. L. Dosetti, *Il simbolo di Nicea e di Constantinopoli* (Rome, 1967).

to their very foundations and down to the simplest people living in them. On the contrary, the question at issue was this: What happens when I myself become a Christian, when I enroll myself under the banner of this Christ and thereby accept him as the authoritative man, as the measure of humanity? What kind of shift in being do I thus accomplish; what attitude to the business of being a man do I adopt? How deep does this process go? What estimate of reality as a whole does it involve?

4. THE CREED AS EXPRESSION OF THE STRUCTURE OF FAITH

To conclude these reflections let us finally draw attention to two factors that also emerge from the text and history of the *Symbolum*.

a. Faith and word

The Creed is a formula that forms the residue of the original dialogue: "Do you believe—I do believe". This dialogue refers for its part to a "We believe" in which the "I" of the "I believe" is not absorbed but allotted its place. Thus in the prehistory of this confession and in its original form, the whole anthropological shape of belief is present as well. It becomes evident that belief is not the result of lonely meditation in which the "I", freed from all ties and reflecting alone on the truth, thinks something out for itself; on the contrary, it is the result of a dialogue, the expression of a hearing, receiving, and answering that guides man through the exchanges of "I" and "You" to the "We" of those who all believe in the same way.

"Faith comes from what is heard", says St. Paul (Rom 10:17). This might seem like a very transient factor, which can change; one might be tempted to see in it purely and simply the result of one particular sociological situation, so that one day it would be right to say instead, "Faith comes from reading" or "from reflection". In reality it must be stated that we have here much more than the reflection of a historical period now past. The assertion "faith comes from what is heard" contains an abiding structural truth about what happens here. It illuminates the fundamental differences between faith and mere philosophy, a difference that does not prevent faith, in its core, from setting the philosophical search for truth in motion again. One could say epigrammatically that faith does in fact come from "hearing", not—like philosophy—from "reflection". Its nature lies in the fact that it is not the thinking out of something that can be thought out and that at the end of the process is then at my disposal as the result of my thought. On the contrary, it is characteristic of faith that it comes from hearing, that it is the reception of something that I have not thought out, so that in the last analysis thinking in the context of faith is always a thinking over of something previously heard and received.

In other words, in faith the word takes precedence over the thought, a precedence that differentiates it structurally from the architecture of philosophy. In philosophy the thought precedes the word; it is after all a product of the reflection that one *then* tries to put into words; the words always remain secondary to the thought and thus in the last resort can always be replaced by other words. Faith, on the other hand, comes to man from outside, and this very fact is fundamental to it. It is—let me repeat—not something thought up by myself; it is something said to me, which hits me as something that has not been thought out and could not be thought out and lays an obligation on me. This double structure of "Do you believe?—I do believe!", this form of the call from outside and the reply to it, is fundamental to it. It is therefore not at all abnormal if, with very few exceptions, we have to say: I did not come to believe through the private search for truth but through a process of reception that had, so to speak, already forestalled me. Faith cannot and should not be a mere product of reflection. The idea that faith really ought to arise through our thinking it up for ourselves and finding it in the process of a purely private search for truth is basically the expression of a definite ideal, an attitude of mind that fails to recognize the intrinsic quality of belief, which consists precisely in being the reception of what cannot be thought out—responsible reception, it is true, in which what is heard never becomes entirely my own property, and the lead held by what is received can never be completely wiped out, but in which the goal must be to make what is received more and more my own, by handing myself over to it as the greater.

Because of this, because faith is not something thought up by me but something that comes to me from outside, its word cannot be treated and exchanged as I please; it is always foreordained, always ahead of my thinking. The positivity of what comes toward me from outside myself, opening up to me what I cannot give myself, typifies the process of belief or faith. Therefore here the fore-given word takes precedence over the thought, so that it is not the thought that creates its own words but the given word that points the way to the thinking that understands. With this primacy of the word and the "positivity" of belief apparent in it goes the social character of belief, which signifies a second difference from the essentially individualistic structure of philosophical thinking. Philosophy is by its nature the work of the solitary individual, who ponders as an individual on truth. A thought, what has been thought out, is something that at any rate seems to belong to me myself, since it comes from me, although no one's thinking is self-supporting; consciously or unconsciously it is intertwined with many other strands. The place where a thought is perfected is the interior of the mind; thus at first it remains confined to me and has an individualistic structure. It only becomes communicable later, when it is put into words, which usually make it only approximately comprehensible to others. In contrast to this the primary factor for belief is, as we have seen, the proclaimed word. While a thought is interior, purely intellectual, the word represents the element that unites us with others. It is the way in which intellectual communication takes place, the form in which the mind is, as it were, human, that is, corporeal and social. This primacy of the word means that faith is focused on community of mind in a quite different way from philosophical thinking. In philosophy, what comes first is the private search for truth, which then, secondarily, seeks and finds traveling companions. Faith, on the other hand, is first of all a call to community, to unity of mind through the unity of the word. Indeed, its significance is, a priori, an essentially social one: it aims at establishing unity of mind through the unity of the word. Only secondarily will it then open the way for each individual's private venture in search of truth.

If in the dialogic structure of faith an image of man is thus defined, we can add that it also brings to light an image of God. Man comes to deal with God in coming to deal with his fellowmen. Faith is fundamentally centered on "You" and "We"; only via this double clamp does it link man with God. The corollary of this is that by the inner structure of faith our relationship to God and our fellowship with man cannot be separated from each other; the relationship to God, to the

"You", and to the "We" are intertwined; they do not stand alongside each other. The same thing could be formulated from a different point of view by saying that God wishes to approach man only through man; he seeks out man in no other way but in his fellow humanity.

Perhaps from this angle it is possible to render comprehensible a state of affairs, at any rate in the inner sanctum of faith, that at first must seem curious and may make the religious attitude of man seem problematical. The phenomenology of religion demonstrates—and we can all test this for ourselves—that there are, or at least appear to be, in religion, as in all other realms of the human spirit, various degrees of endowment. Just as in the field of music we find the creative, the receptive, and finally those who are completely unmusical, so it seems to be in religion, too. Here, too, one meets people who are religiously "talented" and others who are "untalented"; here, too, those capable of direct religious experience and thus of something like religious creativity through a living awareness of the religious world are few and far between. The "mediator" or "founder", the witness, the prophet, or whatever religious history likes to call such men who are capable of direct contact with the divine, remains here, too, the exception. Over against these few, for whom the divine thus becomes undisguised certainty, stand the many whose religious gift is limited to receptivity, who are denied the direct experience of the holy yet are not so deaf to it as to be unable to appreciate an encounter with it through the medium of the man granted such an experience.

At this point one feels forced to object that every man must surely have direct access to God if "religion" is supposed to be a reality that concerns everyone and if everyone has the same demands made upon him by God. Must there not then necessarily be "equality of opportunity", and must not the same certainty be available to everyone? But it will perhaps be evident from our line of argument that this question is misdirected: God's dialogue with men operates only through men's dialogue with each other. The difference in religious gifts that divides men into "prophets" and hearers forces them into speaking to and for one another. The program of the early Augustine, "God and the soul—nothing else", is impracticable; and it is also unchristian. Ultimately religion is not to be found along the solitary path of the mystic but only in the community of proclaiming and hearing. Man's conversation with God and men's conversation with one another are mutually necessary and interdependent. Indeed, perhaps the mystery of God is from the start the most compelling challenge—one that can never be carried to a final conclusion—ever issued to man to take up the dialogue that, however much it may be obstructed and disturbed, causes the *logos* to resound, the real word from which all words proceed and which all words constantly and inchoately attempt to express.

No real dialogue yet takes place where men are still only talking about *something*. The conversation between men comes into its own only when they are trying, no longer to express something, but to express themselves, when dialogue becomes communication. But when this happens, when man brings himself into the conversation, then God, too, is involved in some way or other, for he has been the real theme of controversy between men since the beginning of their history. Moreover, only where man brings himself into the conversation does the *logos* of all being enter, along with the *logos* of human being, into the words of human speech. That is why the testimony of God is inaudible where language is no more than a technique for imparting "something". God does not occur in logistic

calculations.[6] Perhaps the difficulty we find today in speaking about God arises precisely from the very fact that our
language is tending more and more to become pure calcu-
lation, that it is becoming more and more a mere means of
passing on technical information, less and less a means for
our common being to make contact in the *logos*, a process
in which intuitively or deliberately contact is also made
with the ground of all things.

b. Belief as "symbol"

Our consideration of the history of the Apostles' Creed has
led us to the recognition that here, in the baptismal formu-
lary, Christian doctrine stands before us in its original shape
and, thus, also in its primitive form, what we today call
"dogma". Originally there was no such thing as a series of
doctrinal propositions that could be enumerated one after
the other and entered in a book as a well-defined body
of dogmas. Such a notion, which today may be difficult to
resist, would have to be described as a misconception of
the nature of the Christian assent to the God revealed in
Christ. The content of the Christian faith has its inalienable
place in the context of the profession of faith, which is, as
we saw, in the form of assent and renunciation, a conversion, an about-turn of human existence into a new direction of life. In other words, Christian doctrine does not exist
in the form of discrete propositions but in the unity of the
symbolum, as the ancient Church called the baptismal profession of faith. This is probably the moment to look rather

---

[6] Cf. F. G. Jünger, "Sprache und Kalkül", in *Die Künste im technischen Zeit-
alter*, published by the Bavarian Academy of Fine Arts (Darmstadt, 1956),
pp. 86–104.

more closely at the meaning of this word. *Symbolum* comes from *symballein*, meaning in English: to come together, to throw together. The background to the word's etymology is an ancient usage: two corresponding halves of a ring, a staff, or a tablet were used as tokens of identity for guests, messengers, or partners to a treaty. Possession of the corresponding piece entitled the holder to receive a thing or simply to hospitality.[7] A *symbolum* is something that points to its complementary other half and thus creates mutual recognition and unity. It is the expression and means of unity.[8]

Thus in the description of the creed or profession of faith as the *symbolum* we have at the same time a profound interpretation of its true nature. For in fact this is just what the original meaning or aim of dogmatic formulations in the Church was: to facilitate a common profession of faith in God, common worship of him. As *sym-bolum*, it points to the other person, to the unity of spirit in the one Word. To this extent, dogma (or symbol, respectively) is also always, as Rahner has rightly pointed out,[9] essentially an arrangement of words that from a purely intellectual point of view could have been quite different yet, precisely as a form of words, has its own significance—that of uniting people in the community of the confessing word. It is not a piece of doctrine standing isolated in and for itself but is the form of our worship

[7] Cf. J. H. Emminghaus, "Symbol III", in LThK, 2nd ed., 9:1208ff.

[8] In *Plato* the idea of the symbol is expanded into an interpretation of human nature. In the *Symposium* (191d), he describes man himself, in connection with the androgyne myth, as a half that calls for its complementary other half: "Each of us is accordingly only the σύμβολον [symbol, half] of a human being, because we have been cut, like flat-fish, out of a pair. Each of us is always looking for the σύμβολον that belongs to him [for his other half]."

[9] K. Rahner, "Was ist eine dogmatische Aussage?" in *Schriften zur Theologie*, vol. 5 (Einsiedeln, 1962), pp. 54–81, especially 67–72. This whole chapter is much indebted to this important article.

of God, the form of our conversion, which is not only a turn to God but also a turn to one another in the common glorification of God. It is only in this context that Christian doctrine assumes its proper place. It would be fascinating to attempt one day from this point of view a history of the form of ecclesiastical doctrine, from the baptismal dialogue via the conciliar We to the anathema, the Protestant Confessions, and finally the dogma as isolated assertion. Such an investigation would almost certainly throw a great deal of light on the problems involved in the expression of faith and the differing degrees of awareness present in the various attempts.

A further point follows from what we have said: It also means that every man holds the faith only as a *symbolon*, a broken, incomplete piece that can only attain unity and completeness when it is laid together with the others. Only in *symballein*, in fitting together with them, can the *symballein*, the fitting together with God, take place. Faith demands unity and calls for the fellow believer; it is by nature related to a Church. A Church is not a secondary organization of ideas, quite out of accordance with them and hence at best a necessary evil; it belongs necessarily to a faith whose significance lies in the interplay of common confession and worship.

This discovery also points, it is true, in another direction: even the Church herself, as a whole, still holds the faith only as a *symbolon*, as a broken half, which signifies truth only in its endless reference to something beyond itself, to the entirely Other. It is only through the infinitely broken nature of the symbol that faith presses forward as man's continual effort to go beyond himself and reach up to God.

With this, one last thing becomes clear, something that at the same time leads back to the beginning. Augustine relates in his *Confessions* how it was decisive for his own path when

he learned that the famous philosopher Marius Victorinus
had become a Christian. Victorinus had long refused to join
the Church because he took the view that he already possessed in his philosophy all the essentials of Christianity, with
whose intellectual premises he was in complete agreement.[10] Since from his philosophical thinking, he said, he
could already regard the central Christian ideas as his own,
he no longer needed to institutionalize his convictions by
belonging to a Church. Like many educated people both
then and now, he saw the Church as Platonism for the people, something of which he as a full-blown Platonist had no
need. The decisive factor seemed to him to be the idea alone;
only those who could not grasp it themselves, as the philosopher could, in its original form needed to be brought into
contact with it through the medium of ecclesiastical organization. That Marius Victorinus nevertheless one day joined
the Church and turned from Platonist into Christian was an
expression of his perception of the fundamental error implicit
in this view. The great Platonist had come to understand
that a Church is something more and something other than
an external institutionalization and organization of ideas.
He had understood that Christianity is not a system of
knowledge but a way. The believers' "We" is not a secondary addition for small minds; in a certain sense it is the matter itself—the community with one's fellowmen is a reality
that lies on a different plane from that of the mere "idea". If
Platonism provides an *idea* of the truth, Christian belief offers
truth as a *way*, and only by becoming a way has it become
man's truth. Truth as mere perception, as mere idea, remains

---

[10] See the account of Marius Victorinus' conversion and the impression it
made on Augustine in *Confessions*, 8, 2, 3–5; also A. Solignac, "Le Cercle
milanais", in *Les Confessions*, vol. 14 of the (*Œuvres de St. Augustin* [Desclée,
1962]), pp. 529–36.

bereft of force; it only becomes man's truth as a way that makes a claim upon him, that he can and must tread.

Thus belief embraces, as essential parts of itself, the profession of faith, the word, and the unity it effects; it embraces entry into the community's worship of God and, so, finally the fellowship we call Church. Christian belief is not an idea but life; it is, not mind existing for itself, but incarnation, mind in the body of history and its "We". It is, not the mysticism of the self-identification of the mind with God, but obedience and service: going beyond oneself, freeing the self precisely through being taken into service by something not made or thought out by oneself, the liberation of being taken into service for the whole.

PART ONE

GOD

The *Symbolum* begins with the profession of faith in God, who is more precisely described by three predicates: Father— Ruler of all (this is the proper translation of the Greek word *pantokrator*, which we usually render, following the Latin text, by "almighty")—Creator.[1] Consequently our first task is to consider this question: What does it mean when the believer professes his faith in God? This question embraces the further one: What does it signify when this God is characterized by the titles "Father", "Ruler of all", "Creator"?

---

[1] The word "creator" is missing in the original Roman text; but the notion of creation is included in the concept "ruler of all".

Chapter I

PROLEGOMENA TO THE SUBJECT OF GOD

1. THE SCOPE OF THE QUESTION

What in fact is "God" really? In other ages this question may have seemed quite clear and unproblematical; for us it has become a genuine inquiry again. What can this word "God" signify? What reality does it express, and how does the reality concerned make contact with man? If one wished to pursue the question with the thoroughness really needed today, one would first have to attempt an analysis, from the angle of the philosophy of religion, of the sources of religious experience. Such an inquiry would also have to consider how it is that the theme of God has left its stamp on the whole history of humanity and right up to the present can raise such passionate argument—yes, right up to this very moment when the cry that God is dead resounds on every side and when nevertheless, in fact for this very reason, the question of God casts its shadow overpoweringly over all of us.

Where does this idea of "God" really come from? From what roots does it grow? How is it that what is apparently the most superfluous, and, from an earthly point of view, most useless, subject in history has at the same time remained the most insistent one? And why does this subject appear in such fundamentally different forms? So far as this point is concerned, it could of course be demonstrated that in spite of a confusing appearance of extreme variety the subject exists in only three forms (which occur in a number of different variations, of course)—monotheism, polytheism, and atheism, as one can briefly describe the three main paths taken by human history on the question of God. Moreover, we have already noted that even atheism's dismissal of the subject of God is only apparent, that in reality it represents a form of man's concern with the question of God, a form that can express a particular passion about this question and not infrequently does. If we wanted to pursue the fundamental preliminary questions, it would then be necessary to describe the two roots of religious experience to which the manifold forms of this experience can almost certainly be traced back. The peculiar tension existing between them was once defined by van der Leeuw, the well-known Dutch expert on the phenomenology of religion, in the paradoxical assertion that in the history of religion God the Son was there before God the Father.[2] It would be more accurate to say that God the Savior, God the Redeemer appears earlier than God the Creator, and even this clarification must be qualified by the reminder that the formula is not to be taken in the sense of a temporal succession, for which there is no kind of evidence. As far back as we can see in the history of religion the subject always occurs in both forms. Thus the word "before" can only mean that for concrete religious feeling, for the living existential interest, the Savior stands in the foreground as compared with the Creator.

Behind this twofold form in which humanity saw its God stand those two points of departure of religious experience of which we spoke just now. One is the experience of one's own existence, which again and again oversteps its own

[2] G. van der Leeuw, *Phänomenologie der Religion*, 2nd ed. (Tübingen, 1956), p. 103.

bounds and in some form or other, however concealed, points to the entirely Other. This, too, is a process with many layers—as many layers as human existence itself. Bonhoeffer thought, as is well known, that it was time to finish with a God whom we insert to fill the gap at the limit of our own powers, whom we call up when we ourselves are at the end of our tether. We ought to find God, he thought, not, so to speak, in our moments of need and failure, but amid the fullness of earthly life; only in this way could it be shown that God is not an escape, constructed by necessity, which becomes more and more superfluous as the limits of our powers expand.[3] In the story of man's striving for God, both ways exist, and both seem to me equally legitimate. Both the poverty of human existence and its fullness point to God. Where men have experienced existence in its fullness, its wealth, its beauty, and its greatness, they have always become aware that this existence is an existence for which they owe thanks; that precisely in its brightness and greatness it is not what I myself have obtained but the bestowed that comes to meet me, welcomes me with all its goodness before I have done anything, and thus requires of me that I *give* a meaning to such riches and thereby *receive* a meaning. On the other hand, man's poverty has also acted again and again as a pointer to the entirely Other. The question that human existence not only poses but itself *is*, the inconclusiveness inherent in it, the bounds it comes up against and that yet yearn for the unbounded (more or less in the sense of Nietzsche's asser-

[3] Cf. on this point R. Marlé, "Die fordernde Botschaft Dietrich Bonhoeffers", *Orientierung* 31 (1967): 42–46, especially the classical passage from *Widerstand und Ergebung*, ed. Bethge, 12th ed. (Munich, 1964), p. 182: "I should like to speak of God, not at the limits, but in the middle, not in the weaknesses, but in the strength, and thus not alongside death and guilt, but in the life and goodness of man."

tion that all pleasure yearns for eternity yet experiences itself
as a moment), this simultaneity of being limited and of yearn-
ing for the unbounded and open has always prevented man
from resting in himself, made him sense that he is not self-
sufficient but only comes to himself by going outside himself and moving toward the entirely Other and infinitely
greater.

The same thing could be demonstrated in the theme of
loneliness and security. Loneliness is indubitably one of the
basic roots from which man's encounter with God has risen.
Where man experiences his solitariness, he experiences at
the same time how much his whole existence is a cry for the
"You" and how ill-adapted he is to be only an "I" in himself. This loneliness can become apparent to man on various
levels. To start with, it can be comforted by the discovery of
a human "You". But then there is the paradox that, as Claudel says, every "You" found by man finally turns out to be
an unfulfilled and unfulfillable promise;[4] that every "You" is
at bottom another disappointment and that there comes a
point when no encounter can surmount the final loneliness:
the very process of finding and of having found thus becomes
a pointer back to the loneliness, a call to the absolute "You"
that really descends into the depths of one's own "I". But
even here it remains true that it is not only the need born of
loneliness, the experience that no sense of community fills
up all our longing, that leads to the experience of God; it
can just as well proceed from the joy of security. The very
fulfillment of love, of finding one another, can cause man
to experience the gift of what he could neither call up nor

---

[4] P. Claudel, *Le Soulier de Satin*—the great concluding dialogue between
Dona Prouhèze and Rodrigue; see also the whole preceding scene with the
double shadow.

create and make him recognize that in it he receives more than either of the two could contribute. The brightness and joy of finding one another can point to the proximity of absolute joy and of the simple fact of being found that stands behind every human encounter.

All this is just intended to give some idea of how human existence can be the point of departure for the experience of the absolute, which from this angle is seen as "God the Son", as the Savior, or, more simply, as a God related to existence.[5] The other source of religious perception is the confrontation of man with the world, with the powers and the sinister forces he meets in it. Again, it remains true that the cosmos has brought man to the experience of the all-surpassing power that both threatens him and bears him up as much through its beauty and abundance as through its deficiencies, its terrors, and its unfathomability. Here the resulting image is the somewhat vaguer and more distant one crystallized in the image of God the Creator, the Father.

If one were to pursue further the questions here adumbrated one would spontaneously run up against the problem, touched on above, of the three varieties of theism to be found in history—monotheism, polytheism, and atheism. Then, so it seems to me, the underlying unity of these three paths would become apparent, a unity that of course cannot be synonymous with identity and cannot imply that, if one only digs deep enough, everything finally becomes one and foreground differences lose their importance. Such demonstrations of identity, which philosophical thinking might feel tempted to undertake, take no note of the seriousness of human decisions and could certainly not do justice to reality.

---

[5] Cf. on this point A. Brunner, *Die Religion* (Freiburg, 1956), especially pp. 21–94; R. Guardini, *Religion und Offenbarung*, vol. 1 (Würzburg, 1958).

But even if there can be no question of identity, a deeper
look would be able to recognize that the differences between
the three great paths lie elsewhere than is suggested by their
three labels, which declare respectively: "There is one God";
"There are many Gods"; and "There is no God." Between
these three formulas and the professions contained in them
there exists an opposition that cannot be swept aside, but
there also exists a relationship of which the mere words contain no hint. For all three—this could be demonstrated—are
in the last analysis convinced of the unity and oneness of the
absolute. It is not only monotheism that believes in this unity
and oneness; even for polytheism the many gods that it worshipped and in which it placed its hopes were never the absolute itself; even to the polytheist it was clear that somewhere
or other behind the many powers there stood the one Being,
that in the last resort being was either one or at any rate the
eternal strife of two principles opposed to each other from
the beginning.[6] On the other hand, although atheism disputes the recognition of the unity of all being through the
idea of God, this does not mean at all that for the atheist the
unity of being itself is abolished. Indeed, the most influential
form of atheism, namely Marxism, asserts in the strictest form
this unity of being in all that is by declaring all being to be
matter; in this view, granted, the one thing that is being itself
becomes, as matter, completely separated from the earlier
concept of the absolute, which is linked to the idea of God,
but it simultaneously acquires features that make its absoluteness clear and thus once again recall the idea of God.

[6] Cf. J. A. Cuttat, *Begegnung der Religionen* (Einsiedeln, 1956); J. Ratzinger,
"Der christliche Glaube und die Weltreligionen", in *Gott in Welt*, Festschrift
für K. Rahner, vol. 2 (Freiburg, 1964), pp. 287–305; also the material in
P. Hacker, *Prahlada: Werden und Wandlungen einer Idealgestalt*, vols. 1 and 2 (Mainz,
1958).

Thus all three paths are convinced of the unity and uniqueness of the absolute; where they differ is only in their notions of the manner in which man has to deal with the absolute or, alternatively, of how the absolute behaves toward him. If—to treat the question very schematically—monotheism starts from the assumption that the absolute is consciousness, which knows man and can speak to him, for materialism the absolute, being matter, is devoid of all personal predicates and can in no way be brought into contact with the concepts of call and answer; the most one could say is that man himself must liberate what is divine from matter, so that he would then no longer have God behind him as something that had gone before him but only in front of him as something to be creatively effected by him, as his own better future. Finally, polytheism can be closely related to both monotheism and atheism, because the powers of which it speaks imply the oneness of a supporting power, which can be thought of in either way. Thus it would not be difficult to show how in antiquity polytheism went perfectly well with a metaphysical atheism but was also combined with philosophical monotheism.[7]

All these questions are important if one wishes to pursue the subject of God in our present situation today. To deal with them adequately would of course require a great deal

---

[7] One need only point to the fact that ancient philosophy embraced both philosophical atheists (Epicurus, Lucretius, et al.) and philosophical monotheists (Plato, Aristotle, Plotinus), and that both groups were by religion polytheists—a state of affairs that, thanks to the prevailing way of looking at it exclusively from the point of view of the history of philosophy, is seldom given sufficient attention. It is only against this background that one can see clearly the revolutionary nature of the Christian attitude, in which philosophical and religious orientation become identical; cf. on this point, J. Ratzinger, *Volk und Haus Gottes in Augustins Lehre von der Kirche* (Munich, 1954), pp. 2–12 and 218–34.

of time and patience. It must, therefore, suffice here to have
at any rate mentioned them; we shall meet them again and
again if we now go on to consider the fate of the idea of
God in the faith of the Bible, an investigation of which is
demanded by our subject. While we thus follow up further
the problem of God at one quite specific point, we shall
remain confronted with humanity's universal struggle for its
God and open to the full scope of the question.

2. THE PROFESSION OF FAITH
IN THE ONE GOD

Let us therefore return to our point of departure, to the words
of the Creed: I believe in God, the Father, the almighty, the
Creator. This statement, with which Christians have been
professing their faith in God for almost two thousand years,
is the product of a still older history. Behind it stands Israel's
daily profession of faith, the Christian form of which it represents: "Hear, O Israel, Yahweh, thy God, is an only God." [8]
With its first words the Christian creed takes up the creed of
Israel and takes up with it Israel's striving, its experience of
faith, and its struggle for God, which thus becomes an inner
dimension of the Christian faith, which would not exist without this struggle. Quite incidentally we meet here an important law of the history of religion and belief, which always
proceeds by linked steps; there is never complete disconti-
nuity. The faith of Israel is certainly something new in comparison with the faith of the surrounding peoples; nevertheless,

[8] Text of the $Sch^{e}ma$ (as this prayer is called, after the introductory phrase
"Hear, O Israel") in R. R. Geis, *Vom unbekannten Judentum* (Freiburg, 1961),
pp. 22f.

it is not something that has fallen from heaven; it takes shape in the conflict with this faith of other peoples, in the combative selection and reinterpretation that is both continuation and transformation.

"Yahweh, thy God, is an only God"—this fundamental profession, which forms the background to our Creed, making it possible, is in its original sense a renunciation of the surrounding gods. It is a profession in the fullest sense of this word, that is, it is not the registration of one view alongside others but an existential decision. As a renunciation of the gods, it also implies the renunciation both of the deification of political powers and of the deification of the cosmic cycle "Stirb und werde".[9] If one can say that hunger, love, and power are the forces that motivate man, then one can point out, as an extension of this observation, that the three main forms of polytheism are the worship of bread, the worship of love, and the idolization of power. All three paths are aberrations; they make absolutes out of what is not in itself the absolute, and they thereby make slaves of men. They are also, it is true, aberrations in which something is sensed of the power that bears up the universe. Israel's profession is, as we have said, a declaration of war on this threefold worship and thus an event of the greatest importance in the history of man's liberation. As a declaration of war on this threefold worship this profession of faith is at the same time a declaration of war on the multiplication of the divine in general. It is a renunciation—we shall have to look at this more closely later on—of gods of one's own or, in other words, of the deification of one's own possessions, something that is fundamental to polytheism. In this it is simultaneously a renunciation of the attempt to

[9] A quotation from Goethe that means literally "die and become".–TRANS.

keep one's own possessions safe, a renunciation of the fear
that tries to tame the mysterious by worshipping it, and an
assent to the one God of heaven as the power that guarantees everything; it signifies the courage to entrust oneself to
the power that governs the whole world without grasping
the divine in one's hands.

This starting point, which stems from the faith of Israel,
has not been fundamentally changed in the early Christian
creed. Here, too, entry into the Christian community and
the acceptance of its "symbol" signify an existential decision
with serious consequences. For whoever assented to this creed
renounced at the same time the laws of the world to which
he belonged; he renounced the worship of the ruling political power, on which the late Roman Empire rested, he
renounced the worship of pleasure and the cult of fear and
superstition that ruled the world. It was no coincidence that
the struggle over Christianity flared up in the field thereby
defined and grew into a struggle over the whole shape of
public life in the ancient world.

I believe that it is of decisive importance for the correct
assimilation of the Creed today that we should see these events
in their proper context. It is only too easy for us to regard
the Christian refusal, even if it meant the loss of one's life, to
take any part in the cult of the emperor as a piece of fanaticism appropriate to an early period; excusable, perhaps, for
this reason, but certainly not to be imitated today. Christians
rejected even the most harmless forms of the cult, such as
putting one's name down on the list of those contributing to
the cost of a sacrificial victim, and were ready to risk their
lives by such an action. Today, in a case like this, one would
distinguish between the unavoidable act of civic loyalty and
the real religious act, in order to find an acceptable way out
and at the same time to take account of the fact that heroism

cannot be expected of the average man. Perhaps such a distinction is today really possible in certain circumstances as a
result of the decision carried out at the time. In any case it is
important to realize that this refusal was far from being a
piece of narrow-minded fanaticism and that it changed the
world in a way in which it can only be changed by the readi-
ness to suffer. Those events showed that faith is not a matter
of playing with ideas but a very serious business: it says no,
and must say no, to the absoluteness of political power and
to the worship of the might of the mighty in general—"He
has put down the mighty from their thrones" (Lk 1:52); and
in doing so it has shattered the political principle's claim to
totality once and for all. In this sense the profession "There
is only one God" is, precisely because it has itself no political
aims, a program of decisive political importance: through the
absoluteness that it lends the individual from his God, and
through the relativization to which it relegates all political
communities in comparison with the unity of the God who
embraces them all, it forms the only definitive protection
against the power of the collective and at the same time implies
the complete abolition of any idea of exclusiveness in humanity as a whole.

Much the same as has been said about the Christian faith
as the struggle against the worship of power could be demonstrated in the realm of the striving for the true pattern of
human love as against the false worship of sex and Eros, which
was and still is responsible for just as great an enslavement of
humanity as the misuse of power. More than mere imagery
is involved when Israel's fall from faith is depicted again and
again in the prophets by the "image" of adultery. Not only
did these alien cults almost always involve cult prostitution,
so that they could be literally described as "adultery"; these
outward manifestations also revealed their inner tendency.

The unity, finality, and indivisibility of the love between man and woman can in the last analysis only be made a reality and understood in the light of belief in the unity and indivisibility of the love of God. We are beginning to understand more and more clearly today that this concept of love is by no means a philosophically deducible, self-supporting principle and that to a large extent it stands or falls with belief in the one God. We are also coming to understand more and more clearly that the apparent liberation of love and its conversion into a matter of impulse mean the delivery of man to the autonomous powers of sex and Eros, to whose merciless slavery he falls victim just when he is under the illusion that he has freed himself. When he eludes God, the gods put out their hands to grasp him; he can only be liberated by allowing himself to be liberated and by ceasing to try to rely on himself.

No less important than the clarification of the renunciation contained in the Creed is a proper understanding of the assent, the Yes, that it involves; first, simply because the No can only exist by virtue of the Yes, but also because the renunciation of the first few Christian centuries has turned out to be so effective historically that the gods have disappeared irrevocably. To be sure, the *powers* expressed in them have not disappeared, nor has the temptation to regard them as absolutes. Both facts are part of the basic human situation and express the enduring "truth", so to speak, of polytheism; we are threatened no less than the people of ancient times by the tendency to make absolutes of power, bread, and Eros. But even if the gods of those days are still "powers" that try to claim absoluteness, they have irrevocably lost the mask of divinity and must now show themselves unmasked in their true profanity. Here we have a fundamental difference between pre-Christian and post-Christian paganism, which bears the stamp of the Christian rejection of the gods and its power to alter history. This gives all the more urgency to the question that arises in the vacuum in which we now in many respects live: What is the content of the assent that the Christian faith involves?

Chapter II

THE BIBLICAL BELIEF IN GOD

Anyone who wishes to understand the biblical belief in God must follow its historical development from its origins with the patriarchs of Israel right up to the last books of the New Testament. The Old Testament, with which we must consequently begin, itself gives us a thread to guide our labors: basically, it formulated its idea of God in two names, Elohim and Yahweh. These two main names for God reflect the process of being set apart and chosen that Israel underwent in its religious world, and they also throw light on the positive option implicit in this choice and in the progressive reshaping of what had been chosen.

I. THE PROBLEM OF THE STORY OF THE BURNING BUSH

It is probably fair to take as the central text for the Old Testament understanding of God and profession of faith in him the story of the burning bush (Ex 3), in which, with the revelation of the name of God to Moses, the foundation is laid for the idea of God henceforth to prevail in Israel. The text describes the calling of Moses to be the leader of Israel by the God both concealed and revealed in the burning thornbush and the hesitation of Moses, who demands a clear knowledge of his employer and clear proof of his authority. This is the background to the dialogue that has puzzled people ever since:

> Then Moses said to God, "If I come to the people of Israel and say to them, 'The God of your fathers has sent me to you,' and they ask me, 'What is his name?' what shall I say to them?" God said to Moses, "I AM WHO I AM." And he said, "Say this to the people of Israel, 'I AM has sent me to you.' " God also said to Moses, "Say this to the people of Israel, 'The LORD, the God of your fathers, the God of Abraham, the God of Isaac, and the God of Jacob, has sent me to you': this is my name for ever, and thus I am to be remembered throughout all generations." (Ex 3:13–15)

It is clearly the aim of the text to establish the name "Yahweh" as the definitive name of God in Israel, on the one hand, by anchoring it historically in the origins of Israel's nationhood and the sealing of the covenant and, on the other, by giving it a meaning. The latter is accomplished by tracing back the incomprehensible word "Yahweh" to the root *hayah* = to be. From the point of view of the Hebrew consonant system, this is quite possible; but whether it corresponds philologically with the real origin of the name Yahweh is at least questionable. As so often in the Old Testament, it is a question of a theological rather than a philological etymology. It is a matter, not of inquiring into the original linguistic sense, but of giving a meaning here and now. The etymology is in reality a means of establishing a meaningful attitude. This illumination of the name "Yahweh" by the little word "Being" (I AM) is accompanied by a second attempt at clarification consisting of the statement that Yahweh is the God of (Israel's) fathers, the God of Abraham, Isaac, and Jacob. This means that the concept of "Yahweh" is to be enlarged

and deepened by the equation of the God so described with
the God of Israel's fathers, a God who had probably been
addressed for the most part by the names El and Elohim.

Let us try to visualize clearly what kind of image of God
arises in this way. First, what does it mean when the idea of
Being is here brought into play as an interpretation of God?
To the Fathers of the Church, with their background of
Greek philosophy, it seemed a bold and unexpected con-
firmation of their own intellectual past, for Greek philosophy regarded it as its decisive discovery that it had discovered,
behind all the many individual things with which man has
to deal daily, the comprehensive idea of Being, which it
also considered the most appropriate expression of the divine.
Now the Bible, too, seemed to be saying precisely the same
thing in its central text on the image of God. It is not
surprising if this seemed an absolutely amazing confirma-
tion of the unity of belief and thought, and in fact the
Fathers of the Church believed that they had discovered
here the deepest unity between philosophy and faith, Plato
and Moses, the Greek mind and the biblical mind. So complete did they find the identity between the quest of the
philosophical spirit and the acceptance that had occurred
in the faith of Israel that they took the view that Plato
could not have advanced so far on his own but had been
familiar with the Old Testament and borrowed his idea from
it. Thus the central concept of the Platonic philosophy was
indirectly traced back to revelation; people did not dare to
attribute an insight of such profundity to the unaided power
of the human mind.

The text of the Greek Old Testament, which the Fathers
had before them, could very well suggest such an identity of
thought between Plato and Moses, but the dependence is
probably the other way around; the scholars who translated

the Hebrew Bible into Greek were influenced by Greek philosophical thinking and interpreted the text from this angle;
the idea that here the Hellenic spirit and the faith of the
Bible overlapped must already have inspired them; they themselves built the bridge, so to speak, from the biblical concept
of God over to Greek thought if they translated the "I AM
WHO I AM" of verse 14 by "I am he that is". The biblical
name for God is here identified with the philosophical concept of God. The scandal of the name, of the God who names
himself, is resolved in the wider context of ontological thinking; belief is wedded to ontology. For to the thinker it is a
scandal that the biblical God should bear a name. Can this
be more than a reminder of the polytheistic world in which
the biblical faith had at first to live? In a world swarming
with gods Moses could not say, "God sends me", or even
"The God of our fathers sends me." He knew that this meant
nothing, that he would be asked, "Which god?" But the
question is: Could one have ever given the Platonic "Being"
a name and referred to it by this name as a kind of individual? Or is the fact that one can name this God not a sign of
a fundamentally different conception? If one adds that it is
an important detail of the text that one can name God only
because he has named himself, then one only deepens still
further the gulf between this conception and Platonic, absolute Being, the final stage of ontological thinking, which is
not named and names itself still less.

    Are the Greek translations of the Old Testament, then,
and the conclusions that the Fathers drew from it based on
a misunderstanding? Today, not only are the exegetical scholars unanimous that they are, but the dogmatic theologians
emphasize the point strongly and with all the thoroughness
appropriate to a question that exceeds in importance all
other individual problems of exegesis. For example, Emil

Brunner has stated with the utmost firmness that the insertion here of an "equals" sign between the God of faith and the God of the philosophers means turning the biblical idea of God into its opposite. The name, Brunner says, is here replaced by the concept, and the not-to-be-defined is replaced by a definition.[1] But this means that at this one spot the whole patristic exegesis, the ancient Church's faith in God, and the image of God and profession of faith in him to be found in the *Symbolum* come under discussion. Are they a decline into Hellenism, a falling away from the God whom the New Testament names as the Father of Jesus Christ, or do they say again in new conditions what must always be said?

Above all else we must try, if as briefly as possible, to look into the actual findings of exegesis. What does this name Yahweh signify, and what is the meaning of its explanation by the little word "Being"? The two questions are connected but, as we saw, not identical. Let us try first to get a little closer to the first one. Can we still make out at all what the name Yahweh originally means according to its etymological origin? This is almost impossible because we are completely in the dark about its origin. One thing at any rate can be clearly stated: Firm evidence of the name Yahweh before Moses or outside of Israel is lacking; and none of the numerous attempts to clarify the pre-Israelite roots of the name is really convincing. Syllables like *yah, yo, jahw* are known earlier, but so far as we can see today the full form of the name Yahweh first occurs in Israel; its development seems to be the work of Israel's faith, which, not without models but

---

[1] E. Brunner, *Die christliche Lehre von Gott*, vol. 1 of his *Dogmatik* (Zürich, 1960), pp 124–35; cf. J. Ratzinger, *Der Gott des Glaubens und der Gott der Philosophen* (Munich, 1960).

creatively transforming them, here molded its own name for God and, in this name, its own figure of God.[2]

Indeed, today there is again a good deal to be said for the view that the formation of this name was in fact the deed of Moses, who with it brought new hope to his enslaved fellow countrymen: the final development of their own name for God and in it of their own image of God seems to have been the starting point of Israel's nationhood. Even from a purely historical point of view one can say that Israel became a people thanks to God, that it only came to itself through the call of hope signified by the name of God. Of the manifold references to pre-Israelite antecedents of the name Yahweh, which do not need to be discussed here, the best-grounded and most fruitful suggestion seems to me to be the observation made by H. Cazelles, who points out that in the Babylonian kingdom theophorous names occur (that is, personal names containing a reference to God), formed with the word *yaun* or containing the syllable *yau* or *ya*, which has more or less the meaning "mine" or "my God". In the tangle of gods with whom people dealt, this word formation refers to the personal god, that is, the god who is concerned with man and is himself personal and person-centered. It is the God who, as the personal Being, deals with man as man. This indication is noteworthy in that it links up with a central element in Israel's pre-Mosaic faith, with the God-figure whom we are accustomed to describe, following the Bible,

---

[2] That is how it will be expressed from the point of view of the historian. This will not affect the believer's conviction that this "creative transformation" was only possible in the form of a reception of revelation. In any case the creative process is always a process of reception. For the historical aspect, cf. H. Cazelles, "Der Gott der Patriarchen", *Bibel und Leben* 2 (1961): 39–49; O. Eissfeldt, "Jahwe, der Gott der Väter", *Theologische Literaturzeitung* 88 (1963): 481–90; G. von Rad, *Theologie des AT*, vol. 1 (Munich, 1958), pp. 181–88.

as the God of our fathers.[3] The suggested etymology would thus fit in exactly with what the story of the burning bush itself described as the inner assumption of the Yahweh-faith, with the faith of (Israel's) fathers, with the God of Abraham, Isaac, and Jacob. Let us therefore turn our attention for a moment to this figure, without which the meaning of the Yahweh message cannot be understood.

2. THE INTRINSIC ASSUMPTION OF THE BELIEF IN YAHWEH: THE GOD OF [ISRAEL'S] FATHERS

The linguistic and conceptual root of the name Yahweh, a root we thought we recognized in the "personal God" indicated by the syllable *yau*, throws light, not only on the choice made by Israel, which historically set it apart from its religious environment, but also on the continuity with Israel's own early history from the time of Abraham. The God of its fathers had not, it is true, been called Yahweh; when we meet him he bears the names El and Elohim. The patriarchs of Israel were thus able to use as their starting point the El-religion of the surrounding peoples, a religion that is characterized chiefly by the social and personal character of the divinity denoted by the word *El*. The God upon whom they decided is characterized by the fact that, in the language of religious typology, he is a *numen personale* (personal god), not a *numen locale* (local god). What does this mean? Let us try to elucidate briefly what is meant by each phrase. First we should recall that the religious experience of the human race has continually been kindled at holy places, where for some reason or other the "entirely Other", the divine,

---

[3] Cazelles, "Gott der Patriarchen".

becomes especially perceptible to man; a spring, a huge tree, a mysterious stone, or even an unusual happening that occurred at some spot or other, can have this effect. But then the danger immediately arises that in man's eyes the spot where he experienced the divine and the divine itself merge into each other, so that he believes in a special presence of the divine at that particular spot and thinks he cannot find it in equal measure elsewhere: consequently, the spot becomes a holy spot, the dwelling place of the divine. The local connection of the divine thus resulting then also leads, however, by a sort of inner necessity, to its multiplication. Because this experience of the holy occurs not just in *one* spot but in many, while the holy is regarded in each case as confined to the spot concerned, the result is a multitude of local divinities, who thus become at the same time gods of their own respective areas. A faint echo of these tendencies can be noted even now in Christianity: to less enlightened believers the Madonnas of Lourdes, Fatima, or Altötting sometimes seem to be absolutely different beings and by no means simply the same person. But back to our subject! In contrast to the heathen tendency toward the *numen locale*, the locally defined and limited deity, the "God of our fathers" expresses a completely different approach. He is not the god of a place but the god of men: the God of Abraham, Isaac, and Jacob. He is therefore not bound to one spot but is present and powerful wherever man is. In this fashion one arrives at a completely different way of thinking about God. God is seen on the plane of I and You, not on the plane of the spatial. He thus moves away into the transcendence of the illimitable and by this very fact shows himself to be he who is always (not just at one point) near, whose power is boundless. He is not anywhere in particular; he is to be found at any place where man is and where man lets himself be found by him.

By deciding in favor of El, the fathers of Isra-el thus made a choice of the greatest importance: they opted for the *numen personale* as opposed to the *numen locale*, for the personal and person-centered God, who is to be thought of and found on the plane of I and You, not primarily in holy places.[4] This basic characteristic of El remained the one sustaining element, not only of the religion of Israel, but also of the New Testament faith: the emanation of God's personality, the understanding of God on the plane defined by the I-and-You relationship.

To this aspect, by which the intellectual locus of the El-faith is basically defined, a second must be added: El is regarded, not only as the sustainer of personality, as father, creator of creatures, the wise, the king; he is seen also and above all things as the highest God of all, as the greatest power of all, as he who stands above all else. It is unnecessary to emphasize that this second element, too, put its stamp on the whole biblical experience of God. It is not just some power or other, effective somewhere or other, that is chosen; rather, it is that power alone which embraces in itself all power and stands above all individual powers.

Further, attention must be directed to a third element, which likewise persists throughout biblical thinking: this God is the God of the Promise. He is not a force of nature, in whose epiphany the eternal might of nature, the eternal "Stirb und Werde", is demonstrated; he is not a God who orients man to the recurring pattern of the cosmic cycle; rather, he directs man's attention to the coming events toward which his history marches, to a meaning and goal that have a final validity; he is regarded as the God of hope in the future, in a direction that is irreversible.

---

[4] Though it must be pointed out again (as already in n. 2 above) that this sort of decision embraces gift, reception, and, to that extent, revelation.

Finally, it must be pointed out that the El-faith was accepted in Israel chiefly in its extension to "Elohim", an extension that also hints at the process of transformation that even the El-figure needed. It may seem curious that in this way the singular El was replaced by a word (Elohim) that really indicates a plural. We cannot go into the complex details of this process here; suffice it to say that this very development enabled Israel to give better and better expression to God's uniqueness. He is one, but as the exceeding great, entirely Other, he himself transcends the bounds of singular and plural; he lies beyond them. Although in the Old Testament, especially in its early books, there is certainly no kind of revelation of the Trinity, nevertheless in this process there is latent an experience that points toward the Christian concept of the triune God. People realized, if still quite unreflectively, that while God is indeed radically One, he cannot be forced into our categories of singular and plural; rather, he stands above them, so that in the last analysis, even though he is truly one God, he cannot be fitted with complete appropriateness into the category "one". In the early history of Israel (and later on, too—for us especially) this means that at the same time the legitimacy of the question implicit in polytheism is admitted.[5] The plural, when it refers to one God, means, so to speak, "He is everything divine."

---

[5] Cf. Maximus Confessor, *Expositio Orationis Dominicae*, in *Patrologia Graeca* (PG), 90:892: in his view, heathen polytheism and Jewish monotheism are reconciled in the Gospel. "The former is contradictory multiplicity unchecked; the latter is unity without inner riches." Maximus regards them both as equally imperfect and in need of supplementation. But now they reach out beyond themselves to the idea of the tri-une God, which supplements the Jewish concept of unity, "of itself 'narrow and imperfect and almost without substance'", and which "runs the danger of atheism", with the "lively, intellectually engaging multiplicity of Hellenistic religion". Such is Maximus' view according to H. U. von Balthasar, *Cosmic Liturgy: The Universe according to Maximus the*

If one wished to speak appropriately about the "God of our fathers", one would now have to add a reminder of the negation implicit in the Yes that presents itself to us at first in El and Elohim. However, here we must make do with a reference to two catchwords, to two names of gods dominant in the regions around Israel. The Jews rejected the notions of God current in the surrounding areas under the names of Baal (the lord) and Melech, or Moloch (the king). What was renounced here was fertility worship and the local connection of the divine that it brings with it; and the No to the king-god Melech also involved the rejection of a certain social pattern. The God of Israel is not moved away to the aristocratic distance of a king; he is a stranger to the boundless despotism linked in those days with the image of a king—he is the near-at-hand God, who fundamentally can be the God of each and every man. What food for thought this provides! But let us forgo the pleasure of such speculations and return again to our point of departure, to the question of the God of the burning bush.

3. YAHWEH, THE "GOD OF OUR FATHERS" AND THE GOD OF JESUS CHRIST

Since Yahweh, as we have seen, is explained as the "God of our fathers", the Yahweh-faith automatically absorbs the whole context of the faith of Israel's fathers, though this context at the same time acquires a new coherence and a new look. But what is the specifically new element expressed by

---

Confessor, trans. Brian E. Daley from the 3rd German ed. (San Francisco: Ignatius Press and Communio, 2003), p. 313. Cf. also A. Adam, *Lehrbuch der Dogmengeschichte*, vol. 1 (Gütersloh, 1965), p. 368.

the name "Yahweh"? The answers to this question are numerous; the precise meaning of the formulas in Exodus 3 can no
longer be ascertained with certainty. Nevertheless, two aspects
emerge clearly. We have already established that to our way
of thinking the mere fact that God bears a name, and thereby
appears as a kind of individual, is a scandal. But if we look
more closely at the text we are considering the question arises:
Is it, properly speaking, really a name? This question may at
first seem nonsensical, for it is indisputable that Israel knew
the word Yahweh as a name for God. Yet a careful reading
shows that the thornbush scene expounds this name in such
a way that as a name it seems to be absolutely cancelled out;
in any case it moves out of the series of appellations of divinities to which it at first seems to belong. Let us listen once
again carefully. Moses says: "The children of Israel, to whom
you send me, will ask, 'Who is the God who sends you?
What is he called?' What shall I then say to them?" We are
next told that God replied: "I AM WHO I AM". The words
could also be translated, "I am what I am." This really looks
like a rebuff; it seems much more like a refusal to give a
name than the announcement of a name. In the whole scene
there is a sense of displeasure at such importunity: I am just
who I am. The idea that here no name is really given and
that the question is rejected acquires additional probability
when a comparison is made with the two passages that could
be adduced as the best parallels to our text: Judges 13:18 and
Genesis 32:30. In Judges 13:18 a certain Manoah asks the
God who meets him for his name. The answer he is given is:
"Why do you ask my name, seeing it is a secret?" (Another
possible translation is "seeing it is wonderful".) A name is
not given. In Genesis 32:30, it is Jacob who, after his noc-
turnal struggle with the stranger, asks his name and receives
only the discouraging answer, "Why is it that you ask my

name?" Both passages are linguistically and in general construction very closely related to our text, so that it is hardly
disputable that there is also an affinity in the thought. Here
again we have the gesture of repulse. The God with whom
Moses deals in the burning bush cannot give his name in the
same way as the gods round about, who are individual gods
alongside other similar gods and therefore need a name. The
God of the burning bush will not put himself on a level with
them.

In the gesture of rebuff we have come upon here there is
a hint of a God who is entirely different from "the gods".
The explanation of the name Yahweh by the little word "am"
thus serves as a kind of negative theology. It cancels out the
significance of the name as a name; it effects a sort of withdrawal from the only too well known, which the name seems
to be, into the unknown, the hidden. It dissolves the name
into mystery, so that the familiarity and unfamiliarity of God,
concealment and revelation, are indicated simultaneously. The
name, a sign of acquaintance, becomes the cipher for the
perpetually unknown and unnamed quality of God. Contrary to the view that God can here be grasped, so to speak,
the persistence of an infinite distance is in this way made
quite clear. To this extent it was in the last analysis a legitimate development that led people in Israel more and more
to avoid pronouncing this name, to use some sort of periphrasis, so that in the Greek Bible it no longer occurs at all but
is simply replaced by the word "Lord". This development
shows in many ways a more accurate understanding of the
mystery of the burning bush than multifarious learned philological explanations do.

But so far, of course, we have been looking at only one-
half of the subject, for Moses was in fact empowered all the
same to say to the questioners: "I AM has sent me to you"

(Ex 3:14). He has an answer at his disposal, even if it is a
riddle. And can we not, indeed must we not, unriddle it a
bit in a positive sense? Most contemporary biblical scholars
see in the phrase the expression of helpful proximity; they
say that God does not reveal in it—as philosophical thought
tries to—his nature as it is in itself; he reveals himself as a
God for Israel, as a God for man. "I am" is as much as to say
"I am here", "I am here for you"; God's presence for Israel
is emphasized; his Being is expounded, not as Being in itself,
but as a Being-for.[6] Eissfeldt, it is true, considers possible not
only the translation "he helps" but also "he calls into existence; he is the creator"; "he is"; and even "he who is". The
French scholar Edmond Jacob thinks that the name El denotes
life as power, while Yahweh expresses endurance and presence. When God here calls himself "I AM", he is to be
explained, according to Jacob, as he who "is", as Being in
contrast to Becoming, as that which abides and persists in all
passing away. "All flesh is grass, and all its beauty is like the
flower of the field. . . . The grass withers, the flower fades;
but the word of our God will stand for ever" (Is 40:6–8).

The reference to this text indicates a connection that hitherto has probably been given too little attention. To the
Deutero-Isaiah it was a fundamental part of his message that
the things of this world pass away; that men, however force-
fully they behave, are in the end like flowers, which bloom
one day and are cut off and withering away the next, while
in the midst of this gigantic display of transience the God of
Israel "is"—not "becomes". Amid all the becoming and passing away he "is". But this "is" of God, who abides above all
the inconstancy of becoming as the constant one, is not

---

[6] Cf. W. Eichrodt, *Theologie des Alten Testaments*, 2nd ed., vol. 1 (Leipzig,
1939), pp. 92f.; G. von Rad, *Theologie des AT*, p. 184.

proclaimed as something unconnected with anything else. On the contrary, God is at the same time he who grants himself; he is there for us, and from his own firm standing he gives us firmness in our infirmity. The God who "is" is at the same time he who is with *us*; he is not just God in himself; rather, he is our God, the "God of our fathers".

This brings us back to the question that arose at the beginning of our reflections on the story of the burning bush: What is really the relationship between the God of the biblical faith and the Platonic idea of God? Is the God who names himself and has a name, the God who helps and is always there, radically different from the *esse subsistens*, the absolute Being, that is discovered in the lonely silence of philosophical speculation, or what? To deal with this question properly and to grasp the meaning of the Christian notion of God, I think we must look rather more closely both at the biblical idea of God and at the significance of philosophical thinking. To deal first with the Bible, it is important not to isolate the story of the burning bush. We have already seen that it is to be understood primarily against the background of a world saturated with gods, in which it makes Israel's faith visible, both in its continuity and in its efforts to differentiate itself, and at the same time develops it further by adding the many-faceted idea of Being as an intellectual element. The process of interpretation that we encountered in the story does not end with it; in the course of the biblical struggle for God, this process was continually being taken in hand again and carried farther. Ezekiel and especially the Deutero-Isaiah could be described in so many words as the theologians of the name Yahweh; it was not least on this that they based their prophetic preaching. The Deutero-Isaiah is speaking, as is well known, at the end of the Babylonian exile, at a moment when Israel is looking into the future with new hope. The apparently invincible Babylonian power that enslaved Israel has been broken, and Israel, the supposed corpse, is arising out of the ruins. Thus one of the prophets' central ideas is to compare with gods that pass away the God who *is*. "I, Yahweh, the first, and with the last, I am He" (41:4). The last book of the New Testament, the Apocalypse, in a similarly difficult situation, was to repeat this assertion: Before all these powers he stands already, and after them he still stands (Rev 1:4; 1:17; 2:8; 22:13). But let us listen once again to the Deutero-Isaiah: "I am the first and I am the last; besides me there is no god" (44:6). "I am He, I am the first, and I am the last" (48:12). In this context the prophet has coined a new formula, in which the interpretative thread in the story of the burning bush is taken up and given a different emphasis. The formula that in Hebrew seems mysteriously to run simply "I–He" is rendered in Greek, and certainly with accuracy, as "I am" (ἐγώ εἰμι)[7]. In this simple "I am" the God of Israel confronts the gods and identifies himself as the one who *is*, in contrast to those who have been toppled over and pass away. The brief, enigmatic phrase "I am" thus becomes the axis of the prophet's proclamation, expressing his struggle against the gods, his struggle against Israel's despair, and his message of hope and certainty. In face of the worthless pantheon of Babylon and its fallen potentates, the might of Yahweh rises simply, needing no commentary, in the expression "I am", which describes its absolute superiority to all the godly and ungodly powers of this world. The name Yahweh, whose meaning is brought home in such a fashion, thus moves a step farther toward the idea of him

---

[7] On the origin and meaning of this formula, see especially E. Schweizer, *EGO EIMI* (Göttingen, 1939); H. Zimmermann, "Das absolute ἐγώ εἰμι als die neutestamentliche Offenbarungsformel", *Biblische Zeitschrift* 4 (1960): 54–69; E. Stauffer, *Jesus: Gestalt und Geschichte* (Berne, 1957), pp. 130–46.

who "is" in the midst of the ruins of appearance, which has
no endurance.

Let us now take one last step that carries us over into the
New Testament. The line of thought that puts the idea of
God more and more in the light of the idea of Being and
explains God by the simple "I am" occurs once again in St.
John's Gospel, that is, in the last retrospective biblical interpretation of the belief in Jesus, an interpretation that for us
Christians is at the same time the last step in the self-
explanation of the biblical movement in general. John's thinking is directly based on the Wisdom literature and the
Deutero–Isaiah and can only be understood against this background. He makes the "I am" of Isaiah into the central formula of his faith in God, but he does it by making it into the
central formula of his Christology: a process as decisive for
the idea of God as for the image of Christ. The formula that
first occurs in the episode of the burning bush, that at the
end of the Exile becomes the expression of hope and certainty in face of the declining gods and depicts Yahweh's
lasting victory over all these powers, now finds itself here,
too, at the center of the faith, but through becoming testimony to Jesus of Nazareth.

The significance of this process becomes fully visible when
one also realizes that John takes up again, in a much more
striking way than any New Testament author before him,
the heart of the burning bush story: the idea of the name of
God. The notion that God names himself, that it becomes
possible to call on him by name, moves, together with "I
am", into the center of his testimony. In John, Christ is compared with Moses in this respect, too; John depicts him as
the one in whom the story of the burning bush first attains
its true meaning. All chapter 17—the so-called "high priestly
prayer", perhaps the heart of the whole Gospel—centers

around the idea of "Jesus as the revealer of the name of God" and thus assumes the position of New Testament counterpart to the story of the burning bush. The theme of God's name recurs like a *leitmotiv* in verses 6, 11, 12, and 26. Let us take only the two main verses: "I have manifested your *name* to the men whom you gave me out of the world" (v. 6 [emphasis added]). "I made known to them your *name*, and I will make it known, that the love with which you have loved me may be in them, and I in them" (v. 26 [emphasis added]). Christ himself, so to speak, appears as the burning bush from which the name of God issues to mankind. But since in the view of the fourth Gospel Jesus unites in himself, applies to himself, the "I am" of Exodus 3 and Isaiah 43, it becomes clear at the same time that *he himself* is the name, that is, the "invocability" of God. The idea of the name here enters a decisive new phase. The name is, no longer merely a word, but a person: Jesus himself. Christology, or belief in Jesus, is raised to the level of an exposition of the name of God and of what it signifies. This brings us to the point where we must finally deal with an important question affecting the whole discussion of the name of God.

4. THE IDEA OF THE NAME

After all our reflections we must now finally ask in completely general terms: What is a name really? And what is the point of speaking of a name of God? I do not want to undertake a detailed analysis of this question—this is not the place for such an analysis—but simply to try to indicate in a few lines what seem to me to be the essential points. First, we can say that there is a fundamental difference between the purpose of a concept and that of a name. The concept tries to perceive the nature of the thing as it is in itself. The name, on the other hand, does not ask after the nature of the thing as it exists independently of me; it is concerned to make the thing nameable, that is, "invocable", to establish a relation to it. Here, too, the name should certainly fit the thing, but to the end that it comes into relation to me and in this way becomes accessible to me. Let us take an example: If I know of someone that he falls under the concept "man", this is still not enough to enable me to establish a relation to him. Only the name makes him nameable; through the name the other enters into the structure, so to speak, of my fellow humanity; through the name I can call him. Thus the name signifies and effects the social incorporation, the inclusion in the structure of social relations. Anyone who is still regarded only as a number is excluded from the structure of fellow humanity. But the name establishes the relation of fellow humanity. It gives to a being the "invocability" from which coexistence with the namer arises.

This will probably make clear what Old Testament faith means when it speaks of a name of God. The aim is different from that of the philosopher seeking the concept of the highest Being. The concept is a product of thinking that wants to know what that highest Being is like in itself. Not so the name. When God names himself after the self-understanding of faith, he is not so much expressing his inner nature as making himself nameable; he is handing himself over to men in such a way that he can be called upon by them. And by doing this he enters into coexistence with them; he puts himself within their reach; he is "there" for them.

Here, too, is the angle from which it would seem to become clear what it means when John presents the Lord Jesus Christ as the real, living name of God. In him is fulfilled what a

mere name could never in the end fulfill. In him the meaning of the discussion of the name of God has reached its
goal, and so, too, has that which was always meant and
intended by the idea of the name of God. In him—this is
what the evangelist means by this idea—God has really
become he who can be invoked. In him God has entered
forever into coexistence with us. The name is no longer just
a word at which we clutch; it is now flesh of our flesh, bone
of our bone. God is one of us. Thus what had been meant
since the episode of the burning bush by the idea of the
name is really fulfilled in him who as God is man and as man
is God. God has become one of us and so he has become the
truly nameable, standing in coexistence with us.

5. THE TWO SIDES OF THE BIBLICAL CONCEPT OF GOD

If one tries to survey the question as a whole, it becomes
apparent that there are always two components in the biblical concept of God. One side is the element of the personal,
of proximity, of invocability, of self-bestowal, an element that
is heralded in the idea of the "God of our fathers, of Abraham, Isaac, and Jacob", summed up comprehensively in the
giving of the name, and concentrated again later in the idea
of "the God of Jesus Christ". It is always a matter of the God
of men, the God with a face, the personal God; on him were
focused continuity, the choice and the decision of the faith
of the patriarchs, from which a long yet straight road leads to
the God of Jesus Christ.

On the other side is the fact that this proximity, this acces-
sibility, is the free gift of the One who stands above space
and time, bound to nothing and binding everything to himself. The element of timeless power is characteristic of this

God; it becomes concentrated more and more emphatically
in the idea of Being, of the enigmatic and profound "I am".
As time went on, Israel visibly tried to interpret something
of this second element to the surrounding peoples, to impress
on them the special character, the "otherness" of its faith. It
placed the "is" of God over against the becoming and passing away of the world and its gods—gods of the earth, of
fertility, of one nation. It contrasted the God of heaven, standing over all, to whom everything belongs and who belongs
to no one, with the various particular gods. It insisted emphatically that its God was not a national god of Israel in the way
that every people had its own deity. Israel insisted that it had
no god of its own but only the God of all people and of the
whole universe; it was convinced that precisely for this reason it alone worshipped the real God. I do not have God
until I no longer have any god of my own but only trust the
God who is just as much the next man's God as mine, because
we both belong to him.

The paradox of the biblical faith in God consists in the
conjunction and unity of the two elements just described, in
the fact, therefore, that Being is accepted as a person, and
the person accepted as Being itself, that only what is hidden
is accepted as the One who is near, only the inaccessible as
the One who is accessible, the one as the One who exists for
all men and for whom all exist. At this point let us break off
our analysis of the biblical idea of God and take up again on
a broader basis the question of the relationship between faith
and philosophy, between faith and understanding, which we
came up against at the start and which now poses itself to us
again at the end.

Chapter III

THE GOD OF FAITH AND THE GOD
OF THE PHILOSOPHERS

I. THE DECISION OF THE EARLY CHURCH
IN FAVOR OF PHILOSOPHY

The choice made in the biblical image of God had to be
made once again in the early days of Christianity and the
Church; at bottom it has to be made afresh in every spiritual
situation and thus always remains just as much a task as a gift.
The early Christian proclamation of the gospel and the early
Christian faith found themselves once again in an environment teeming with gods and thus once again facing the problem with which Israel had been confronted in its original
situation and in its debate with the great powers of the exilic
and postexilic period. Again it was a question of stating which
God the Christian faith really had in mind. It is true that the
early Christian decision could base itself on the whole preceding struggle, especially on the last phase of it, on the words
of the Deutero-Isaiah and the Wisdom literature, on the step
that had been taken in the Greek translation of the Old Testament, and finally on the writings of the New Testament,
especially St. John's Gospel. It was in the wake of this whole
series of events that early Christianity boldly and resolutely
made its choice and carried out its purification by deciding
for the God of the philosophers and *against* the gods of the
various religions. Wherever the question arose as to which

god the Christian God corresponded, Zeus perhaps or Hermes or Dionysus or some other god, the answer ran: To none of them. To none of the gods to whom you pray but solely and alone to him to whom you do not pray, to that highest being of whom your philosophers speak. The early Church resolutely put aside the whole cosmos of the ancient religions, regarding the whole of it as deceit and illusion, and explained its faith by saying: When we say God, we do not mean or worship any of this; we mean only Being itself, what the philosophers have expounded as the ground of all being, as the God above all powers—that alone is our God. This proceeding involved a choice, a decision, no less fateful and formative for ages to come than the choice of El and *yah* as opposed to Moloch and Baal had been in its time, with the subsequent development of the two into Elohim and toward Yahweh, the idea of Being. The choice thus made meant opting for the *logos* as against any kind of myth; it meant the definitive demythologization of the world and of religion.

Was this decision for the *logos* rather than the myth the right one? To find the answer to this we must keep in view all our previous reflections on the inner development of the biblical concept of God, the last stages of which had in essentials already determined that the position to be taken up by Christianity in the Hellenistic world should be this one. On the other side, it must be noted that the ancient world itself knew the dilemma between the God of faith and the God of the philosophers in a very pronounced form. Between the mythical gods of the religions and the philosophical knowledge of God there had developed in the course of history a stronger and stronger tension, which is apparent in the criticism of the myths by the philosophers from Xenophanes to Plato, who even thought of trying to replace the classical Homeric mythology with a new mythology appropriate to the *logos*. Contemporary scholarship is coming to see more and more clearly that there are quite amazing parallels in chronology and content between the philosophers' criticism of the myths in Greece and the prophets' criticism of the gods in Israel. It is true that the two movements start from completely different assumptions and have completely different aims; but the movement of the *logos* against the myth, as it evolved in the Greek mind in the philosophical enlightenment, so that in the end it necessarily led to the fall of the gods, has an inner parallelism with the enlightenment that the prophetic and Wisdom literature cultivated in its demythologization of the divine powers in favor of the one and only God. For all the differences between them, both movements coincide in their striving toward the *logos*. The philosophical enlightenment and its "physical" view of Being pressed the mythological semblance farther and farther back, though certainly without doing away with the religious form of the worship of the gods. The ancient religion did eventually break up because of the gulf between the God of faith and the God of the philosophers, because of the total dichotomy between reason and piety. That no success was achieved in uniting the two, that reason and piety moved farther and farther apart, and the God of faith and the God of the philosophers were separated from each other, meant the inner collapse of the ancient religion. The Christian religion would have to expect just the same fate if it were to accept a similar amputation of reason and were to embark on a corresponding withdrawal into the purely religious, as advocated by Schleiermacher and present, paradoxically enough, in a certain sense in Schleiermacher's great critic and opponent Karl Barth.

The opposing fates of myth and Gospel in the ancient world, the end of myth and the victory of the Gospel, are fundamentally to be explained, from the point of view of intellectual history, by the opposing relationship established in either instance between religion and philosophy, between faith and reason. The paradox of ancient philosophy consists, from the point of view of religious history, in the fact that intellectually it destroyed myth but simultaneously tried to legitimize it afresh as religion; in other words, that from the religious point of view it was not revolutionary but, at the most, evolutionary, that it treated religion as a question of the regulation of life, not as a question of truth. Paul, following the Wisdom literature, has described this circumstance in his Epistle to the Romans (1:18–31) in the language of the prophetic sermon (or Old Testament Wisdom discourse) with perfect accuracy. The reference to this mortal fate of the ancient religion, and to the paradox implicit in the separation of truth and piety, occurs in the Book of Wisdom, chapters 13–15. Paul recapitulates in a few verses what is said there in some detail, accounting for the fate of the ancient religion by the division between *logos* and myth: "For what can be known about God is plain to them, because God has shown it to them.... [But] although they knew God they did not honor him as God or give thanks to him.... [They] exchanged the glory of the immortal God for images resembling mortal man or birds or animals or reptiles" (Rom 1:19–23).

Religion did not go the way of the *logos* but lingered in myths already seen to be devoid of reality. Consequently its decline was inevitable; this followed from its divorce from the truth, a state of affairs that led to its being regarded as a mere *institutio vitae*, that is, as a mere contrivance and an outward form of life. The Christian position, as opposed to this situation, is put emphatically by Tertullian when he says with splendid boldness: "Christ called himself truth, not custom." [1] In my view this is one of the really great assertions of patristic theology. In it the struggle of the early Church, and the abiding task with which the Christian faith is confronted if it is to remain itself, is summed up with unique conciseness. The idolization of the *consuetudo Romana*, of the "tradition" of the city of Rome, which had made its own customs into a self-sufficient code of behavior, was challenged by the truth and its claim to uniqueness. Christianity thus put itself resolutely on the side of truth and turned its back on a conception of religion satisfied to be mere outward ceremonial that in the end can be interpreted to mean anything one fancies.

Another observation may help to clarify the point. The ancient world had finally tried to face up to the dilemma of its religion, to its divorce from the truth of the knowledge attained through philosophy, by adopting the idea of three theologies: physical, political, and mythical theology. It had justified the separation of myth and *logos* by consideration for the feelings of the people and consideration for the good of the state, insofar as a mythical theology permitted the simultaneous existence of a political theology. In other words, it had in fact weighed truth against custom, usefulness against truth. The exponents of the Neoplatonic philosophy went a step farther, by interpreting myth ontologically, expounding it as symbolic theology and thus trying via interpretation to reconcile it with the truth. But what can go on existing only through interpretation has in reality ceased to exist. The

---

[1] "Dominus noster Christus veritatem se, non consuetudinem cognominavit." *De virginibus velandis* I, 1, in *Corpus Christianorum seu nova Patrum collectio* (CChr) 2:1209.

human mind rightly turns to the truth itself, not to what by means of devious interpretation can be shown to be reconcilable with the truth, though no longer containing any truth itself.

Both procedures have something frighteningly contemporary about them. In a situation in which the truth of the Christian approach seems to be disappearing, the struggle for Christianity has brought to the fore again the two very methods that ancient polytheism employed to fight—and lose—its last battle. On one side, we have the retreat from the truth of reason into a realm of mere piety, mere faith, mere revelation; a retreat that in reality bears a fatal resemblance, whether by design or accident and whether the fact is admitted or not, to the ancient religion's retreat before the *logos*, to the flight from truth to beautiful custom, from nature to politics. On the other side, we have an approach I will call for short "interpreted Christianity": the stumbling blocks in Christianity are removed by the interpretative method, and, as part of the process of thus rendering it unobjectionable, its actual content is written off as dispensable phraseology, as a periphrasis not required to say the simple things now alleged, by complicated modes of exposition, to constitute its real meaning.

In contrast to all this, the original Christian option was something quite different. The Christian faith opted, we have seen, against the gods of the various religions and in favor of the God of the philosophers, that is, against the myth of custom and in favor of the truth of Being itself and nothing else. Hence the accusation made against the early Church that her adherents were atheists; this reproach arose out of the fact that the early Church did indeed reject the whole world of the ancient religion, declaring none of it to be acceptable and sweeping the whole system aside as empty custom that was contrary to the truth.

The God of the philosophers, however, who was left over, was not regarded by the ancient world as having any religious significance but as an academic extrareligious reality. To leave only him standing and to profess faith in him alone and in nothing else seemed like lack of religion, as a denial of religion, as atheism. The suspicion of atheism with which early Christianity had to contend makes its intellectual orientation, its decision against *religio* and custom devoid of truth, its option in favor of the truth of Being clearly apparent.

2. THE TRANSFORMATION OF THE GOD
OF THE PHILOSOPHERS

Of course, the other side of the picture must not be overlooked. By deciding exclusively in favor of the God of the philosophers and logically declaring this God to be the God who speaks to man and to whom one can pray, the Christian faith gave a completely new significance to this God of the philosophers, removing him from the purely academic realm and thus profoundly transforming him. This God who had previously existed as something neutral, as the highest, culminating concept; this God who had been understood as pure Being or pure thought, circling around forever closed in upon itself without reaching over to man and his little world; this God of the philosophers, whose pure eternity and unchangeability had excluded any relation with the changeable and transitory, now appeared to the eye of faith as the God of men, who is not only thought of all thoughts, the eternal mathematics of the universe, but also *agape*, the power of creative love. In this sense there does exist in the Christian faith what Pascal experienced on the night when he wrote on a slip of paper that he henceforth kept sewn in

the lining of his jacket the words: "Fire. 'God of Abraham,
God of Isaac, God of Jacob', not 'of the philosophers and
scholars'." [2] He had encountered the burning bush experience, as opposed to a God sinking back completely into the
realm of mathematics, and had realized that the God who is
the eternal geometry of the universe can only be this because
he is creative love, because he is the burning bush from which
a name issues forth, through which he enters the world of
man. So in this sense there is the experience that the God of
the philosophers is quite different from what the philosophers had thought him to be, though he does not thereby
cease to be what they had discovered; that one only comes
to know him properly when one realizes that he, the real
truth and ground of all Being, is at one and the same time
the God of faith, the God of men.

In order to see the transformation undergone by the philosophical concept of God through being equated with the
God of faith, one need only look at any passage in the Bible
that speaks of God. Let us take quite at random Luke 15:1–
10, the parables of the lost sheep and the lost drachma. The
point of departure is the irritation felt by the scribes and
Pharisees at the fact that Jesus sat down to eat with sinners.
In reply comes the story of the man who owns a hundred
sheep, loses one of them, goes after it, looks for it and finds
it, and rejoices more than over the ninety-nine for which he
never needed to search. The story of the lost drachma that,
when found again, causes more joy than the one that was

[2] The text of the "Mémorial", as this slip of paper is called, is quoted in R.
Guardini, *Christliches Bewusstsein*, 2nd ed. (Munich, 1950), pp. 47f.; on p. 23
there is a facsimile, reduced in size, of the original; see also Guardini's analysis,
on pp. 27–61. This is supplemented and corrected by H. Vorgrimler, "Marginalien zur Kirchenfrömmigkeit Pascals", in J. Daniélou and H. Vorgrimler,
Sentire ecclesiam (Freiburg, 1961), pp. 371–406.

never lost tends in the same direction: "Just so, I tell you, there will be more joy in heaven over one sinner who repents than over ninety-nine righteous persons who need no repentance" (15:7). This parable, in which Jesus depicts and justifies his activity and his task as the emissary of God, involves not only the relations between God and man but also the question of who God himself is.

If we try to answer the question on the basis of this passage, we shall have to say that the God whom we encounter here appears to be, as in so many passages of the Old Testament, highly anthropomorphic, highly unphilosophical; he has emotions as a man does, he rejoices, he seeks, he waits, he goes to meet. He is not the unfeeling geometry of the universe, neutral justice standing above things undisturbed by a heart and its emotions; he *has* a heart; he stands there like a person who loves, with all the capriciousness of someone who loves. Thus in this passage the transformation of purely philosophical thinking becomes clear, and it becomes apparent how far we still are fundamentally from this identification of the God of faith and the God of the philosophers, how incapable we are of catching up with it, and how badly our basic image of God and our understanding of the Christian reality come to grief *on this very point*.

Most people today still admit in some form or other that there probably is some such thing as a "supreme being". But people find it an absurd idea that this being should concern himself with man; we have the feeling—for it happens again and again even to those who try to believe— that this sort of thing is the expression of a naïve anthropomorphism, of a primitive mode of thought comprehensible in a situation in which man still lived in a small world, in which the earth was the center of all things and

God had nothing else to do but look down on it. But, we think, in an age when we know how infinitely different things are, how unimportant the earth is in the vast universe and consequently how unimportant that little speck of dust, man, is in comparison with the dimensions of the cosmos—in an age like this it seems an absurd idea that this supreme being should concern himself with man, his pitiful little world, his cares, his sins, and his non-sins. But although we may think that in this way we are speaking about God in an appropriately divine manner, in reality we are in fact thinking of him in a very petty and only too human way, as if he had to be selective so as not to miss the overview. We thereby imagine him as a consciousness like ours, which has limits, must somewhere or other call a halt, and can never embrace the whole.

In contrast to such limited notions, the aphorism with which Hölderlin prefaced his *Hyperion* will serve to recall the Christian image of the true greatness of God: "Non coerceri maximo, contineri tamen a minimo, divinum est" (Not to be encompassed by the greatest, but to let oneself be encompassed by the smallest—that is divine). The boundless spirit who bears in himself the totality of Being reaches beyond the "greatest", so that to him it is small, and he reaches into the smallest, because to him nothing is too small. Precisely this overstepping of the greatest and reaching down into the smallest is the true nature of absolute spirit. At the same time we see here a reversal in value of maximum and minimum, greatest and smallest, that is typical of the Christian understanding of reality. To him who as spirit upholds and encompasses the universe, a spirit, a man's heart with its ability to love, is greater than all the milky ways in the universe. Quantitative criteria become irrelevant; other orders of magnitude become visible, according to which the infinitely small is the truly embracing and truly great.[3]

From this angle yet another prejudice is unmasked as a prejudice. It always seems to us in the last analysis self-evident that the infinitely great, the absolute spirit, cannot be emotion and feeling but only pure cosmic mathematics. We unthinkingly assume that pure thought is greater than love, while the message of the Gospel, and the Christian picture of God contained in it, corrects philosophy and lets us know that love is higher than mere thought. Absolute thought is a kind of love; it is not unfeeling idea, but creative, because it is love.

To sum up, we can say that, in the deliberate connection with the God of the philosophers made by the Christian faith, purely philosophical thinking was transcended on two fundamental points:

a. *The philosophical God is essentially self-centered*, thought simply contemplating itself. The God of faith is basically defined by the category of relationship. He is creative fullness encompassing the whole. Thereby a completely new picture of the world, a completely new world order is established: the highest possibility of Being no longer seems to be the detachment of him who exists in himself and needs only

---

[3] The origin of the "epitaph on Loyola" quoted by Hölderlin has been explained by H. Rahner, "Die Grabschrift des Loyola", in *Stimmen der Zeit*, year 72, vol. 139 (February 1947): 321–37: the saying comes from the great work *Imago primi saeculi Societatis Jesu a Provincia Flandro–Belgica eiusdem Societatis repraesentata* (Antwerp, 1640). On pages 280–82 of this work there is an *elogium sepulchrale* on St. Ignatius by an unknown young Flemish Jesuit from which the saying is taken; cf. also Hölderlin, *Werke*, vol. 3, ed. by F. Beissner, special edition for the Wissenschaftliche Buchgesellschaft, Darmstadt (Stuttgart, 1965), pp. 346f. The same idea occurs in a large number of impressive late Jewish texts; cf. on this aspect P. Kuhn, *Gottes Selbsterniedrigung in der Theologie der Rabbinen* (Munich, 1968), especially pp. 13–22.

himself. On the contrary, the highest mode of Being includes the element of relationship. It is hardly necessary to say what a revolution it must mean for the direction of man's existence when the supreme Being no longer appears as absolute, enclosed autarchy but turns out to be at the same time involvement, creative power, which creates and bears and loves other things . . .

b. The philosophical God is pure thought: he is based on the notion that thought and thought alone is divine. The God of faith, as thought, is also love. His image is based on the conviction that to love is divine.

The *logos* of the whole world, the creative original thought, is at the same time love; in fact this thought is creative because, as thought, it is love, and, as love, it is thought. It becomes apparent that truth and love are originally identical; that where they are completely realized they are not two parallel or even opposing realities but one, the one and only absolute. At this point it also becomes possible to glimpse the starting point of the confession of faith in the tri-une God, to which we shall return later.

3. THE REFLECTION OF THE QUESTION IN THE TEXT OF THE CREED

In the Apostles' Creed, the point of departure of our reflections, the paradoxical unity of the God of faith and the God of the philosophers, on which the Christian image of God rests, is expressed in the juxtaposition of the two attributes "Father" and "Almighty" ("Lord of all"). The second title— *panto-krator* in Greek—points back to the Old Testament "Yahweh Zebaoth" (Sabaoth), the meaning of which can no longer be fully elucidated. Literally translated, it means something like "God of hosts", "God of powers"; it is sometimes rendered in the Greek Bible by "Lord of powers". For all the uncertainties about its origin, we can at any rate see that this word is intended to describe God as the Lord of heaven and earth; it was probably intended above all to define him, in opposition to the Babylonian religion of the stars, as the Lord to whom the stars, too, belong, alongside whom the stars cannot exist as independent divine powers: the stars are not gods, but *his* tools, at his disposal like a warlord's armies. Thus the word *pantokrator* has at first a cosmic significance; later it also has a political sense, describing God as the Lord of all lords.[4] By calling God simultaneously "Father" and "Almighty", the Creed has joined together a family concept and the concept of cosmic power in the description of the one God. It thereby expresses accurately the whole point of the Christian image of God: the tension between absolute power and absolute love, absolute distance and absolute proximity, between absolute Being and a direct affinity with the most human side of humanity, the interplay of maximum and minimum of which we spoke just now.

The word "Father", which in its reference point here still remains quite open, at the same time links the first article of the Creed to the second; it points forward to Christology and thus harnesses the two sections together in such a way that what is said of God only becomes fully comprehensible when one at the same time looks over at the Son. For example, what "almightiness" and "lordship of all" mean only becomes clear from a Christian point of view in the crib and the Cross. It is only here, where the God who is recognized

---

[4] Kattenbusch 2:526; P. van Imschoot, "Heerscharen", in H. Haag, *Bibellexikon* (Einsiedeln, 1951), pp. 667–69. In the second edition (1968), p. 684, the article has been drastically shortened.

as Lord of all has voluntarily chosen the final degree of powerlessness by delivering himself up to his weakest creature,
that the Christian concept of the almightiness of God can be
truly formulated. At this point simultaneously a new concept of power and a new concept of lordship and dominion
are born. The highest power is demonstrated as the calm
willingness completely to renounce all power; and we are
shown that it is powerful, not through force, but only through
the freedom of love, which, even when it is rejected, is
stronger than the exultant powers of earthly violence. Here
and only here does that revaluation of criteria and dimensions that made itself heard earlier in the antithesis of maximum and minimum finally come into its own.

Chapter IV

FAITH IN GOD TODAY

After all we have said, what does it mean today when a man says, in the words of the Church's Creed, "I believe in God"? Anyone who utters these words makes first and foremost a decision about values and emphasis in this world that is certainly comprehensible as truth (and, indeed, in a qualified sense must be regarded as a decision for the truth) but in the last analysis can only be attained in the decision and as decision. What thus takes place is also a decision in the sense that a separation is made between various possibilities. What Israel had to do in the early days of its history, and the Church had to do again at the beginning of her career, must be done afresh in every human life. Just as in those days the verdict had to be delivered against the possibilities symbolized by Moloch and Baal, against custom and in favor of truth, so the Christian statement "I believe in God" is always a process of separation, of acceptance, of purification, and of transformation. Only in this way can the Christian confession of faith in the one God be maintained in the passing ages. But in what directions does this process point today?

1. THE PRIMACY OF THE LOGOS

Christian faith in God means first the decision in favor of the primacy of the *logos* as against mere matter. Saying "I believe that God exists" also implies opting for the view that the *logos*—that is, the idea, freedom, love—stands not merely at the end but also at the beginning, that it is the originating and encompassing power of all being. In other words, faith means deciding for the view that thought and meaning do not just form a chance by-product of being; that, on the contrary, all being is a product of thought and, indeed, in its innermost structure is itself thought.

To that extent faith means in a specific sense deciding for the truth, since, to faith, being itself is truth, comprehensibility, meaning, and all this does not simply represent a secondary product of being that arose at some point or other but could have no structural, authoritative meaning for reality as a whole.

This decision in favor of the intellectual structure of the kind of being that emerges from meaning and understanding includes the belief in creation. This means nothing else than the conviction that the objective mind we find present in all things, indeed, as which we learn increasingly to understand things, is the impression and expression of subjective mind and that the intellectual structure that being possesses and that we can *re*-think is the expression of a creative *pre*-meditation, to which they owe their existence.

To put it more precisely, in the old Pythagorean saying about the God who practices geometry there is expressed that insight into the mathematical structure of being which learns to understand being as having been thought, as intellectually structured; there is also expressed the perception that even matter is not simply non-sense that eludes understanding, that it too bears in itself truth and comprehensibility that make intellectual comprehension possible. In our time, through the investigation of the mathematical construction of matter and the way it can be conceived and evaluated in mathematical terms, this insight has gained an amazing solidity. Einstein said once that in the laws of nature "an intelligence so superior is revealed that in comparison all the significance of human thinking and human arrangements is a completely worthless reflection."[1]

This surely means that all our thinking is, indeed, only a rethinking of what in reality has already been thought out beforehand. It can only try in a paltry way to trace over that being-thought which things are and to find truth in it. The mathematical understanding of the world has here discovered, through the mathematics of the universe, so to speak, the "God of the philosophers"—with all its problems, as is shown when Einstein over and over again rejects the concept of a personal God as "anthropomorphic", ascribing it to the "religion of fear" and the "religion of morality", with which he contrasts, as the only appropriate attitude, the "cosmic religiosity" that to him expresses itself in "enraptured wonder at the harmony of the laws of nature", in a "deep faith in the rationality of the structure of the world", and in the "longing for understanding, if only of a pale reflection of the intelligence revealed in this world".[2]

Here we have before us the whole problem of belief in God. On the one side, there is the transparency of being, which as being-thought points to a process of thinking; on the other, we have the impossibility of bringing this thinking of being into relation with man. It becomes easy to see

[1] A. Einstein, *Mein Weltbild*, ed. by C. Seelig (Zürich, Stuttgart, and Vienna, 1953), p. 21.

[2] Ibid., pp. 18–22. In the section entitled "The Necessity for an Ethical Culture" (pp. 22–24) there are signs of a loosening of the previously intimate connection between scientific knowledge and religious wonder; his perception of the specifically religious seems to have been somewhat sharpened by previous tragic experiences.

the barrier to equating the "God of faith" and the "God of
the philosophers" constituted by a narrow and insufficiently
pondered concept of person.

Before we try to make any progress on this point, I should
like to cite another similar statement by a scientist. James
Jeans once said: "We discover that the universe shows traces
of a planning and controlling power that has something in
common with our own individual minds, not, so far as we
have yet discovered, feeling, morality, or aesthetic capacity,
but the tendency to think in a way that, for lack of a better
word, we have called geometry." [3] This is the same thing all
over again: the mathematician discovers the mathematics of
the cosmos, the being-thought-ness of things; but no more.
He discovers only the God of the philosophers.

But is this really surprising? Can the mathematician who
looks at the world mathematically find anything else but mathematics in the universe? Should not one rather ask him
whether he has not himself at some time or other looked at
the world in a way that is other than mathematical? Whether,
for example, he has never seen an apple tree in blossom and
wondered why the process of fertilization by the interplay
between bees and tree is not effected otherwise than through
the roundabout way of the blossom, thus including the completely superfluous wonder of beauty, which again, of course,
can only be understood by cooperation, by relying on that
which is already beautiful even without us? When Jeans opines
that this kind of thing has so far not been discovered in the
mind of which he speaks, one can confidently say to him
that it will indeed never be discovered by physics and cannot
be, because in its investigations it abstracts, in accordance

[3] Quoted in W. von Hartlieb, *Das Christentum und die Gegenwart*, Stifter-
bibliothek, vol. 21 (Salzburg, 1953), pp. 18f.

with its nature, from the aesthetic feeling and from the moral attitude, questions nature from a purely mathematical point of view, and consequently can also catch sight only of the mathematical side of nature. The answer depends quite simply on the question. Yet the man who seeks a view of the whole will have to say: In the world we find present, without doubt, objective mathematics; but we also find equally present in the world unparalleled and unexplained wonders of beauty, or, to be more accurate, there are events that appear to the apprehending mind of man in the form of beauty, so that he is bound to say that the mathematician responsible for these events has displayed an unparalleled degree of creative imagination.

If we summarize the observations we have strung together in a sketchy and fragmentary fashion we can say: The world is objective mind; it meets us in an intellectual structure, that is, it offers itself to our mind as something that can be reflected upon and understood. From this follows the next step. To say "*Credo in Deum*—I believe in God" expresses the conviction that objective mind is the product of subjective mind and can only exist at all as the declension of it, that, in other words, being-thought (as we find it present in the structure of the world) is not possible without thinking.

It may be useful to clarify and confirm this statement by inserting it—again only in broad strokes—into a kind of self-criticism of historical reason. After two and a half thousand years of philosophical thinking it is no longer possible for us to speak blithely about the subject itself as if so many different people had not tried to do the same thing before us and come to grief. Moreover, when we survey the acres of shattered hypotheses, vainly applied ingenuity, and empty logic that history shows us, we might well lose all heart in the quest for the real, hidden truth that transcends the obvious.

Yet the situation is not quite so hopeless as it must appear at first sight, for in spite of the almost endless variety of opposing philosophical paths that man has taken in his attempts to think out being, in the last analysis there are only a few basic ways of explaining the secret of being. The question to which everything finally leads could be formulated like this: In all the variety of individual things, what is, so to speak, the common stuff of being—what is the one being behind the many "things", which nevertheless all "exist"? The many answers produced by history can finally be reduced to two basic possibilities. The first and most obvious would run something like this: Everything we encounter is in the last analysis stuff, matter; *this* is the only thing that always remains as demonstrable reality and, consequently, represents the real being of all that exists—the materialistic solution. The other possibility points in the opposite direction. It says: Whoever looks thoroughly at matter will discover that it is being-thought, objectivized thought. So it cannot be the ultimate. On the contrary, before it comes thinking, the idea; all being is ultimately being-thought and can be traced back to mind as the original reality; this is the "idealistic" solution.

To reach a verdict we must ask still more precisely: What is matter, really? And what is mind? Abbreviating drastically, we could say that we call "matter" a being that does not itself comprehend being, that "is" but does not understand itself. The reduction of all being to matter as the primary form of reality consequently implies that the beginning and ground of all being is constituted by a form of being that does not itself understand being; this also means that the understanding of being only arises as a secondary, chance product during the course of development. This at the same time also gives us the definition of "mind": it can be described as being that understands itself, as being that is present to itself. The idealistic solution to the problem of being accordingly signifies the idea that all being is the being-thought by one single consciousness. The unity of being consists in the identity of the one consciousness, whose impulses constitute the many things that are.

The Christian belief in God is not completely identical with either of these two solutions. To be sure, it, too, will say, being is being-thought. Matter itself points beyond itself to thinking as the earlier and more original factor. But in opposition to idealism, which makes all being into moments of an all-embracing consciousness, the Christian belief in God will say: Being is being-thought—yet not in such a way that it remains only thought and that the appearance of independence proves to be mere appearance to anyone who looks more closely. On the contrary, Christian belief in God means that things are the being-thought of a creative consciousness, of a creative freedom, and that the creative consciousness that bears up all things has released what has been thought into the freedom of its own, independent existence. In this it goes beyond any mere idealism. While the latter, as we have just established, explains everything real as the content of a single consciousness, in the Christian view what supports it all is a creative freedom that sets what has been thought in the freedom of its own being, so that, on the one hand, it is the being-thought of a consciousness and yet, on the other hand, is true being itself.

This also clarifies the heart of the creation concept: the model from which creation must be understood is not the craftsman but the creative mind, creative thinking. At the same time it becomes evident that the idea of freedom is the characteristic mark of the Christian belief in God as opposed to any kind of monism. At the beginning of all being it puts not just some kind of consciousness but a creative freedom that creates further freedoms. To this extent one could very well describe Christianity as a philosophy of freedom. For Christianity, the explanation of reality as a whole is not an all-embracing consciousness or one single materiality; on the contrary, at the summit stands a freedom that thinks and, by thinking, creates freedoms, thus making freedom the structural form of all being.

2. THE PERSONAL GOD

If Christian belief in God is first of all an option in favor of the primacy of the *logos*, faith in the preexisting, world-supporting reality of the creative meaning, it is at the same time, as belief in the personal nature of that meaning, the belief that the original thought, whose being-thought is represented by the world, is not an anonymous, neutral consciousness but rather freedom, creative love, a person. Accordingly, if the Christian option for the *logos* means an option for a personal, creative meaning, then it is at the same time an option for the primacy of the particular as against the universal. The highest is not the most universal but, precisely, the particular, and the Christian faith is thus above all also the option for man as the irreducible, infinity-oriented being. And here once again it is the option for the primacy of freedom as against the primacy of some cosmic necessity or natural law. Thus the specific features of the Christian faith as opposed to other intellectual choices of the human mind now stand out in clear relief. The position occupied by a man who utters the Christian *Credo* becomes unmistakably clear.

Moreover, it can be shown that the first option—for the primacy of the *logos* as opposed to mere matter—is not possible without the second and third, or, to be more accurate, the first, taken on its own, would remain mere idealism; it is only the addition of the second and third options—primacy of the particular, primacy of freedom—that marks the watershed between idealism and Christian belief, which now denotes something different from mere idealism.

Much could be said about this. Let us content ourselves with the indispensable elucidations by first asking what it really means to say that this *logos*, whose thought is the world, is a person and that therefore faith is the option in favor of the primacy of the particular over the universal. In the last analysis, the answer can be put quite simply: It means nothing else than that the creative thinking we found to be the precondition and ground of all being is truly conscious thinking and that it knows not only itself but also its whole thought. It means further that this thinking not only knows but loves; that it is creative because it is love; and that, because it can love as well as think, it has given its thought the freedom of its own existence, objectivized it, released it into distinct being. So the whole thing means that this thinking knows its thought in its distinct being, loves it and, loving, upholds it. Which brings us back to the saying to which our reflections keep leading: Not to be encompassed by the greatest, but to let oneself be encompassed by the smallest—that is divine.

But if the *logos* of all being, the being that upholds and encompasses everything, is consciousness, freedom, and love, then it follows automatically that the supreme factor in the world is not cosmic necessity but freedom. The implications of this are very extensive. For this leads to the conclusion that freedom is evidently the necessary structure of the world, as it were, and this again means that one can only comprehend the world as incomprehensible, that it must be incomprehensibility. For if the supreme point in the world's design is a freedom that upholds, wills, knows, and loves the whole world as freedom, then this means that together with freedom the incalculability implicit in it is an essential part of the world. Incalculability is an implication of freedom; the world can never—if this is the position—be completely reduced to mathematical logic. With the boldness and greatness of a world defined by the structure of freedom there comes also the somber mystery of the demonic, which emerges from it to meet us. A world created and willed on the risk of freedom and love is no longer just mathematics. As the arena of love it is also the playground of freedom and also incurs the risk of evil. It accepts the mystery of darkness for the sake of the greater light constituted by freedom and love.

Once again it becomes evident here how the categories of minimum and maximum, smallest and greatest, change in a perspective of this sort. In a world that in the last analysis is not mathematics but love, the minimum is a maximum; the smallest thing that can love is one of the biggest things; the particular is more than the universal; the person, the unique and unrepeatable, is at the same time the ultimate and highest thing. In such a view of the world, the person is not just an individual, a reproduction arising by the diffusion of the idea into matter, but, precisely, a "person". Greek thought always regarded the many individual creatures, including the many individual human beings, only as individuals, arising out of the splitting up of the idea in matter. The reproductions are thus always secondary; the real thing is the one and universal. The Christian sees in man, not an individual, but a person; and it seems to me that this passage from individual to person contains the whole span of the transition from antiquity to Christianity, from Platonism to faith. This definite being is not at all something secondary, giving us a fragmentary glimpse of the universal, which is the real. As the minimum it is a maximum; as the unique and unrepeatable, it is something supreme and real.

From this follows one last step. If it is the case that the person is more than the individual, that the many is something real and not something secondary, that there exists a primacy of the particular over the universal, then oneness is not the unique and final thing; plurality, too, has its own and definitive right. This assertion, which follows by an inner necessity from the Christian option, leads of its own accord to a transcending of the concept of a God who is mere oneness. The internal logic of the Christian belief in God compels us to go beyond mere monotheism and leads to the belief in the triune God, who must now, in conclusion, be discussed.

Chapter V

BELIEF IN THE TRIUNE GOD

Our previous reflections have brought us to the point at which
the Christian profession of faith in the one God passes over by
a kind of inner necessity to the profession of faith in the triune
God. On the other hand, we cannot overlook the fact that we
are now touching a realm in which Christian theology must
be more aware of its limits than it has often been in the past; a
realm in which any false forthrightness in the attempt to gain
too precise a knowledge is bound to end in disastrous fool-
ishness; a realm in which only the humble admission of igno-
rance can be true knowledge and only wondering attendance
before the incomprehensible mystery can be the right profession of faith in God. Love is always *mysterium*—more than one
can reckon or grasp by subsequent reckoning. Love itself—
the uncreated, eternal God—*must* therefore be in the highest
degree a mystery—"the" *mysterium* itself.

Yet—despite the necessary moderation of reason, which
here is the only way in which thinking can remain true to
itself and to its task—the question must be posed: What is
really meant by the profession of faith in the triune God? We
cannot here attempt—as we really should in order to reach a
satisfactory answer—to trace the individual stages by which
it developed or even to display the individual formulas in
which faith strove to protect it from misinterpretation. A
few indications must suffice.

a. The point of departure of the belief in the triune God

The doctrine of the Trinity did not arise out of speculation about God, out of an attempt by philosophical thinking to figure out what the fount of all being was like; it developed out of the effort to digest historical experiences. The biblical faith was concerned at first—in the Old Covenant—with God, who was encountered as the Father of Israel, the Father of the peoples, the Creator of the world and its Lord. In the formative period of the New Testament comes a completely unexpected event in which God shows himself from a hitherto unknown side: in Jesus Christ one meets a man who at the same time knows and professes himself to be the Son of God. One finds God in the shape of the ambassador who is completely God, not some kind of intermediary being, yet with us says to God "Father". The result is a curious paradox: on the one hand, this man calls God his Father and speaks to him intimately as to a person facing him; if this is not to be a piece of empty theatricality but truth, which alone befits God, then Christ must be someone other than this Father to whom *he* speaks and to whom *we* speak. But, on the other hand, he is himself the real proximity of God coming to meet us, God's mediation to us, and that precisely because he himself is God as man, in human form and nature, God-with-us ("Emmanuel"). His mediation would indeed basically cancel itself out and become a separation instead of a mediation if he were someone other than God, if he were an intermediate being. He would then be guiding us, not toward God, but away from him. It thus turns out that as mediator he is God himself and "man himself"—both with equal reality and totality. But this means that God meets me

here, not as Father, but as Son and as my brother, whereby—
both incomprehensibly and quite comprehensibly—a duality appears in God: God as "I" and "You" in one. This new
experience of God is followed finally by a third, the experience of the Spirit, the presence of God in us, in our innermost being. And again it turns out that this "Spirit" is not
simply identical either with the Father or the Son, nor is he
yet a third thing erected between God and us; it is the manner in which God gives himself to us, in which he enters
into us, so that he is *in* man yet, in the midst of this "indwell-
ing", is infinitely *above* him.

We can thus observe that the Christian faith first comes to
deal with God in this triple shape in the course of its historical development, as a matter of sheer fact. It is clear that
it had to begin straightaway to consider how these different
pieces of data were to be reconciled with each other. It had
to ask itself how these three forms of historical encounter
with God were related to the particular reality of God himself. Is the triplicity of the form in which God is experienced perhaps only his historical mask, in which he approaches
man in different roles yet always as the One? Does this triplicity only tell us something about man and the various modes
of his relationship to God, or does it shed light on what God
is like in himself? If today we might swiftly feel inclined to
regard only the former as conceivable and with that to consider all the problems solved, before taking refuge in such a
solution we ought to make ourselves aware of the scope of
the question. The point at issue here is whether man in his
relations with God is only dealing with the reflections of his
own consciousness or whether it is given to him to reach
out beyond himself and to encounter God himself. In either
case the consequences are far-reaching. If the first hypoth-
esis is true, then prayer, too, is only an occupation of man

with himself; there are no more grounds for worship, strictly speaking, than there are for prayers of petition—and this inference is in fact drawn to an increasing degree. This renders all the more pressing the question of whether it does not rest in the end on comfortable thinking that takes the line of least resistance without asking too many questions. For if the other answer is the correct one, worship and prayer are not only possible; they are commanded, that is, they are a postulate of the being "man" who is open to God.

Anyone who sees the profundity of the question will at the same time understand the passionate nature of the struggle that was fought out around it in the ancient Church; he will understand that anything but hair-splitting and formula-worship was involved, as a superficial view might easily suggest. Indeed, he will realize that the strife of those days is flaring up afresh today in just the same form—the one constant struggle of man for God and for himself—and that we cannot endure as Christians if we think it permissible to make it easier for ourselves today than it was then. Let us anticipate the answer found in those days to the parting between the path of faith and a path bound to lead to the mere appearance of faith: God *is* as he *shows* himself; God does not show himself in a way in which he is not. On this assertion rests the Christian relation with God; in it is grounded the doctrine of the Trinity; indeed, it *is* this doctrine.

b. The guiding motives

What led to this conclusion? Three basic attitudes were decisive. The first could be described as faith in man's immediate proximity to God, the belief that the man who comes to deal with Christ meets in his fellow man Jesus, who as a fellow man is attainable and accessible to him, who is God

himself, not some hybrid being intervening. The concern in
the early Church about the true divinity of Jesus springs from
the same root as the concern about his true humanity. Only
if he was really a man like us can he be *our* mediator, and
only if he is really God, like God, does the mediation reach
its goal. It is not at all difficult to see that the fundamental
decision of monotheism, the previously described equation
of the God of faith with the God of the philosophers, here
comes into the question and becomes exceptionally acute:
Only the God who, on the one hand, is the real ground of
the world and, on the other, totally the One near to us can
be the goal of a piety devoted to the truth. Thus the second
basic attitude has already been described by implication: the
unyielding loyalty to a strictly monotheistic decision, to the
confession, "There is only *one* God." Care had to be taken
at all costs not to erect again, via the mediator, a whole region
of middle beings and, with it, a region of false gods where
man worships what is not God.

The third basic attitude could be described as the effort to
give the story of God's dealings with man its due and to take
it seriously. This means that when God appears as Son, who
says "You" to the Father, it is not a play produced for man,
not a masked ball on the stage of human history, but the
expression of reality. The idea of a divine show had been
canvassed in the ancient Church by the Monarchians. The
three Persons, they maintained, were three "roles" in which
God shows himself to us in the course of history. Here it
must be mentioned that the word *persona* and its Greek equivalent, *prosopon*, belong to the language of the theater. They
denoted the mask that made the actor into the embodiment
of someone else. It was as a result of considerations of this
sort that the word was first introduced into the language of
Christianity and so transformed by the Christian faith itself

in the course of a severe struggle that out of the word arose the idea of the person, a notion alien to antiquity.

Others—the so-called Modalists—thought that the three forms of God were three *modi*, ways, in which our consciousness perceives God and explains him to itself. Although it is true that we only know God as he is reflected in human thought, the Christian faith held firmly to the view that in this reflection it is *him* that we know. Even if we are not capable of breaking *out* of the narrow bounds of our consciousness, God can nevertheless break *into* this consciousness and show himself in it. All the same, it need not be denied that the efforts of the Monarchians and Modalists resulted in noteworthy progress toward a correct conception of God; after all, the language of Christianity adopted the terminology they developed, and in the profession of faith in the three *Persons* in God it is still at work today. That the word *prosopon* or *persona* could not at once express the whole scope of what there is to express here was not, after all, their fault. The enlargement of the bounds of human thinking necessary to absorb intellectually the Christian experience of God did not come of its own accord. It demanded a struggle, in which even error was fruitful; here it followed the basic law that everywhere governs the human mind in its advances.

c. *The hopelessness of the solutions*

In the light of what we have already said, the whole struggle of the first few centuries, with its many ramifications, can be traced back to the inadequacy of two paths, which had more and more to be recognized as dead ends: Subordinationism and Monarchianism. Both solutions *seem* logical; yet with their seductive simplifications both destroy the whole. The

teaching of the Church, as it comes to us in the doctrine of
the triune God, means at bottom renouncing any solution
and remaining content with a mystery that cannot be plumbed
by man. In truth this profession of faith is the only real way
to renounce the arrogance of "knowing all about it", which
makes smooth solutions with their false modesty so tempting.

So-called Subordinationism escapes from the dilemma by
saying: God himself is only a single being; Christ is not God
but only a being particularly close to God. This removes the
difficulty, but the consequence—as we explained at length a
little earlier—is that man is cut off from God himself and
confined, so to speak, to the antechamber. God becomes a
sort of constitutional monarch; faith deals, not with him,
but only with his ministers.[1] Anyone who is not content
with this, who really believes in the Lordship of God, in the
"greatest" in the smallest, will have to hold fast to the belief
that God *is* man, that the being of God and man intermin-
gle, and will thus adopt with the belief in Christ the starting
point of the doctrine of the Trinity.

Monarchianism, whose solution we have touched on earlier, solves the dilemma by proceeding in the opposite direction. It, too, holds firmly to the oneness of God but at the same
time also takes seriously the God who meets us, the God who
comes toward us, first as Creator and Father, then, in Christ,
as Son and Redeemer, and finally as Holy Spirit. But these three
figures are regarded only as masks of God that tell us something about ourselves but nothing about God himself. Tempting as such an approach seems, in the end it leads back to a
situation in which man is only circling around in himself and
not penetrating to God's own reality. The subsequent history

---

[1] E. Peterson, *Theologische Traktate* (Munich, 1951), pp. 45–147; for monotheism as a political problem, see especially pp. 52f.

of Monarchianism in modern thinking has only confirmed this once again. Hegel and Schelling, in their efforts to interpret Christianity philosophically and to rethink philosophy from Christian premises, went back to this early Christian attempt at a philosophy of Christianity and hoped by starting from here to make the doctrine of the Trinity intelligible and useful, to elevate it in its allegedly pure philosophical sense into the true key to all understanding of Being. Obviously we cannot try here to give an overall evaluation of these attempts, the most stimulating so far made, to adapt the Christian faith in intellectual terms. All we can do is indicate how they, too, like Monarchianism (and Modalism), run up again, for all practical purposes, against a dead end.

The point of departure of this whole approach remains the idea that the doctrine of the Trinity is the expression of the historical side of God and, therefore, of the way in which God appears in history. Inasmuch as Hegel and—in a different way—Schelling push this idea to its logical conclusion, they reach the point where they no longer distinguish this process of the historical self-revelation of God from a God quietly resting in himself behind it all; instead, they now understand the process of history as the process of God himself. The historical form of God, then, is the gradual self-realization of the divine; thus, while history is the process of the *logos*, even the *logos* is only real as the process of history. In other words, this means that it is only gradually in the course of history that the *logos*—the meaning of all being—brings itself forth to itself. Thus the "historicization" of the doctrine of the Trinity, as contained in Monarchianism, now becomes the "historicization" of God. This again signifies that meaning is no longer simply the creator of history; instead, history becomes the creator of meaning, and the latter becomes its creation. From this vantage point Karl Marx merely continued resolutely this line of thinking by asserting that if meaning does not precede man, then it lies in the future, which man himself must bring about by his own struggles.

It thus becomes clear that the logic of Monarchianism is just as unhelpful to faith as Subordinationism is. For such a view does away with the confrontation of freedoms, so essential to faith; it also does away with the dialogue of love and its incalculability; and it does away with the "personal" structure of meaning, with its interplay of greatest and smallest, of the world-encompassing meaning and the creature in quest of meaning. All this—the personal element, the dialogue, the freedom, and the love—is merged into the inevitability of the one process of reason. But something else, too, comes to light here: the radical attempt to fathom the doctrine of the Trinity, the thoroughly logical approach that ends in the "historicization" of the *logos* itself and, with the comprehension of God, also wants to abolish mystery and comprehend the history of God, to construct it itself according to its own logic—this grandiose attempt to lay hands on the logic of the *logos* itself leads us back to a mythology of history, to the myth of a God who brings himself to birth historically. The attempt at total logic ends in illogicality, in the self-dissolution of logic into myth.

The history of Monarchianism also has another side to it that must at least be briefly mentioned here. Even in its early Christian form and then again in its revival by Hegel and Marx, it has a decidedly political tinge; it is "political theology". In the ancient Church it served the attempt to give the imperial monarchy a theological foundation; in Hegel it becomes the apotheosis of the Prussian state, and in Marx a program of action to secure a sound future for humanity. Conversely, it could be shown how in the old Church the victory of belief in the Trinity over Monarchianism signified a victory over the political abuse of theology: the ecclesiastical belief in the

Trinity shattered the politically usable molds, destroyed the potentialities of theology as a political myth, and disowned the misuse of the Gospel to justify a political situation.[2]

d. The doctrine of the Trinity as negative theology

If one surveys the whole question it is possible to observe that the ecclesiastical doctrine of the Trinity can be justified first and foremost on the negative side, as a demonstration of the hopelessness of all other approaches. Indeed, perhaps this is all we can really accomplish here. The doctrine of the Trinity would in that case be essentially negative—the only remaining way to reject all attempts to fathom the subject, a sort of cipher for the insolubility of the mystery of God. It would become questionable if, for its part, it were to result in a simple, positive desire for knowledge. If the painful history of the human and Christian striving for God proves *anything*, it surely proves this: that any attempt to reduce God to the scope of our own comprehension leads to the absurd. We can only speak rightly about him if we renounce the attempt to comprehend and let him be the uncomprehended. Any doctrine of the Trinity, therefore, cannot aim at being a perfect comprehension of God. It is a frontier notice, a discouraging gesture pointing over to unchartable territory. It is not a definition that confines a thing to the pigeonholes of human knowledge, nor is it a concept that would put the thing within the grasp of the human mind.

This character of allusion, in which the concept becomes a mere hint, and comprehension a mere reaching out toward

[2] Ibid., pp. 102ff. Peterson's concluding remark (p. 147, n. 168) is also important: "The concept of 'political theology' was introduced, so far as I know, by Carl Schmitt, *Politische Theologie* (Munich, 1922)... We have tried here, by means of a concrete example, to demonstrate the theological impossibility of a 'political theology'."

the incomprehensible, could be accurately mapped by the ecclesiastical formulas themselves and their early history. Every one of the main basic concepts in the doctrine of the Trinity was condemned at one time or another; they were all adopted only after the frustration of a condemnation; they are accepted only inasmuch as they are at the same time branded as unusable and admitted simply as poor stammering utterances—and no more.[3] The concept of *persona* (or *prosopon*) was once condemned, as we have seen; the crucial word that in the fourth century became the standard of orthodoxy, *homoousios* (= of one substance with the Father), had been condemned in the third century; the concept of "proceeding" has a condemnation behind it—and so one could go on. One must say, I think, that these condemnations of the later formulas of faith form an intimate part of them: it is only through the negation, and the infinite indirectness implicit in it, that they are usable. The doctrine of the Trinity is only possible as a piece of baffled theology, so to speak.

A further observation should be added. When one looks at the history of the dogma of the Trinity as it is reflected in a present-day manual of theology, it looks like a graveyard of heresies, whose emblems theology still carries around with it like the trophies from battles fought and won. But such a view does not represent a proper understanding of the matter, for all the attempted solutions that in the course of a long struggle were finally thrown out as dead ends and, hence, heresies are not just mere gravestones to the vanity of human

---

[3] The history of the *homoousios* will suffice to illustrate the point; see the summary by A. Grillmeier, in LThK, 2nd ed., 5:467f.; and also the survey of the history of trinitarian dogma in A. Adam, *Lehrbuch der Dogmengeschichte*, vol. 1 (Gütersloh, 1965), pp. 115–254 (p. 349, n. 13). On the subject of man's stammering before God, cf. the beautiful story "Das Stammeln" from the Chassidic stories in M. Buber, *Werke*, vol. 3 (Munich, 1963), p. 334.

endeavor, monuments that confirm how often thinking has come to grief and at which we can now look back in retrospective—and, in the last analysis, fruitless—curiosity. On the contrary, every heresy is at the same time the cipher for an abiding truth, a cipher we must now preserve with other simultaneously valid statements, separated from which it produces a false impression. In other words, all these statements are not so much gravestones as the bricks of a cathedral, which are, of course, only useful when they do not remain alone but are inserted into something bigger, just as even the positively accepted formulas are valid only if they are at the same time aware of their own inadequacy.

The Jansenist Saint-Cyran once made the thought-provoking remark that faith consists of a series of contradictions held together by grace.[4] He thereby expressed in the realm of theology a discovery that today in physics, as the law of complementarity, belongs to the realm of scientific thought.[5] The physicist is becoming increasingly aware today that we cannot embrace given realities—the structure of light, for example, or of matter in general—in *one* form of experiment and so in *one* form of statement; that, on the contrary, from different sides we glimpse different aspects, which cannot be traced back to each other. We have to take the two together—say, the structure of particle and wave—without

[4] Quoted by H. Dombois, "Der Kampf um das Kirchenrecht", in H. Asmussen and W. Stählin, *Die Katholizität der Kirche* (Stuttgart, 1957), pp. 285–307. The quotation is on p. 297.

[5] H. Dombois, ibid., points out that Niels Bohr, who introduced the notion of complementarity in physics, referred for his part to theology—to the complementarity of God's justice and mercy; cf. N. Bohr, *Atomtheorie und Naturbeschreibung* (Berlin, 1931); *Atomphysik und menschliche Erkenntnis* (Braunschweig, 1958). Further references and literature are provided by C. F. von Weizsäcker in his article "Komplementarität", in *Die Religion in Geschichte und Gegenwart* (RGG), 3:1744f.

being able to find a comprehensive explanation—as a provisional assessment of the whole, which is not accessible to us as a unified whole because of the restrictions implicit in our point of view. What is true here in the physical realm as a result of the limitations in our ability to observe is true in an incomparably greater degree of the spiritual realities and of God. Here, too, we can always look from *one* side and so grasp only one particular aspect, which seems to contradict the other, yet only when combined with it is a pointer to the whole, which we are incapable of stating or grasping. Only by circling round, by looking and describing from different, apparently contrary angles can we succeed in alluding to the truth, which is never visible to us in its totality.

The intellectual approach of modern physics may offer us more help here than Aristotelian philosophy was able to give. Physicists know today that one can only talk about the structure of matter by approaching the subject from various angles. They know that the position of the observer at any one time affects the result of his investigation of nature. Why should we not be able to understand afresh, on this basis, that in the question of God we must not look, in the Aristotelian fashion, for an ultimate concept encompassing the whole but must be prepared to find a multitude of aspects that depend on the position of the observer and that we can no longer survey as a whole but only accept alongside each other, without being able to say the final word on the subject? We meet here the hidden interplay of faith and modern thought. That present-day physicists are stepping outside the structure of Aristotelian logic and thinking in this way is surely an effect already of the new dimension that Christian theology has opened up, of its need to think in "complementarities".

In this connection I should like to mention briefly two other aids to thought provided by physics. E. Schrödinger has defined the structure of matter as "parcels of waves" and thereby hit upon the idea of a being that has no substance but is purely actual, whose apparent "substantiality" really results only from the pattern of movement of superimposed waves. In the realm of matter such a suggestion may well be physically, and in any case philosophically, highly contestable. But it remains an exciting simile for the *actualitas divina*, for the fact that God is absolutely "in act" [and not "in potency"], and for the idea that the densest being—God— can subsist only in a multitude of relations, which are not substances but simply "waves", and therein form a perfect unity and also the fullness of being. We shall have to consider this idea more fully later on; it is already formulated to all intents and purposes in St. Augustine, when he develops the idea of the pure act-existence (the "parcel of waves").

But first let me mention the second aid to understanding provided by science. We know today that in a physical experiment the observer himself enters into the experiment and only by doing so can arrive at a physical experience. This means that there is no such thing as pure objectivity even in physics, that even here the result of the experiment, nature's answer, depends on the question put to it. In the answer there is always a bit of the question and a bit of the questioner himself; it reflects not only nature in itself, in its pure objectivity, but also gives back something of man, of what is characteristically ours, a bit of the human subject. This too, *mutatis mutandis*, is true of the question of God. There is no such thing as a mere observer. There is no such thing as pure objectivity. One can even say that the higher an object stands in human terms, the more it penetrates the center of individuality; and the more it engages the beholder's individuality, then the smaller the possibility of the mere distancing involved in pure objectivity. Thus,

wherever an answer is presented as unemotionally objective, as a statement that finally goes beyond the prejudices
of the pious and provides purely factual, scientific information, then it has to be said that the speaker has here fallen
victim to self-deception. This kind of objectivity is quite
simply denied to man. He cannot ask and exist as a mere
observer. He who tries to be a mere observer experiences
nothing. Even the reality "God" can only impinge on the
vision of him who enters into the experiment with God—
the experiment that we call faith. Only by entering does
one experience; only by cooperating in the experiment does
one ask at all; and only he who asks receives an answer.

Pascal set this out in his famous argument of the wager
with an almost uncanny clarity and an acuteness verging on
the unbearable. The verbal strife with the unbelieving inter-
locutor has finally reached the point at which the latter admits
that he must make a choice about God. But he would like to
avoid the leap, to possess a mathematical certainty: "Is there
no way of illuminating the darkness and of seeing the face of
the cards?" "Yes, Scripture and all the other testimony of
religion." "Yes, but my hands are tied and my lips are
closed. . . . I am so made that I cannot believe. What am I to
do?" "So you admit that your inability to believe does not
come from reason; on the contrary, reason leads you to belief;
the reason for your refusal lies elsewhere. There is therefore
no point in trying to convince you any further by piling up
the proofs of the existence of God; you must above all fight
against your passions. You would like to reach faith, but you
do not know the way? You want to cure yourself of unbelief,
and you ask for a remedy? Take a lesson from those who
were earlier racked by doubts like yourself. . . . Follow the
way by which they began; by acting as if they believed, by
taking holy water, by having Masses said, and so on. This

will bring you quite naturally to believe and will stupefy you." [6]

In this curious passage, this much at any rate is right: the mere neutral curiosity of the mind that wants to remain uninvolved can never enable one to see—even in dealing with a human being, and much less in dealing with God. The experiment with God cannot take place without man.

Certainly it is true here, even more than it is in physics, that anyone who enters into the experiment of belief receives an answer that reflects not only God but also his own questioning and that, through the refraction of his own personality, lets us know something about God. Even dogmatic formulas such as "one being in three Persons" include this refraction of the human element; they reflect in this case the man of late antiquity, whose questions and experiments are governed by the categories of late antique philosophy, which provide him with his observation post. Indeed, we must go a step farther: that we put any questions or make any experiments at all is due to the fact that God for his part has agreed to the experiment, has entered into it himself as man. Through the human refraction of this one man we can thus come to know more than the mere man; in him who is both man and God, God has demonstrated his humanity and in the man has let himself be experienced.

[6] B. Pascal, *Pensées*, fragment 233 (ed. Brunschvicg, pp. 137f.). Cf. Brunschvicg, p. 333, n. 53, who, contrary to V. Cousin, shows that to Pascal *s'abêtir* (stupefy) means: "retourner à l'enfance, pour atteindre les vérités supérieures qui sont inaccessibles à la courte sagesse des demi-savants". On this basis, Brunschvicg can say in Pascal's sense: "Rien n'est plus conforme à la raison que le désaveu de la raison" (Nothing is in more conformity with reason than the disavowal of reason). Pascal speaks here, not, as Cousin thought he did, as a sceptic, but out of the conviction and certainty of the believer; cf. also H. Vorgrimler, "Marginalien zur Kirchenfrömmigkeit Pascals", in J. Daniélou and H. Vorgrimler, *Sentire ecclesiam* (Freiburg, 1961), pp. 383f.

2. POSITIVE SIGNIFICANCE

The inner limitation of the doctrine of the Trinity in the
sense of a negative theology, upon which we have tried to
throw some light in the foregoing discussion, cannot mean
all the same that its formulas remain impenetrable, empty
verbal constructs. They can and must be understood as meaningful statements, representing, it is true, references to the
ineffable, not its adaptation to our mental world. To conclude our reflections on the doctrine of the Trinity we shall
now try to elucidate the signpost character of these references by means of three theses.

Thesis No. 1

*The paradox "una essentia tres personae"—one Being in three
Persons—is associated with the question of the original meaning of
unity and plurality.*

What is meant by this is best illustrated by a glance at the
background of pre-Christian Greek thought against which
faith in the triune God emerges. To ancient thought, only
unity (that is, oneness) is divine; plurality seems in contrast
to be secondary, the disintegration of unity. It proceeds from
disintegration and tends toward it. The Christian confession
of faith in God as the Three-in-One, as he who is simultaneously the *monas* and the *trias*, absolute unity and fullness,
signifies the conviction that divinity lies beyond our categories of unity and plurality. Although to us, the nondivine, it
is one and single, the one and only divine as opposed to all
that is not divine; nevertheless in itself it is truly fullness and
plurality, so that creaturely unity and plurality are both in
the same degree a likeness and a share of the divine. Not
only unity is divine; plurality, too, is something primordial

and has its inner ground in God himself. Plurality is not just disintegration that sets in outside the divinity; it does not arise simply through the intervention of the *dyas*, of disintegration; it is not the result of the dualism of two opposing powers; it corresponds to the creative fullness of God, who himself stands above plurality and unity, encompassing both.[7] So at bottom the belief in the Trinity, which recognizes the plural in the unity of God, is the only way to the final elimination of dualism as a means of explaining plurality alongside unity; only through this belief is the positive validation of the many given a definitive base. God stands above singular and plural. He bursts both categories.

This has a further important consequence. To him who believes in God as tri-une, the highest unity is not the unity of inflexible monotony. The model of unity or oneness toward which one should strive is consequently not the indivisibility of the atom, the smallest unity, which cannot be divided up any further; the authentic acme of unity is the unity created by love. The multi-unity that grows in love is a more radical, truer unity than the unity of the "atom".

Thesis No. 2

The paradox "una essentia tres personae" is a function of the concept of person and is to be understood as an intrinsic implication of the concept of person.

Inasmuch as Christian faith acknowledges God, the creative meaning, as person it acknowledges him as knowledge, word, and love. But the profession of faith in God as a person necessarily includes the acknowledgment of God as relatedness,

[7] Cf. on this point W. Kern, "Einheit-in-Manningfaltigkeit", in *Gott in Welt* (essays presented to K. Rahner), vol. 1 (Freiburg, 1964), pp. 207–39; see also what we said on p. 125, n. 5, about Maximus Confessor.

as communicability, as fruitfulness. The unrelated, unrelatable, absolutely One could not be person. There is no such thing as person in the categorical singular. This is already apparent in the words in which the concept of person developed: the Greek word *prosopon* means literally "look toward"; with the prefix *pros* (toward), it includes the notion of relatedness as an integral part of itself. It is the same with the Latin *persona* = "sounding through"; again, the *per* = "through ... to" expresses relatedness, this time in the form of communication through speech. In other words, if the absolute is person, it is not an absolute singular. To this extent the overstepping of the singular is implicit in the concept of person. Of course, we shall have to say at the same time that the acknowledgment that God is a person in the guise of a triple personality explodes the naïve, anthropomorphic concept of person. It declares in a sort of cipher that the personality of God infinitely exceeds the human kind of personality; so that the concept of person, illuminating as it is, once again reveals itself as an inadequate metaphor.

Thesis No. 3

The paradox "una essentia tres personae" is connected with the problem of absolute and relative and emphasizes the absoluteness of the relative, of that which is in relation.

a. Dogma as speech form

Let us try to feel our way to this idea by means of the following reflections. If faith has expressed the three-in-oneness of God since the fourth century in the formula "one Being—three Persons", this distribution of the concepts is first of all largely just a form of words.[8] The only thing certain at first was that the element of oneness, that of three-ness, and the complete simultaneity of both in the all-embracing dominance of oneness had all to be expressed. That the two things were allotted to the concepts of sub-stance and person, as they were, is in a certain sense acci-dental; in the last resort it is only a case of ensuring that both are put into words and not left to individual whim, which at bottom could always dissipate and destroy the thing itself as well as the words. In face of this discovery one is not entitled to go too far in the direction of taking these words as the only possible ones and deducing that the matter can be stated only in this way and in no other. That would mean a failure to recognize the negative character of the language of the-ology, the purely tentative fashion in which it speaks.

b. The concept of person

On the other hand, it remains true that this speech form is more than just a final decision to cling to some string of letters or other. In the struggle over the language of the pro-fession of faith, the struggle over the thing itself was settled, so that in this language, inadequate as it may be, contact with the reality does take place. We can say from the history of ideas that it was here that the reality "person" was first fully sighted; the only way that the concept and idea of "person" dawned on the human mind was in the struggle over the Christian image of God and the interpretation of the figure

---

[8] Cf. the article by K. Rahner mentioned above: "Was ist eine dogmatische Aussage?" in *Schriften zur Theologie*, vol. 5 (Einsiedeln, 1962), pp. 54–81, espe-cially 67–72.

of Jesus of Nazareth. If we try to test the intrinsic suitability of our formula while bearing these points in mind, we find that it was imposed by two basic premises. First, it was clear that, seen absolutely, God is only One, that there is not a plurality of divine principles. Once this has been established, it is also clear that the oneness lies on the plane of substance; consequently the three-ness that must also be mentioned is not to be sought here. It must therefore exist on a different level, on that of relation, of the "relative".

This result was also recommended above all by the evidence of the Bible. Here one met the fact that God seems to converse with himself. There is a "We" in God—the Fathers found it on the very first page of the Bible in the words "Let us make man" (Gen 1:26); there are an "I" and a "You" in him—the Fathers found this in the Psalms ("The Lord said to my lord": Ps 110:1) as well as in Jesus' conversations with the Father. The discovery of the dialogue within God led to the assumption of the presence in God of an "I" and a "You", an element of relationship, of coexistent diversity and affinity, for which the concept of *persona* absolutely dictated itself. It thereby acquired, over and above its theatrical and literary significance, a new depth of meaning without losing the vagueness that made it suitable for such a use.[9]

With the insight that, seen as substance, God is One but that there exists in him the phenomenon of dialogue, of differentiation, and of relationship through speech, the category of *relatio* gained a completely new significance for Christian thought. To Aristotle, it was among the "accidents", the chance

[9] Cf. C. Andresen, "Zur Entstehung und Geschichte des trinitarischen Personbegriffs", *Zeitschrift für die neutestamentliche Wissenschaft* 52 (1961): 1–38; J. Ratzinger, "Zum Personverständnis in der Dogmatik", in J. Speck, *Das Personverständnis in der Pädagogik und ihren Nachbarwissenschaften* (Münster, 1966), pp. 157–71.

circumstances of being, which are separate from substance, the sole sustaining form of the real. The experience of the God who conducts a dialogue, of the God who is not only *logos* but also *dia-logos*, not only idea and meaning but speech and word in the reciprocal exchanges of partners in conversation—this experience exploded the ancient division of reality into substance, the real thing, and accidents, the merely circumstantial. It now became clear that the dialogue, the *relatio*, stands beside the substance as an equally primordial form of being.

With that, the wording of the dogma was to all intents and purposes settled. It expresses the perception that God as substance, as "being", is absolutely one. If we nevertheless have to speak of him in the category of triplicity, this does not imply any multiplication of substances but means that in the one and indivisible God there exists the phenomenon of dialogue, the reciprocal exchange of word and love. This again signifies that the "three Persons" who exist in God are the reality of word and love in their attachment to each other. They are not substances, personalities in the modern sense, but the relatedness whose pure actuality ("parcel of waves"!) does not impair the unity of the highest being but fills it out. St. Augustine once enshrined this idea in the following formula: "He is not called Father with reference to himself but only in relation to the Son; seen by himself he is simply God." [10] Here the decisive point comes beautifully to light. "Father" is purely a concept of relationship. Only in being for the other is he Father; in his own being in himself he is simply God. Person is the pure relation of being related, nothing else. Relationship is not something extra added to the person, as it is with us; it only exists at all as relatedness.

---

[10] Augustine, *Enarrationes in Psalmos 68*, p. 1, 5, in CChr 39:905 (*Patrologia Latina* [PL] 36:845).

Expressed in the imagery of Christian tradition, this means that the first Person does not beget the Son as if the act of begetting were subsequent to the finished Person; it *is* the act of begetting, of giving oneself, of streaming forth. It is identical with the act of self-giving. Only as this act is it person, and therefore it is not the giver but the act of giving, "wave" not "particle" . . . In this idea of relatedness in word and love, independent of the concept of substance and not to be classified among the "accidents", Christian thought discovered the kernel of the concept of person, which describes something other and infinitely more than the mere idea of the "individual". Let us listen once again to St. Augustine: "In God there are no accidents, only substance and relation."[11] Therein lies concealed a revolution in man's view of the world: the sole dominion of thinking in terms of substance is ended; relation is discovered as an equally valid primordial mode of reality. It becomes possible to surmount what we call today "objectifying thought"; a new plane of being comes into view. It is probably true to say that the task imposed on philosophy as a result of these facts is far from being completed—so much does modern thought depend on the possibilities thus disclosed, without which it would be inconceivable.

c. The connection back to biblical thought and the question of Christian existence

But let us return to our question. The reflections just described can easily give the impression that one has here arrived at

---

[11] Cf. *De Trinitate* 5, 5, 6 (PL 42:913f.): "In Deo autem nihil quidem secundum accidens dicitur, quia nihil in eo mutabile est; nec tamen omne quod dicitur, secundum substantiam dicitur . . . quod tamen relativum non est accidens, quia non est mutabile." See also on the whole question M. Schmaus, *Katholische Dogmatik*, 3rd ed., vol. 1 (Munich, 1948), pp. 425–32 (§58).

the outermost point of speculative theology, which in elaborating on what is found in Scripture has moved far away from Scripture and lost itself in purely philosophical speculation. It will be all the more surprising to hear that closer inspection discloses that here the most extreme speculation leads directly back to biblical thought. For at bottom the ideas just outlined are to a large extent already present in Johannine thought, albeit expressed in different concepts and with a somewhat different aim. A brief indication will have to suffice. In St. John's Gospel Christ says of himself: "The Son can do nothing of his own accord" (5:19 and 30). This seems to rob the Son of all power; he has nothing of his own; precisely because he is the Son he can only *operate* by virtue of him to whom he owes his whole existence. What first becomes evident here is that the concept "Son" is a concept of relation. By calling the Lord "Son", John gives him a name that always points away from him and beyond him; he thus employs a term that denotes essentially a relatedness. He thereby puts his whole Christology into the context of the idea of relation. Formulas like the one just mentioned only emphasize this; they only, as it were, draw out what is implicit in the word "son", the relativity it contains. On the face of it, a contradiction arises when the same Christ says of himself in St. John: "I and the Father are one" (10:30). But anyone who looks more closely will see at once that in reality the two statements are complementary. In that Jesus is called "Son" and is thereby made "relative" to the Father, and in that Christology is ratified as a statement of relation, the automatic result is the total reference of Christ back to the Father. Precisely because he does not stand in *himself*, he stands in *him*, constantly one with him.

What this signifies, not just for Christology, but for the illumination of the whole meaning of being a Christian at all, comes to light when John extends these ideas to

Christians, who proceed from Christ. It then becomes apparent that he explains by Christology what the Christian's situation really is. We find here precisely the same interplay of
the two series of statements as before. Parallel to the formula
"The Son can do nothing of his own accord", which illumines
Christology from the son concept as a doctrine of relativity,
is the statement about those who belong to Christ, the disciples: "Apart from me you can do nothing" (Jn 15:5). Thus
Christian existence is put with Christ into the category of
relationship. And parallel to the logic that makes Christ say,
"I and the Father are one", we find here the petition "that
they may be one, even as we are one" (17:11 and 22). The
significant difference from Christology comes to light in the
fact that the unity of Christians is expressed, not in the indic-
ative, but in the form of a prayer.

Let us now try briefly to consider the significance of the
line of thought that has become visible. The Son as Son, and
insofar as he is Son, does not proceed in any way from himself and so is completely one with the Father; since he is
nothing beside him, claims no special position of his own,
confronts the Father with nothing belonging only to him,
makes no reservations for what is specifically his own, therefore he is completely equal to the Father. The logic is compelling: If there is nothing in which he is just he, no kind of
fenced-off private ground, then he coincides with the Father,
is "one" with him. It is precisely this totality of interplay
that the word "Son" aims at expressing. To John, "Son" means
being from another; thus, with this word he defines the being
of this man as being from another and for others, as a being
that is completely open on both sides, knows no reserved
area of the mere "I". When it thus becomes clear that the
being of Jesus as Christ is a completely open being, a being
"from" and "toward", which nowhere clings to itself and
nowhere stands on its own, then it is also clear at the same

time that this being is pure relation (not substantiality) and, as pure relation, pure unity. This fundamental statement about Christ becomes, as we have seen, at the same time the explanation of Christian existence. To John, being a Christian means being like the Son, becoming a son; that is, not standing on one's own and in oneself, but living completely open in the "from" and "toward". Insofar as the Christian is a "Christian", this is true of him. And certainly such utterances will make him realize to how small an extent he is a Christian.

It seems to me that this illuminates the ecumenical character of the passage from a quite unexpected angle. Everyone knows, it is true, that Jesus' "high priestly prayer" (Jn 17), of which we are speaking, is the basic charter of all efforts for the unity of the Church. But do we not often take far too superficial a view of it? Our reflections have shown that Christian unity is first of all unity with Christ, which becomes possible where insistence on one's own individuality ceases and is replaced by pure, unreserved being "from" and "for". From such being with Christ, which enters completely into the openness of the one who willed to hold on to nothing of his own individuality (cf. also Phil 2:6f.), follows the complete "at-one-ness"—"that they may be one, even as we are one". All not-at-one-ness, all division, rests on a concealed lack of real Christliness, on a clinging to individuality that hinders the coalescence into unity.

I think it is not unimportant to note how the doctrine of the Trinity here passes over into an existential statement, how the assertion that relation is at the same time pure unity becomes transparently clear to us. It is the nature of the trinitarian personality to be pure relation and so the most absolute unity. That there is no contradiction in this is probably now evident. And one can understand from now on more clearly than before that it is not the "atom", the indivisible

smallest piece of matter,[12] that possesses the highest unity;
that, on the contrary, pure oneness can only occur in the
spirit and embraces the relatedness of love. Thus in Christianity the profession of faith in the oneness of God is just as
radical as in any other monotheistic religion; indeed, only in
Christianity does it reach its full stature. But it is the nature
of Christian existence to receive and to live life as relatedness
and, thus, to enter into that unity which is the ground of all
reality and sustains it. This will perhaps make it clear how
the doctrine of the Trinity, when properly understood, can
become the reference point of theology that anchors all other
lines of Christian thought.

Let us turn here once again to St. John's Gospel, which
offers the decisive assistance. One can well say that the line
we have indicated forms the dominant one in his theology.
As well as in the "Son" idea it appears especially in two further christological concepts that must at least be briefly outlined here for the sake of completeness. These are the idea of
the "mission" and the description of Jesus as the "Word"
(*logos*) of God. "Mission" theology is again theology of being
as relation and of relation as mode of unity. There is a well-
known late Jewish saying: "The ambassador of a man is like
the man himself." [13] Jesus appears in St. John as the Father's
ambassador, in whom is really fulfilled what all other ambas-
sadors can only aim at asymptotically: he really loses his own
identity in the role of ambassador; he is nothing but the ambassador who represents the other without interposing his own
individuality. And so, as the true ambassador, he is one with
him who sends him. Once again, through the concept of the
mission, being is interpreted as being "from" and as being

[12] Cf. the short survey of the history of the concept "atom" by C. F. von
Weizsäcker, in RGG 1:682–86.
[13] Quoted in K. H. Schelkle, *Jüngerschaft und Apostelamt* (Freiburg, 1957),
p. 30.

"for"; once again being is conceived as absolute openness without reservation. And again we find the extension to Christian existence in the words, "As the Father has sent me, even so I send you" (13:20; 17:18, 20:21). In the classification of this existence as mission it is again expounded as being "from" and "for", as relatedness and hence as unity. Finally, a remark on the concept of *logos* would also be appropriate. When John characterizes the Lord as *Logos* he is employing a term widely current in both Greek and Jewish thought and taking over with it a series of ideas implicit in it that are in this way transferred to Christ. But perhaps one can say that the new element that John has added to the *logos* concept lies not least in the fact that, to him, *logos* does not mean simply the idea of the eternal rationality of being, as it did essentially in Greek thought. By its application to Jesus of Nazareth, the concept of *logos* acquires a new dimension. It no longer denotes simply the permeation of all being by meaning; it characterizes this man: he who is here is "Word". The concept of *logos*, which to the Greeks meant "meaning" (*ratio*), changes here really into "word" (*verbum*). He who is here is Word; he is consequently "spoken" and, hence, the pure relation between the speaker and the spoken to. Thus *logos* Christology, as "word" theology, is once again the opening up of being to the idea of relationship. For again it is true that "word" comes essentially "from someone else" and "to someone else"; word is an existence that is entirely way and openness.

Let us round off the whole discussion with a passage from St. Augustine that elucidates splendidly what we mean. It occurs in his commentary on St. John and hinges on the sentence in the Gospel that runs, "Mea doctrina non est mea"—"My teaching is not mine, but his who sent me" (7:16). Augustine has used the paradox in this sentence to illuminate the paradoxical nature of the Christian image of

God and of Christian existence. He asks himself first whether
it is not a sheer contradiction, an offense against the elementary rules of logic, to say something like "Mine is not mine."
But, he goes on to ask, digging deeper, what, then, is the
teaching of Jesus that is simultaneously his and not his? Jesus
is "word", and thus it becomes clear that his teaching is he
himself. If one reads the sentence again with this insight, it
then says: I am by no means just I; I am not mine at all; my
I is that of another. With this we have moved on out of
Christology and arrived at ourselves: "Quid tam tuum quam
tu, quid tam non tuum quam tu"—What is so much yours
as yourself, and what is so little yours as yourself?[14] The
most individual element in us—the only thing that belongs
to us in the last analysis—our own "I", is at the same time
the least individual element of all, for it is precisely our "I"
that we have neither from ourselves nor for ourselves. The
"I" is simultaneously what I have completely and what least
of all belongs to me. Thus here again the concept of mere
substance (= what stands in itself!) is shattered, and it is made
apparent how being that truly understands itself grasps at the
same time that *in* being itself it does not belong to itself; that
it only comes to itself by moving away from itself and finding its way back as relatedness to its true primordial state.

Such thoughts do not make the doctrine of the Trinity
unmysteriously comprehensible, but they do help, I think,
to open up a new understanding of reality, of what man is
and of what God is. Just when we seem to have reached the
extreme limit of theory, the extreme of practicality comes
into view: talking about God discloses what man is; the most
paradoxical approach is at the same time the most illuminating and helpful one.

[14] Augustine, *In Ioannis Evangelium tractatus* 29, 3 (on Jn 7:16), in CChr
36:285.

PART TWO

JESUS CHRIST

Chapter I

"I BELIEVE IN JESUS CHRIST, HIS ONLY SON, OUR LORD"

A. THE PROBLEM OF FAITH IN JESUS TODAY

It is only in the second section of the Creed that we come up against the real difficulty—already considered briefly in the introduction—about Christianity: the profession of faith that the man Jesus, an individual executed in Palestine round about the year 30, the *Christus* (anointed, chosen) of God, indeed God's own Son, is the central and decisive point of all human history. It seems both presumptuous and foolish to assert that one single figure who is bound to disappear farther and farther into the mists of the past is the authoritative center of all history. Although faith in the *logos*, the meaningfulness of being, corresponds perfectly with a tendency in the human reason, this second article of the Creed proclaims the absolutely staggering alliance of *logos* and *sarx*, of meaning and a single historical figure. The meaning that sustains all being has become flesh; that is, it has entered history and become one individual in it; it is no longer simply what encompasses and sustains history but a point in it. Accordingly the meaning of all being is first of all no longer to be found in the sweep of mind that rises above the individual, the limited, into the universal; it is no longer simply given in the world of ideas, which transcends the individual and is reflected in it only in a fragmentary fashion;

it is to be found in the midst of time, in the countenance of
one man. One is reminded of the moving conclusion of Dante's
Divine Comedy, where, looking on the mystery of God, in the
midst of that "all-powerful love which, quiet and united, leads
around in a circle the sun and all the stars", the poet discovers
in blissful wonder his own likeness, a human countenance.[1] The
transformation of the path from being to meaning that results
from this will have to be considered later. For the time being,
let us note that alongside the union of the God of faith and the
God of the philosophers, which we recognized in the first article as the basic assumption and structural form of the Christian faith, a second, no less decisive alliance appears, namely,
that of the *logos* and *sarx*, of word and flesh, of faith and history. The historical man Jesus is the Son of God, and the Son
of God is the man Jesus. God comes to pass for man through
men, nay, even more concretely, through *the* man in whom the
quintessence of humanity appears and who for that very reason is at the same time God himself.

Perhaps it is already clear at this point that even in the paradox of word and flesh we are faced with something meaningful and in accordance with the *logos*. Yet at first this article
of faith represents a stumbling block for human thinking. In
this have we not fallen victim to an absolutely staggering kind
of positivism? Can we cling at all to the straw of one single historical event? Can we dare to base our whole existence, indeed
the whole of history, on the straw of one happening in the great
sea of history? Such a notion, which even in itself is an adventurous one and seemed equally improbable to both ancient and
Asiatic thought, is rendered still more difficult in the intellectual climate of modern times, or at any rate rendered difficult

[1] *Paradiso* XXXIII, 127, to the end. See the decisive passage in V, 130ff.:
"Dentro da sè del suo colore istesso / Mi parve pinta della nostra effige / Per
che il mio viso in lei tutto era messo."

in a different way, by the fashion in which history is now dealt with by scholars: that is to say, by the historico-critical method. This means that the encounter with history is affected by the same sort of problem that has arisen in the search for being and for the ground of being as a result of the methods employed by physics and of the scientific approach to the investigation of nature. We have seen in our reflections on this subject that physics has renounced the discovery of being itself and confines itself to the "positive", to what can be proved. The impressive gain in precision thus made has to be paid for by a renunciation of truth that in the end can go so far that behind the prison bars of positivism, being, truth itself, disappears, ontology becomes visibly more impossible, and even philosophy has to yield in large measure to phenomenology, to the investigation of mere appearances.

A very similar position threatens to arise in the encounter with history. The methods of physics are followed as far as they possibly can be, though a limit is set to the process by the fact that history cannot carry verification, which forms the core of the modern scientific approach, to the point of repetition, on which the unique certainty of scientific statements rests. The historian is denied this satisfaction; past history cannot be reenacted, and verification must be content with the demonstrable soundness of the evidence on which the historian bases his view. The consequence of this methodical approach is that—as in natural science—only the "phenomenal" or outer surface of what has happened comes into view. But this "phenomenal" aspect, that is, the surface that can be checked by documentary evidence, is more questionable than the positivism of physics from two points of view. It is more questionable, first, because it has to rely on the availability of documents, that is, on chance statements, while physics at any rate always has the necessary material realities before it. It is also more questionable because the expression of the human element in the written evidence is less accurate than the self-expression of nature; its reflection of human depths is inadequate and often positively conceals them; and its interpretation involves man and his personal mode of thinking far more extensively than the interpretation of physical phenomena does. Accordingly, although one must agree that the imitation of scientific methods in the realm of history undoubtedly heightens the accuracy of its assertions, on the other hand, it cannot be overlooked that here, too, this approach involves a grievous loss of truth that is even more extensive than it is in physics. Just as in physics being retires behind appearance, so here to a large extent the only past events that are still accepted as valid are those that are presented as "historical", that is, tested and passed by historical methods. It is quite often forgotten that the full truth of history eludes documentary verification just as much as the truth of being escapes the experimental approach. So it must be said that historical science in the narrowest sense of the term not only reveals but also conceals history. The automatic result is that it can see the man Jesus all right but can only with difficulty discover the Christ in him, which as a truth of history cannot simply be checked as right or wrong by reference to the documentary evidence.

B. JESUS THE CHRIST: THE BASIC FORM OF THE CHRISTOLOGICAL PROFESSION OF FAITH

I. THE DILEMMA OF MODERN THEOLOGY: JESUS OR CHRIST?

It is hardly surprising, after all we have said, that the more the barrier of historical science tends to divide faith and history, the more theology seeks to escape in one way or the other from the dilemma of the simultaneous existence of both. Thus today we meet here and there the attempt to establish Christology securely on the historical plane, to make it visible in spite of everything, by this method of the "accurate" and demonstrable;[2] or the very much simpler enterprise of straightforwardly reducing it to the demonstrable.[3] The first course cannot succeed because, as we have seen, the "historical" in the strict sense of the word denotes a mode of thought that restricts investigation to the phenomenon (the demonstrable) and thus can no more produce faith than physics can produce the profession of belief in God. But the second course can bring no satisfaction because the whole of what happened then cannot be grasped in this fashion, and what is offered as a statement of fact is in reality the expression of a personal view, not the pure result of historical research.[4] So these efforts are being accom-

---

[2] This is the approach of the group centered round W. Pannenberg; cf. W. Pannenberg, *Grundzüge der Christologie*, 2nd ed. (Gütersloh, 1966), especially definition no. 23: "It is therefore the task of Christology to base on the history of Jesus the true perception of his significance...."

[3] This was the approach of earlier liberal theology; cf. its classical expression in A. von Harnack, *Das Wesen des Christentums*, new ed. by R. Bultmann (Stuttgart, 1950) [English trans.: *What Is Christianity?* (*Lectures 1899–1900*), trans. by T. B. Saunders, 1958].

[4] This was pointed out with all possible emphasis by A. Schweitzer in his *Geschichte der Leben-Jesu-Forschung* (Tübingen, 1906) [Eng. trans., *The Quest of the Historical Jesus*, 1922], which thus also drew a provisional line under this enterprise. Let me just quote the following *locus classicus* in this work: "There is nothing more negative than the result of the research into the life of Jesus. The Jesus of Nazareth who appeared upon the scene as the Messiah, proclaimed the morality of the kingdom of God, founded the kingdom of heaven upon earth, and died to consecrate his work never existed. He is a figure sketched by rationalism, brought to life by liberalism, and clothed by modern theology with historical scholarship. This image has not been destroyed from outside; it has collapsed internally, shaken and riven by the actual historical problems" (quoted from W. G. Kümmel, *Das Neue Testament: Geschichte der Erforschung seiner Probleme* [Freiburg and Munich, 1958], p. 305).

panied more and more by a third, the attempt to escape the
dilemma of the historical altogether and to leave it behind as
superfluous. This already happens on a grand scale in Hegel;
and however much Bultmann's work differs from that of Hegel,
he shares this same tendency. It is certainly not quite the same
thing whether one confines oneself to the idea or the kerygma,
but the difference is not quite so sweeping as the exponents of
kerygma theology themselves seem to assume.[5]

The dilemma of the two courses—on the one hand, that
of transposing or reducing Christology to history and, on
the other, that of escaping history completely and abandoning it as irrelevant to faith—could be quite accurately summarized in the two alternatives by which modern theology
is vexed: Jesus or Christ? Modern theology begins by turning away from Christ and taking refuge in Jesus as a figure
who is historically comprehensible, only to make an about-
turn at the climax of this movement—in Bultmann—and
flee in the opposite direction back to Christ, a flight, however, that at the present moment is already starting to change
back into the new flight from Christ to Jesus.

Let us try to follow this zig-zag movement of modern
theology a little more closely, because by doing so we shall
come nearer to the heart of the matter. The first tendency—
flight from Christ to Jesus—produced Harnack's *Wesen des
Christentums* at the beginning of the [twentieth] century, a
book that offers a form of Christianity drenched in the pride
and optimism of reason, the Christianity to which liberalism
had reduced the original Creed by a process of "purification". One of the crucial sentences in this work runs thus:

---

[5] This becomes quite clear in Bultmann's last great utterance on the question of Jesus: *Das Verhältnis der urchristlichen Christusbotschaft zum historischen
Jesus* (Heidelberg, 1960); and still more in the work of his disciple H. Braun,
to whom, however, he often draws near in the book mentioned.

"Not the Son but only the Father belongs in the Gospel as Jesus preached it." [6] How simple, how liberating this seems! Where faith in the Son had divided people—Christians from non-Christians, Christians of different denominations from one another—knowledge of the Father can unite. While the Son belongs only to a few, the Father belongs to all, and all to him. Where faith has parted people, love can bind them together. Jesus versus Christ, and this means "away from dogma, onward to love". According to Harnack, what caused the decisive rupture was the fact that the preaching Jesus, who told all men of their common father and so made them brothers, had been turned into the preached Jesus, who then demanded faith and became dogma: Jesus had proclaimed the undoctrinal message of love, and therein lay the great revolution with which he had split the armor of pharisaical orthodoxy, replacing intolerant right-thinking with the simplicity of trust in the Father, of the brotherhood of man, and of the call to one love. For this had been substituted the doctrine of the God-man, of the "Son", and so patience and brotherly love, which is salvation, had been replaced by a doctrine of salvation, which can only signify the contrary and has unleashed conflict upon conflict, cleavage after cleavage. So the watchword is obvious: back past the preached Christ, the object of the divisive belief, to the preaching Jesus, back to the summons to the unifying power of love under the one Father with all our brothers. One certainly cannot deny that these are impressive and stirring assertions, which cannot be lightly dismissed. And yet—while Harnack was still proclaiming his optimistic message about Jesus, those who

---

[6] New impression, 1950, p. 86. In the 56th–60th thousand (1908), Harnack endorsed this statement emphatically in a note (183) ("I have nothing to alter in it") and at the same time emphasized that it is obviously only true of the gospel "as Jesus preached it", not "as Paul and the evangelists preached it".

were to bury his work were already knocking at the door. At
the very same time proof was produced that the plain Jesus
of whom he spoke was a romantic dream, a *Fata Morgana* of
the historian, a mirage induced by thirst and longing that
dissolved as he approached it.

So Bultmann resolutely chose the other path. The only
thing that is important about Jesus, he says, is the fact of his
having existed; for the rest, faith does not rest on such uncer-
tain hypotheses, which can yield no historical certainty, but
only on the verbal happening of the preaching of the Gospel, through which closed human existence is opened up to
its true nature. But is an empty event any easier to swallow
than one filled with content? Is anything gained when the
question of who, what, and how this Jesus was is dismissed as
meaningless and man is tied instead to a mere verbal event?
The latter certainly takes place, for it is *preached*; but this way
its authenticity and content of reality remain extremely
dubious.

Such questions enable us to understand why it is that more
and more people are fleeing back from the pure kerygma
and from the pale ghost of the historical Jesus to the most
human of all human beings, whose humanity seems to them
in a secularized world like the last shimmer of the divine left
after the "death of God". This is what is happening today in
the "death of God" theology, which tells us that, although
we no longer have God, Jesus remains to us as the symbol of
trust that gives us courage to go on.[7] In the midst of a world
emptied of God, his humanity is to be a sort of proxy for the
God who can no longer be discovered. But how uncritical

[7] See the survey by G. Hasenhüttl, "Die Wandlung des Gottesbildes" in
Theologie im Wandel (Tübingen festschrift), ed. by J. Ratzinger and J. Neu-
mann (Munich, 1967), pp. 228–53; W.H. van de Pol, *Das Ende des konven-
tionellen Christentums* (Vienna, 1967), pp. 438–43.

here are those who before were so critical that they were only willing to accept a theology without God, just so as not to appear old-fashioned in the eyes of their progressive contemporaries! Perhaps one should really put the question a bit earlier and consider whether a gravely uncritical attitude is not already reflected in the attempt to pursue theology—the science of God—without God. We do not need to argue about that here; so far as our question is concerned, it is at any rate certain that we cannot undo the work of the last forty years and that the way back to a mere Jesus is irrevocably barred. The attempt to outflank historical Christianity and out of the historian's retorts to construct a pure Jesus by whom one should then be able to live is intrinsically absurd. Mere history creates no present; it only confirms what happened in the past. In the last analysis, therefore, the romantic approach to Jesus is just as devoid of value for the present or future as the flight to the pure verbal event was bound to be.

Yet the shuttle movement of the modern mind between Jesus and Christ, the main stages of which in the present [twentieth] century I have just tried to sketch, was not entirely wasted. I believe that it can even become a very useful pointer to something, namely, to the fact that the one (Jesus) cannot exist without the other (Christ), that, on the contrary, one is bound to be continually pushed from one to the other because in reality Jesus only subsists as the Christ and the Christ only subsists in the shape of Jesus. We must advance a step farther and—before we do any reconstructing, which, after all, can only produce reconstructions, that is, supplementary artificial creations—we must simply try to understand what is stated by the Christian faith, which is not a reconstruction or a theory but a present, a living reality. After all, perhaps we should put more trust in the presence of the faith, which has endured for centuries and by its very nature had no other

aim but that of understanding—understanding who and what
this Jesus really was—than in the activity of reconstruction,
which goes its own way, aloof from reality; at the very least
one must try for once to appreciate clearly what this faith
really says.

2. THE CREED'S IMAGE OF CHRIST

The Creed, which we are following in this book as a representative summary of the faith, formulates its faith in Jesus in
the quite simple phrase "and [I believe] in Christ Jesus". The
most striking thing about it for us is that, as in St. Paul's preferred usage, the word Christ, which was originally not a name
but a title ("Messiah"), is put first.[8] It can be shown that the
Christian community at Rome, which formulated our Creed,
was still completely aware of the significance of the word's content. The transformation into a mere proper name, as we perceive the word today, was certainly completed at a very early
period, but here "Christ" is still used as the definition of what
this Jesus is. The fusion with the name Jesus is well advanced,
it is true; we stand here at the last stage, so to speak, in the change
of meaning of the word Christ.

Ferdinand Kattenbusch, the great student of the Apostles'
Creed, illustrates the process with a neat example from his own
time (1897): he points to the comparison with the phrase
"Kaiser Wilhelm". The words "Kaiser" and "Wilhelm" go so
closely together that the title "Kaiser" had itself already become
almost a part of the name; yet everyone was still aware that the
word was not just a name but denoted a function.[9] The phrase

[8] Though not in the usual English version—TRANS.
[9] Kattenbusch 2:491; cf. pp. 541–62.

"Christ Jesus" is an exactly similar case and shows just the same development: Christ is a title and yet also already part of the unique name for the man from Nazareth. This fusion of the name with the title, the title with the name, is far from being just another example of history's forgetfulness. On the contrary, it spotlights the very heart of that process of understanding that faith went through with regard to the figure of Nazareth. For what faith really states is precisely that with Jesus it is not possible to distinguish office and person; with him, this differentiation simply becomes inapplicable. The person *is* the office; the office *is* the person. The two are no longer separable. Here there is no private area reserved for an "I" that remains in the background behind the deeds and actions and thus at some time or other can be "off duty"; here there is no "I" separate from the work; the "I" *is* the work, and the work *is* the "I".

Jesus did not leave behind him (again, as the faith expressed in the Creed understood it) a body of teaching that could be separated from his "I", as one can collect and evaluate the ideas of great thinkers without going into the personalities of the thinkers themselves. The Creed offers no teachings of Jesus; evidently no one even conceived the—to us—obvious idea of attempting anything like this, because the operative understanding pointed in a completely different direction. Similarly, as faith understood the position, Jesus did not perform a work that could be distinguished from his "I" and depicted separately. On the contrary, to understand him as the Christ means to be convinced that he has put himself into his word. Here there is no "I" (as there is with all of us) that utters words; he has identified himself so closely with his word that "I" and word are indistinguishable: he *is* word. In the same way, to faith, his work is nothing else than the unreserved way in which he merges himself into this very work; he performs *himself* and gives *himself*; his work is the giving of himself.

Karl Barth once expressed this perception on the part of faith in the following way:

> Jesus is absolutely the bearer of an office. Thus, thus, he is not first a man and then also bearer of this office as well. . . . There exists no neutral humanity of Jesus. . . . The remarkable words of Paul at 2 Corinthians 5:16, 'Even if we have known Christ according to the flesh, we know him thus no longer now', could be spoken also in the name of all four evangelists. [They] were totally uninterested in everything that this man did outside of his office as Messiah and thus in whatever he might have been and have done apart from the carrying-out of this office. . . . Even when they relate of him that he was hungry and thirsty, that he became tired and rested and slept, that he loved, mourned, became angry and indeed wept, they touch accompanying circumstances in which, however, there nowhere became visible a personality that was autonomous over against its work, with interests, inclinations and emotions of its own. . . . His being as a man is his work.[10]

In other words, faith's decisive statement about Jesus lies in the indivisible unity of the two words "Jesus Christ", a unity that conceals the experience of the identity of existence and mission. In this sense one can certainly speak of a "functional Christology": the whole being of Jesus is a function of the "for us", but the function, too, is—for this very reason—all being.[11]

---

[10] K. Barth, *Kirchliche Dogmatik* III, 2 (Zürich, 1948), pp. 66–69; quoted from H. U. von Balthasar, "Two Modes of Faith" in *Explorations in Theology*, vol. 3: *Creator Spirit* (San Francisco: Ignatius Press, 1993), pp. 85–102; 76–91; quote on p. 100. Balthasar's whole contribution should be compared with this citation.

[11] H. U. von Balthasar, "Two Modes of Faith", especially p. 100; Balthasar, *Explorations in Theology*, vol. 1: *The Word Made Flesh* (San Francisco: Ignatius Press, 1989), pp. 11–68, especially 30ff. and 52ff.

As a fitting conclusion one could indeed assert that, thus understood, the teaching and the deeds of the historical Jesus are not as such important but that the mere fact of his having existed is sufficient—so long as one realizes that this "fact" implies the whole reality of the person who as such is his own teaching, who as such coincides with his deeds and thereby possesses his unparalleled individuality and uniqueness. The person of Jesus *is* his teaching, and his teaching is he himself. Christian faith, that is, faith in Jesus as the Christ, is therefore truly "personal faith". What this means can really be understood only from this standpoint. Such faith is not the acceptance of a system but the acceptance of this person who is his word; of the word as person and of the person as Word.

3. THE POINT OF DEPARTURE OF FAITH IN JESUS: THE CROSS

What has been said so far will be clarified if we go back a step farther, past the Apostles' Creed, to the origin of the Christian faith as a whole. Today we can establish with some certainty that the birthplace of the faith in Jesus as the Christ, that is, the birthplace of "Christ"-ian faith as a whole, is the Cross. Jesus himself did not proclaim himself directly as the Christ ("Messiah"). Although this statement is certainly somewhat surprising to us, it now emerges with some clarity from the frequently confusing quarrels of the historians; it cannot be eluded even if, indeed, especially if, one confronts with an appropriately critical attitude the hasty process of subtraction current in present-day research into Jesus. So Jesus did not call himself unequivocally the Messiah (Christ); the man who gave him this name was Pilate, who for his part associated himself with the accusation of the Jews by giving in to this accusation and proclaiming Jesus on the Cross, in an execution notice drawn up in all the international languages of the day, as the executed king (= Messiah, *Christus*) of the Jews. This execution notice, the death sentence of history, became with paradoxical unity the "profession of faith", the real starting point and taproot of the Christian faith, which holds Jesus to be the Christ: as the crucified criminal, this Jesus is the Christ, the King. His crucifixion is his coronation; his kingship is his surrender of himself to men, the identification of word, mission, and existence in the yielding up of this very existence. His existence is thus his word. He *is* word because he is love. From the Cross faith understands in increasing measure that this Jesus did not just do and say *something*; that in him message and person are identical, that he is all along what he says. John needed only to draw the final straightforward inference: if that is so—and this is the christological basis of his Gospel—then this Jesus Christ is "word"; but a person who not only *has* words but *is* his word and his work, who is the *logos* ("the Word", meaning, mind) itself; that person has always existed and will always exist; he is the ground on which the world stands—if we ever meet such a person, then he is the meaning that comprises us all and by which we are all sustained.

The unfolding of the understanding that we call faith thus happens in such a way that Christians first hit upon the identification of person, word, and work through the Cross. Through it they recognized the really and finally decisive factor, in the presence of which all else becomes of secondary importance. For this reason their profession of faith could be restricted to the simple association of the words Jesus and Christ—this combination said it all. Jesus is seen from the Cross, which speaks louder than any words: he *is* the Christ—no more need be said. The crucified "I"

of the Lord is such an abundant reality that all else can
retire into the background. A second step was then taken,
and, from the understanding of Jesus thus acquired, people
looked back at his words. When the community began to
think back like this, it was forced to note, to its amaze-
ment, that the same concentration on his "I" was to be
found in the words of Jesus; that his message itself, studied
retrospectively, is such that it always leads to and flows into
this "I", into the identity of word and person. Finally John
was able to take one last step and link the two movements.
His Gospel is, as it were, the thorough reading of the words
of Jesus from the angle of the person and of the person
from the words. That he treats "Christology", the assertion
of faith in the Christ, as the message of the story of Jesus
and, vice-versa, the story of Jesus as Christology indicates
the complete unity of Christ and Jesus, a unity that is and
remains formative for the whole further history of faith.[12]

4. JESUS THE CHRIST

It will probably be clear from what has been said in what
sense and to what point one can follow Bultmann's movement. There does exist such a thing as a concentration on
the fact of Jesus' existence, a fusion of the fact of Jesus with
faith in the Christ—his most characteristic word is indeed
he himself. But this does mean skating rather swiftly over
the question posed by Harnack. What about the opposite of

[12] Cf. the illuminating remarks of E. Käsemann, in *Exegetische Versuche und
Besinnungen*, vol. 2 (Göttingen, 1964), p. 47. Käsemann points out that the
mere fact that John sets down his kerygma in the form of a gospel says a great
deal.

Christology, the message about the Father-God, about the love of all men that oversteps and surmounts the boundaries of faith? Has it been swallowed up in a christological dogmatism? In this attempt to redefine the faith of early Christendom and of the Church of all ages has the important element brought to the fore by liberal theology not been pushed into the background again and overlaid by a faith that causes love to be forgotten? That this can happen, and has indeed happened more than once in history, we are well aware. But that it corresponds to the intention of this conception of faith must be most emphatically denied.

For anyone who recognizes the Christ in Jesus, and only in him, and who recognizes Jesus as the Christ, anyone who grasps the total oneness of person and work as the decisive factor, has abandoned the exclusiveness of faith and its antithesis to love; he has combined both in one and made their mutual separation unthinkable. The hyphen between Jesus and Christ, the inseparability of person and work, the identity of one man with the act of sacrifice—these also signify the hyphen between love and faith. For the peculiarity of Jesus' "I", of his person, which now certainly moves right into the center of the stage, lies in the fact that this "I" is not at all something exclusive and independent but rather is Being completely derived from the "Thou" of the Father and lived for the "You" of men. It is identity of *logos* (truth) and love and thus makes love into the *logos*, the truth of human existence. The essence of the faith demanded by a Christology so understood is consequently entry into the universal openness of unconditional love. For to believe in a Christ so understood means simply to make love the content of faith, so that from this angle one can perfectly well say, love is faith.

This corresponds with the picture sketched by Jesus in his great parable of the Last Judgment (Mt 25:31–46): the profession of faith in Christ demanded by the Lord when he sits in judgment is explained as the discovery of Christ in the least of men, in those who need my help. From here onward, to profess one's faith in Christ means to recognize the man who needs me as the Christ in the form in which he comes to meet me here and now; it means understanding the challenge of love as the challenge of faith. The apparent reinterpretation here—in Matthew 25—of the christological profession of faith into the unconditionality of human service and mutual help is not to be regarded, after what we have said, as an escape from otherwise prevailing dogma; it is in truth the logical consequence of the hyphen between Jesus and Christ and, therefore, comes right from the heart of Christology itself. For this hyphen—let me repeat—is at the same time the hyphen between faith and love. Therefore it is also true that faith that is not love is not a really *Christian* faith; it only seems to be such—a fact that must redound both against any doctrinalistic misunderstanding of the Catholic concept of faith and against the secularization of love that proceeds in Luther from the notion of justification exclusively by faith.[13]

---

[13] Cf. P. Hacker, *Das Ich im Glauben bei Martin Luther* (Graz, 1966), especially the section "Säkularisierung der Liebe", pp. 166–74. Hacker shows there with an abundance of textual references that Luther as reformer (i.e., from about 1520 onward) assigns love to the "outward life", to "the use of the second table", to life not with God but "with men", and thus to the realm of the profane, to what is called today "pure worldliness", and therefore to the "righteousness of the law". He thus secularizes it and excludes it from the realm of grace and salvation. Hacker is thereby able to demonstrate convincingly that Gogarten's program of secularization can quite rightly claim to be based on Luther. It is clear that at this point Trent had to draw a firm dividing line and that where the secularization of love is retained the dividing line continues to run as it did before. On Gogarten, see A. V. Bauer's survey and evaluation of his work in *Freiheit zur Welt (Säkularisation)* (Paderborn, 1967).

C. JESUS CHRIST—TRUE GOD AND TRUE MAN

1. THE FORMULATION OF THE QUESTION

Let us return once again to the christological question in the narrower sense, so that what we have said does not rest as mere assertion or even seem like an attempt to take refuge in a modern interpretation. We had established that the Christian Yes to Jesus affirms that he is the Christ, that is, the one in whom person and work are identical; from this point we then came up against the unity of faith and love. Inasmuch as Christian faith leads us away from all mere ideas, from any independent body of teaching, to the "I" of Jesus, it leads toward an "I" that is complete openness, all "Word", all "Son". We had also already considered the fact that the concepts "word" and "son" are intended to convey the dynamic character of this existence, its pure *actualitas*. Word never stands on its own; it comes from someone, is there to be heard, and is therefore meant for others. It can only subsist in this totality of "from" and "for". We had discovered the same meaning in the concept "son", which signifies a similar tension between "from" and "for". We could accordingly summarize the whole in the formula, "Christian faith is not centered on ideas but on a person, an 'I', and on one that is defined as 'word' and 'son', that is, as 'total openness'." But this now leads to a double consequence, in which the drama of faith in Christ (in the sense of a faith in Jesus as *Christ*, that is, as Messiah) and its necessary historical development into the scandal of faith in the Son (as faith in the true divinity of Jesus) come to light. For if this is the case, if this "I" is believed in as pure openness, as total being derived from the Father; if with its whole existence it is "son"—*actualitas* of

pure service; if—in other words—this existence not only *has*
but *is* love—must it not then be identical with God, who
alone is love? Is Jesus, the Son of God, not then himself God?
Is it not true that "the Word was with God, and the Word
was God" (Jn 1:1)? But the opposite question also arises, so
that we must say: If this man is all he does, if he stands behind
all he says, if he is all for others and yet in such self-
abandonment still completely with himself; if he is the one
who in losing himself has found himself (cf. Mk 8:35), is he
not the most human of men, the fulfillment of the whole
concept of humanity? Is it then permissible to resolve Christology (= study of Christ) into theology (= study of God)?
Must we not much rather claim Jesus enthusiastically as *man*
and treat Christology as humanism and anthropology? Or
should the real man, precisely because he *is* wholly and properly such, be God, and God be the real man? Ought it to be
possible for the most radical humanism and faith in the God
who reveals himself to meet and even merge here?

I think it is clear that these questions, whose tremendous
import shook the Church of the first five centuries, emerge
quite simply from the christological confession of faith itself;
that period's dramatic wrestling with these questions led in the
ecumenical councils of those days to the answering of *all three
questions* in the affirmative. This triple Yes forms the content
and final shape of the classical christological dogma, which was
only trying in this way to be completely loyal to the straightforward original confession of faith in Jesus as the "Christ".
In other words, developed christological dogma acknowledges that the radical Christship of Jesus presupposes the Sonship and that the Sonship includes the Godship; only if it is thus
understood does it remain "*logos*-like", that is, a rational statement; without this logical consistency, one sinks into myth. But
it also acknowledges no less resolutely that in the radicality of

his service Jesus is the most human of men, the true man, and it thus subscribes to the coincidence of theology and anthropology a correspondence in which ever since then the truly exciting part of Christ-ian faith has resided.

But yet again a question arises. Even if one must admit the soundness of the argument just expounded and thus simply recognize the intrinsic logic of the dogma, there yet remains the all-important step of looking at the facts. Have we not perhaps raised ourselves aloft on a splendid system of ideas but left reality behind us, so that the indisputable coherence of the system is of no use to us because the foundation is missing? In other words, we must ask whether the findings of the Bible and its critical illumination of the facts empower us to conceive the Sonship of Jesus in the way we have just done and in the way christological dogma does. Today the answer usually given to this question is an ever more decided and self-evident No; to many people the Yes seems to have sunk to a precritical position hardly worth noting any more. I should like to try to show, on the contrary, that one not only can but must answer with Yes if one is not to slip either into rationalistic trivialities or mythological son-ideas that were long ago surpassed and overcome by biblical faith in the Son and the way it was expounded in the early Church.[14]

2. A MODERN STOCK IDEA OF THE "HISTORICAL JESUS"

We must proceed slowly. Who was Jesus of Nazareth really? What view did he take of himself? According to the stock idea, which today, as the vulgarized form of modern theology,

[14] Naturally this does not mean taking up again by way of an appendix the attempt, already rejected as impossible, at a historical construction of faith; what we *are* concerned with is demonstrating the historical legitimacy of faith.

is beginning to gain wide currency,[15] things happened like this. This historical Jesus is to be visualized as a sort of prophetic teacher who appeared on the scene in the eschatologically overheated atmosphere of the late Judaism of his time and preached, in accordance with this eschatologically pregnant situation, the proximity of the Kingdom of God. This had been at first an assertion to be understood in an entirely temporal sense: The Kingdom of God, the end of the world, was now coming very soon. But the "now" had received so much emphasis in Jesus' words that, for anyone who looked deeper, the element of "future" could no longer be regarded as the essential one, which seemed rather to reside—even if Jesus himself was thinking of a future, of a Kingdom of God—in the call to make a decision: Man's whole duty was to the "now" that thrust itself upon him at any particular time.

Let us not pause to wonder how such an empty message, which is alleged to reflect a better understanding of Jesus than he had himself, could have ever meant anything to anyone. Let us rather hear what is supposed to have happened next. For reasons that can no longer be properly established, Jesus was condemned to death and died a failure. Afterward, in a way that can no longer be clearly perceived, the belief in a Resurrection arose, the notion that he lived on or at any rate still signified something. Gradually this belief increased, and the idea developed—an idea that can be shown to have arisen in other places in a similar way—that Jesus would return in the future as the Son of Man, Messiah. The next step was

[15] When we speak here of a "vulgarized form of modern theology", this in itself implies that in specialized fields of research things are seen in varying lights and often in detail quite differently. But the impasses remain the same, and for this reason there is no validity in the popular excuse that "it is not quite so simple as that."

finally to project this hope back on to the historical Jesus, put it on his own lips, and reinterpret him accordingly. The picture was now rearranged to make it look as if Jesus had proclaimed himself as the coming Son of Man or Messiah. Very quickly—according to our stock idea—the tidings passed over from the Semitic world into the Hellenistic world. This had the following consequences. In the Jewish world Jesus had been explained along Jewish lines (Son of Man, Messiah). In the Hellenistic area these categories were incomprehensible, and consequently Hellenistic patterns of thought were pressed into service. The Semitic notions, Son of Man and Messiah, were replaced by the Hellenistic idea of the "divine person" or "God-man" (θεῖος ἀνήρ) and the figure of Jesus was thus rendered comprehensible.

But the "God-man" in the Hellenistic sense was characterized chiefly by two qualities: he was a miracle worker, and he was of divine origin. The latter idea means that in some way or other God is his Father; it is precisely his half-divine, half-human origin that makes him a God-man, a divine man. The consequence of the utilization of the category of divine man was that the attributes just described above had also to be transferred to Jesus. So people now began to portray him as a miracle worker; the "myth" of the Virgin Birth was created for the same reason. The latter, for its part, led afresh to the description of Jesus as the Son of God, since God now appeared in mythical style as his Father. In this fashion the Hellenistic interpretation of Jesus as a "divine man", together with the inevitable accompanying phenomena, finally transformed the phenomenon of proximity to God, which had been characteristic of Jesus, into the "ontological" notion of descent from God. The faith of the early Church then advanced along these mythical lines up to the final ratification of the whole in the dogma of Chalcedon, with its concept of the ontological Divine Sonship of Jesus. With the idea of the ontological origin of Jesus from God, the myth was turned by this Council into dogma and surrounded with so much abstruse learning that in the end it was raised to the status of shibboleth of orthodoxy; the starting point was thus finally stood on its head.

To anyone accustomed to think historically, the whole theory is absurd, even if today hordes of people believe it; for my part I must confess that, quite apart from the Christian faith and simply from my acquaintance with history, I find it preferable and easier to believe that God became man than that such a conglomeration of hypotheses represents the truth. In the space at our disposal here we cannot, I fear, go into the details of the historical problems involved; this would demand a very comprehensive and tedious investigation. Instead, we must (and are entitled to) confine ourselves to the crucial point around which the whole question revolves: the Divine Sonship of Jesus. If one goes to work carefully from a linguistic point of view and does not mix together things that it would be convenient to find cohering, the following points can be established.

3. THE CLAIM OF CHRISTOLOGICAL DOGMA

a. The question of the "divine man"

The concept of the divine man or God-man (θεῖος ἀνήρ) occurs *nowhere* in the New Testament. Conversely, *nowhere* in antiquity is the "divine man" described as the "Son of God". These are two important facts. Historically the two concepts are in no way connected; they have nothing to do with each other either in language or content. The Bible is not familiar with the divine man, nor is antiquity familiar, in the realm of divine men, with the idea of "Son of God". Indeed, recent researches show in addition that even the concept of the "divine man" can hardly be attested in the pre-Christian period but only turns up later.[16] But even apart from this observation, the fact remains that the title Son of God and the things implicit in it cannot be explained from the content of the title and idea of the divine man; from a historical point of view, the two patterns of thought are completely alien to each other and had no contact with each other.

b. Biblical terminology and its relation to dogma

Within the language of the New Testament, a rigorous distinction must be made between the designation "Son of God" and the simple designation "the Son". To anyone who does not proceed with linguistic precision, the two seem to mean just the same thing. The two descriptions do indeed in a certain sense have something to do with each other; but originally they belong to quite different contexts, have different origins, and express different things.

i. "Son of God." The expression "Son of God" stems from the "king" theology of the Old Testament, which itself rests on the demythologization of oriental "king" theology and expresses its transformation into the "Chosen People" theology of Israel. The classical example of this procedure (that is, of the borrowing of ancient oriental "king" theology and its biblical demythologization into the idea of election) is provided by Psalm 2:7, and thus by the text that at the same time became one of the points of departure of christological

---

[16] W. v. Martitz, "υἱός im Griechischen", in *Theologisches Wörterbuch zum NT*, ed. Kittel and Friedrich, 8:335–40, esp. 339f.

thinking. In this verse the following oracle is delivered to the king of Israel: "I will tell of the decree of the LORD: He said to me, 'You are my son, today I have begotten you. Ask of me, and I will make the nations your heritage, and the ends of the earth your possession.' " This dictum, which belongs in the context of the enthronement of the kings of Israel, stems, as we have said, from ancient oriental coronation rites, in which the king was declared the son begotten of God, though the full scope of the notion of begetting seems to have been retained only in Egypt. There the king was regarded as a being mythically begotten by God, while in Babylon the same ritual was largely demythologized and the idea that the king was the son of God was already conceived as the conferment of a legal sanction.[17]

When the formula was taken over by the Davidic court, the mythological sense was certainly set aside completely. The idea of a physical begetting of the king by the Godhead is replaced by the notion that the king becomes son here and now; the act of procreation consists in the act of election by God. The king is son, not because he has been begotten by God, but because he has been chosen by God. The reference is not to a physical event but to the power of the divine will that creates new being. In the idea of sonship so conceived, the whole theology of the Chosen People is now also concentrated. In older passages of the Bible (Ex 4:22, for example) Israel as a whole had been called Yahweh's firstborn, beloved son. When in the age of the kings this description is transferred to the ruler, this means that in him, the successor of David, Israel's vocation is summed up; that he stands for Israel and unites in himself the mystery of the promise, the call, the love that rests upon Israel.

[17] Cf. H.J. Kraus, *Psalmen*, vol. 1 (Neukirchen, 1960), pp. 18ff. (on Ps 2:7).

Then there is a further point. The application of the oriental ritual of coronation to the king of Israel, as it occurs in
the psalm, must have seemed like a cruel mockery in face of
the actual situation of Israel. When people called out to
Pharaoh or to the king of Babylon at his enthronement, "The
nations are your heritage, and the ends of the earth your
possession; you shall break them with a rod of iron, and dash
them in pieces like a potter's vessel", there was some sense in
it. Such words corresponded to these kings' claims to world
power. But when what was meaningful for the great powers
of Babylon and Egypt is applied to the king on Mount Zion,
it turns into pure irony, for the kings of the earth do not
tremble before him; on the contrary, he trembles before them.
Mastery of the world, declared as it was by a petty prince,
must have sounded almost ridiculous. To put it another way,
the mantle of the psalm, borrowed from oriental coronation
ritual, was far too big for the shoulders of the real king on
Mount Zion. So it was historically inevitable that this psalm,
which seen from the angle of the present must have appeared
almost unbearable, should grow more and more into a profession of hope in him of whom it would one day really be
true. This means that the "royal" theology, which had first
been transformed from a theology of begetting into one of
election, now went through a further change and turned from
a theology of election into a theology of hope in the king to
come. The coronation oracle became more and more a reiter-
ation of the promise that one day that king would come of
whom it could rightly be said: "You are my son, today I have
begotten you. Ask of me, and I will make the nations your
heritage."

At this point the new application of the passage by the
original Christian community begins. The words of the psalm
were probably first applied to Jesus in the framework of the

belief in his Resurrection. The event of Jesus' awakening from the dead, in which this community believed, was conceived by the first Christians as the moment at which the happenings of Psalm 2 had become a factual reality. The paradox is certainly no less striking here, for to believe that he who died on Golgotha is at the same time he to whom *these* words are addressed seems an extraordinary contradiction. What does this application of the psalm mean? It means that people know that Israel's royal hope is fulfilled in him who died on the Cross and, to the eye of faith, rose again from the dead. It implies the conviction that to him who died on the Cross, to him who renounced all earthly power (and this must be heard against the background of the talk about kings trembling and being broken with a rod of iron!), to him who laid aside the sword and, instead of sending others to their death (as earthly kings do), himself went to his death for others, to him who saw the meaning of human existence, not in power and self-assertion, but in existing utterly for others—who indeed was, as the Cross shows, existence for others—to him and to him alone God has said, "You are my son, today I have begotten you." In the crucified Christ those who believe see what the meaning of that oracle, what the meaning of being chosen is: not privilege and power for oneself, but service to others. In him it becomes clear what the meaning of the story of being chosen, what the true meaning of kingship is. It has always aimed at standing for others, at being "representation". The "representation", the standing as proxy for others, now acquires a changed meaning. It is of him, the complete failure, who no longer has an inch of ground under his feet as he hangs from the Cross, for whose garments lots are drawn and who himself seems to be abandoned by God, that the oracle speaks: "You are my son; today—on *this* spot—I have begotten you. Ask of me, and I will make the nations your heritage and the ends of the earth your possession."

The Son of God idea that in this way and in this form—the explanation of Cross and Resurrection by Psalm 2—entered into the profession of faith in Jesus of Nazareth has truly nothing to do with the Hellenistic idea of the divine man and is not to be explained in any way from it. On the contrary, it is the second stage in the demythologization of the oriental concept of kingship, an idea already partly demythologized in the Old Testament. It defines Jesus as the true heir to the universe, as heir to the promise in which Davidic theology culminates. At the same time it becomes evident that the idea of the king, which to this extent is transferred to Jesus in the title of "son", becomes intertwined with the idea of the servant. As king he is a servant, and as the servant of God he is king. This interplay, so fundamental to belief in Christ, is adumbrated in the Old Testament and anticipated linguistically in the Greek translation of it. The word *pais*, which the latter uses to denote the servant of God, can also mean "child"; in the light of the Christ event this ambiguity must have become a pointer to the way in which the two roles coincide in Jesus.[18]

The interchangeability of son and servant, of glory and service, that thus resulted, signifying a completely new interpretation of the concepts both of king and son, probably received its most magnificent formulation in the Epistle to the Philippians (2:5–11), that is, in a text still springing solely from the soil of Palestinian Christianity. The passage in question points to the basic example of the attitude of Jesus Christ, who did not jealously cling to the equality with God that is proper to him but accepted the humble position of servant,

---

[18] Cf. the important article by J. Jeremias, "παῖς θεοῦ", in *Theologisches Wörterbuch zum NT*, 5:653–713, especially p. 702f.

right to the point of complete self-emptying; the word *exinanivit* used here by the Latin text points to this translation, to the assertion that he "emptied" himself and, surrendering existence for himself, entered into the pure movement of the "for". But precisely therein, the passage goes on to say, he has become the lord of all, of the whole cosmos, before whom the latter performs the *proskynesis*, the rite and act of submission, which is due to the real king alone. The willing subject thus appears as the true ruler; he who humbled himself to the utter abasement of emptying himself of his own being is for that very reason the ruler of the world. What we had already discovered in our reflections on the triune God appears again here at the end of a different train of reasoning: he who does not cling to himself but is pure relatedness coincides in this with the absolute and thus becomes lord. The Lord before whom the universe bows is the slaughtered Lamb, the symbol of existence that is pure act, pure "for". The cosmic liturgy, the adoring homage of the universe, centers round this Lamb (Rev 5).

But let us return once again to the question of the title "Son of God" and its position in the ancient world. For we must, after all, observe that there was in fact *one* linguistic and objective parallel to it in the Graeco-Roman world. The only thing is that this parallel did not consist in the idea of the "divine man", which simply has nothing to do with it. The only real ancient parallel to the description of Jesus as the Son of God (which expresses a new understanding of power, kingship, election, indeed, of humanity) occurs in the description of Emperor Augustus as "son of God" (Θεου υἱός = *Divi* [*Caesaris*] *filius*).[19] Here we do indeed encounter the exact phrase with which the New Testament

---

[19] Cf. W. v. Martitz, "υἱός im Griechischen", pp. 330ff., 336.

describes the significance of Jesus of Nazareth. In the cult of the Roman emperor, and not before, we see the return in late antiquity, in conjunction with the oriental concept of monarchy, of the title "son of God", which otherwise did not exist and could not exist simply because of the many possible meanings of the word "god".[20] It reappears only with the return of the oriental concept of monarchy from which the designation stems. In other words, the title "son of god" belongs to the political theology of Rome and thus refers to the same basic context that also gave rise, as we have seen, to the New Testament "Son of God". Both usages proceed in fact, if independently and by different paths, from the same native soil and point back to one and the same source. So both in the ancient East and again in imperial Rome, the title "son of God" is—let us be quite clear about this—a piece of political theology. In the New Testament the phrase has been transferred to another dimension of thought as a result of its reinterpretation in Israel by a theology of election and hope. So from the same root completely different things grew up; and the conflict— soon to become unavoidable—between the acknowledgment of *Jesus* as the Son of God and the acknowledgment of the *emperor* as the son of God represented for all practical purposes a clash between demythologized myth and myth that has remained myth. The Roman god-emperor, with his all-embracing claims, could certainly not allow, alongside his own pretensions, the continued existence of the transformed "king" and "emperor" theology that lives on in faith in Jesus as the Son of God. To that extent *martyria*

---

[20] For this reason similar formulas always contain some determinant. Cf. the material in W. Bauer, *Wörterbuch zum NT*, 5th ed. (Berlin, 1958), pp. 1649ff., and in W. v. Martitz, "υἱός im Griechischen".

(testimony) was bound to turn into *martyrium*, the challenge to the self-deification of political power.[21]

ii. "The Son." Jesus' own description of himself as "the Son" is something quite distinct from the concept "son of God" that we have just discussed. This phrase, "the Son", has a different linguistic history and belongs to a different kind of language, namely, that of the coded parable, which Jesus employed in the wake of Israel's prophets and teachers of wisdom. And here again the phrase is to be located, not in the public preaching, but in Jesus' conversations with the inner circle of disciples. Its real source is probably to be found in Jesus' prayers; it forms the natural corollary to his new mode of addressing God, *Abba*.[22] Joachim Jeremias has shown by means of careful analyses that the few words that have been handed down to us by the Greek New Testament in Jesus' mother tongue, Aramaic, form a particularly good key to his original mode of speech. They struck those who heard them as so surprisingly new, and mirrored so well the special quality of the Lord, his uniqueness, that they were remembered word for word; in them we can still hear him, as it were, speaking in his own voice.

Among the few small treasures in which the original Christian community preserved Jesus' Aramaic words untranslated, because they seemed a particularly striking reflection of his personality, is the form of address *Abba*—"Father". It differs from the way in which it was possible to address God

---

[21] Cf. on this the important materials in A. A. T. Ehrhardt, *Politische Metaphysik von Solon bis Augustin*, 2 vols. (Tübingen, 1959); E. Peterson, "Zeuge der Wahrheit", in *Theologische Traktate* (Munich, 1951), pp. 165–224; N. Brox, *Zeuge und Märtyrer* (Munich, 1961).

[22] This has been convincingly demonstrated by F. Hahn, *Christologische Hoheitstitel*, 3rd ed. (Göttingen, 1966), pp. 319–33; see also the important observations of J. Jeremias, in *Abba: Studien zur neutestamentlichen Theologie und Zeitgeschichte* (Göttingen, 1966), pp. 15–67.

as Father in the Old Testament as well, inasmuch as *Abba*
is a term of intimate familiarity (comparable with the
word "Papa", if rather more elevated);[23] the intimacy implicit
in the word excluded for the Jew the possibility of using it
in reference to God; such a close approach was not seemly in
man. That Jesus prayed in this way, that he used this word in
his converse with God, thereby expressing a new form of
intimacy with God belonging only to him personally—this
was what gripped the first Christians and caused them to
preserve the word as it originally sounded.

But this form of address finds its intrinsically appropriate
corollary, as we have already indicated, in Jesus' description
of himself as Son. The two words together express the distinctive way in which Jesus prayed, his awareness of God,
into which, in however restrained a fashion, he let his closest
circle of friends have an insight. If, as we have seen, the title
"Son of God" is taken from Jewish Messianology and is thus
a phrase with a rich historical and theological content, here
we are confronted with something quite different, something infinitely simpler and at the same time infinitely more
personal and more profound. Here we see into Jesus' experience of prayer, into the nearness to God that, while distinguishing his relations with God from those of all other
men, yet does not aim at any kind of exclusiveness but is
designed to include the others in its own relationship to God.
It wishes to incorporate them, as it were, in its own kind of

---

[23] J. Jeremias, *Abba*, pp. 58–67. Jeremias here amends his own earlier view—
according to which *Abba* was merely a childish stammer—in the *Theologisches
Wörterbuch zum NT*, 5:984f.; but the fundamental perception remains valid:
"To the Jewish way of thinking it would have been disrespectful and therefore
unthinkable to address God with this familiar word. It was something new and
unheard of that Jesus should have dared to take this step.... The 'Abba' of
Jesus' prayers reveals the very heart of his relationship to God."

attitude to God, so that with Jesus and in him they can say *Abba* to God just as he does: no set distance shall separate them any longer; they are to be embraced in that intimacy that in Jesus is reality.

St. John's Gospel puts this self-description of Jesus, which in the first three Gospels occurs only in a few places (at moments when the disciples are being instructed) at the heart of its picture of Jesus; this corresponds with the basic tendency of this text, which is much more "inward" in character than the other three Gospels. Jesus' own description of himself as "the Son" now becomes the guiding thread of the depiction of the Lord; and at the same time, as the Gospel progresses, the full meaning of the phrase is unfolded. Since the most important aspects of this have already been covered in our consideration of the doctrine of the Trinity, it will be sufficient here if we just remind ourselves briefly of the conclusions at which we arrived there.

To John, the description of Jesus as Son is not the expression of any power of his own claimed by Jesus but the expression of the total relativity of his existence. When Jesus is put completely into this category, this means that his existence is explained as completely relative, nothing other than "being from" and "being for", coinciding precisely in this total relativity with the absolute. In this the title "Son" is identical with the designations "the Word" and "the one sent". And when John describes the Lord in the words of God's dictum in Isaiah [chapters 41ff.], "I am", again the same thing is meant, the total unity with the "I am" that results from an attitude of complete surrender. The heart of this Son-Christology of John's, the basis of which in the synoptic Gospels and through them in the historical Jesus (*Abba!*) was made plain earlier, lies accordingly in what became clear to us at the outset as being the starting point of all Christology:

in the identity of work and being, of deed and person, of the total merging of the person in his work and in the total coincidence of the doing with the person himself, who keeps back nothing for himself but gives himself completely in his work.

To that extent it can indeed be maintained that in John there is an "ontologization", a reaching back to the being behind the "phenomenal" character of the mere happening. It is no longer simply a question of speaking about the work, the doings, sayings, and teaching of Jesus; on the contrary, it is now established that at bottom his teaching is he himself. He as a totality is Son, Word, and mission; his activity reaches right down to the ground of being and is one with it. And it is precisely in this unity of being and doing that his special character lies. This radicalization of the statement, this inclusion of the ontological element, does not imply, to anyone who can see the context and the background, any sacrifice of the earlier conclusions; above all, it does not imply replacing the Christology of service with any kind of triumphalist Christology of glorification, which would not know what to do with the crucified and serving man and would like to invent instead another ontological myth about God. On the contrary, anyone who has properly understood the train of ideas must see that the earlier aspect is now grasped in its full profundity. The "servant" aspect is no longer explained as a deed, behind which the person of Jesus remains aloof; it is made to embrace the whole existence of Jesus, so that his *being* itself is service. And precisely because this being, as a totality, is nothing but service, it is sonship. To that extent it is not until this point that the Christian revaluation of values reaches its final goal; only here does it become fully clear that he who surrenders himself completely to service for others, to complete selflessness and self-emptying, literally *becomes* these things—that this very person is the true man, the man of the future, the coinciding of man and God.

This leads to the next step: the meaning of the dogmas of Nicaea and Chalcedon becomes evident. These dogmas were intended to express nothing else than this identity of service and being, in which the whole content of the prayer relationship "*Abba*–Son" comes to light. These dogmatic formulations with their so-called ontological Christology are not prolongations of mythical notions of begetting. Anyone who makes that assumption only proves that he has no idea of the Council of Chalcedon, of the real meaning of ontology, or even of the mythological concepts opposed to them. These declarations were not developed out of mythological notions of origin but out of the Johannine testimony, which for its part simply represents the prolongation of Jesus' converse with the Father and of Jesus' existence for men to the point of sacrificing himself on the Cross.

If one pursues these connections further, it is not difficult to see that the "ontology" of the fourth Gospel and of the old creeds embraces a much more radical "actualism" than anything appearing today under the label "actualism". I shall content myself with one example, a statement of Bultmann's on the question of Jesus' Sonship: "Just as the ἐκκλησία, the eschatological community, is only ever really ἐκκλησία as an event, so too Christ's Lordship, his Godhood, is in any case only an event." [24] In this form of actualism, the real *being* of the man Jesus remains static behind the event of "being God" and "being Lord", like the being of any man, fundamentally untouched by the event and only the chance kindling point at which it comes to pass that for someone as he hears the Word an actual encounter with God himself becomes reality. And just as the being of Jesus remains static behind

[24] *Glauben und Verstehen*, vol. 2 (Tübingen, 1952), p. 258. Cf. G. Hasenhüttl, *Der Glaubensvollzug: Eine Begegnung mit R. Bultmann aus katholischem Glaubensverständnis* (Essen, 1963), p. 127.

the event, so the being of man, too, can be affected by the divine only "now and then", by something in the realm of events. Here, too, the encounter with God only comes to pass in the momentary flash of an event; the "being" is excluded from the meeting. Theology of this sort seems to me to display a kind of despair in face of what *is*; it leaves no hope that being itself could ever become act.

The Christology of John and of the Church's Creed, in contrast, goes much farther in its radicalism, inasmuch as it acknowledges being itself as act and says, "Jesus is his work." Then there is no man behind it all to whom nothing has really happened. His being is pure *actualitas* of "from" and "for". But precisely because this "being" is no longer separable from its *actualitas*, it coincides with God and is at the same time the exemplary man, the man of the future, through whom it becomes evident how very much man is still the coming creature, a being still, so to speak, waiting to be realized; and what a short distance man has even now progressed toward being himself. When this is understood, it also becomes clear why phenomenology and existential analyses, helpful as they are, cannot suffice for Christology. They do not reach deep enough, because they leave the realm of real "being" untouched.

D. THE DIFFERENT PATHS TAKEN BY CHRISTOLOGY

1. THEOLOGY OF THE INCARNATION AND THEOLOGY OF THE CROSS

The insights so far acquired also provide access to those basic assertions of Christology that still remain to be considered.

In the history of the Christian faith two divergent lines of approach to the contemplation of Jesus have appeared again and again: the theology of the Incarnation, which sprang from Greek thought and became dominant in the Catholic tradition of East and West, and the theology of the Cross, which based itself on St. Paul and the earliest forms of Christian belief and made a decisive breakthrough in the thinking of the Reformers. The former talks of "being" and centers around the fact that here a man *is* God and that, accordingly, at the same time God is man; this astounding fact is seen as the all-decisive one. All the individual events that followed pale before this one event of the one-ness of man and God, of God's becoming man. In face of this they can only be secondary; the interlocking of God and man appears as the truly decisive, redemptive factor, as the real future of man, on which all lines must finally converge.

The theology of the Cross, on the other hand, will have nothing to do with ontology of this kind; it speaks instead of the event; it follows the testimony of the early days, when people inquired, not yet about *being*, but about the *activity* of God in the Cross and Resurrection, an activity that conquered death and pointed to Jesus as the Lord and as the hope of humanity. The differing tendencies of these two theologies result from their respective approaches. The theology of the Incarnation tends toward a static, optimistic view. The sin of man may well appear as a transitional stage of fairly minor importance. The decisive factor, then, is not that man is in a state of sin and must be saved; the aim goes far beyond any such atonement for the past and lies in making progress toward the convergence of man and God. The theology of the Cross, on the other hand, leads rather to a dynamic, topical, anti-world interpretation of Christianity, which understands Christianity only as a discontinuously but constantly appearing breach in the self-confidence and self-assurance of man and of his institutions, including the Church.

Anyone at all familiar with these two great historical forms of Christian self-comprehension will certainly not be tempted to try his hand at a simplifying synthesis. The two fundamental structural forms of "Incarnation" theology and "Cross" theology reveal polarities that cannot be surmounted and combined in a neat synthesis without the loss of the crucial points in each; they must remain present as polarities that mutually correct each other and only by complementing each other point toward the whole. Nevertheless, our reflections may perhaps have given us a glimpse of that ultimate unity which makes these polarities possible and prevents them from falling apart as contradictions. For we have found that the *being* of Christ ("Incarnation" theology!) is *actualitas*, stepping beyond oneself, the exodus of going out from self; it is, not a being that rests in itself, but the act of being sent, of being son, of serving. Conversely, this "doing" is not just "doing" but "being"; it reaches down into the depths of being and coincides with it. This being is exodus, transformation. So at this point a properly understood Christology of being and of the Incarnation must pass over into the theology of the Cross and become one with it; conversely, a theology of the Cross that gives its full measure must pass over into the Christology of the Son and of being.

2. CHRISTOLOGY AND THE DOCTRINE OF REDEMPTION

From the position thus gained it is at last possible to perceive also the operation of another antithesis erected by history; it is in fact closely related to the one we have just considered. In the course of the historical development of faith in Christ, two aspects of it, which people became accustomed to call

"Christology" and "soteriology", visibly parted company. The former term came to denote the doctrine of the being of Jesus, which was treated more and more as a self-contained ontological exception and thus transformed into an object of speculation concerning something special, incomprehensible, and confined to Jesus alone. Soteriology then came to denote the doctrine of the redemption: after dealing with the ontological crossword puzzle—the question of how man and God could in Jesus be one—people went on to inquire quite separately about what Jesus had really done and how the effect of his deed impinges on us. That the two questions parted company, that the person and his work were made the subjects of separate inquiries and treatises, led to both problems becoming incomprehensible and insoluble. A brief inspection of the manuals of dogmatic theology is sufficient to confirm how complicated the theories dealing with both problems were, because it had been forgotten that they can only be understood when considered together. Let me just recall the form that the doctrine of redemption most often takes in the Christian consciousness. It is based on the so-called "satisfaction theory", which was developed by St. Anselm of Canterbury on the threshold of the Middle Ages and molded the Western consciousness more and more exclusively. Even in its classical form it is not devoid of one-sidedness, but when considered in the vulgarized form that has to a great extent shaped the general consciousness, it looks cruelly mechanical and less and less feasible.

Anselm of Canterbury (ca. 1033–1109) had been concerned to deduce the work of Christ by a train of necessary reasons (*rationibus necessariis*) and thus to show irrefutably that this work *had* to happen in the precise way in which it in fact did. The main lines of his argument may be summarized as follows: By man's sin, which was aimed against God, the order of justice was violated beyond measure and God infinitely offended. Behind this is the idea that the measure of the offense is determined by the status of the offended party; if I offend a beggar, the consequences are not the same as they would be if I offended a head of state. The importance of the offense varies according to the addressee. Since God is infinite, the offense to him implicit in humanity's sin is also infinitely important. The right that has been violated to such an extent must be restored, because God is a God of order and justice; indeed, he is justice itself. But the measure of the offense demands an infinite reparation, which man is not capable of making. He can offend infinitely—his capacity extends that far—but he cannot produce an infinite reparation; what he, as a finite being, gives will always be only finite. His powers of destruction extend farther than his capacity to reconstruct. Thus between all the reparations that man may attempt and the greatness of his guilt there remains an infinite gulf he can never bridge. Any gesture of expiation can only demonstrate his powerlessness to close the infinite gulf that he himself opened up.

Is order to be destroyed forever, then, and man to remain eternally imprisoned in the abyss of his guilt? At this point Anselm moves on to the figure of Christ. His answer runs thus: God himself removes the injustice; not (as he could have done) by a simple amnesty, which cannot after all overcome from inside what has happened, but through another expedient: the infinite Being himself becomes man and then as a man—who belongs to the race of the offenders yet possesses the power, denied to man, of infinite reparation—makes the required expiation. Thus the redemption takes place entirely through grace and at the same time entirely as restoration of the right. Anselm thought he had thereby given a compelling answer to the difficult question of "Cur Deus homo?", the wherefore of the Incarnation and the Cross.

His view has put a decisive stamp on the second millennium of Western Christendom, which takes it for granted that Christ had to die on the Cross in order to make good the infinite offense that had been committed and in this way to restore the order that had been violated.

Now it cannot be denied that this theory takes account of crucial biblical and human insights; anyone who studies it with a little patience will have no difficulty in seeing this. To that extent it will always command respect as an attempt to synthesize the individual elements in the biblical evidence in one great all-embracing system. It is not hard to see that, in spite of all the philosophical and juridical terminology employed, the guiding thread remains that truth which the Bible expresses in the little word "for", in which it makes clear that we as men live not only directly from God but from one another and, in the last analysis, from the One who lived for all. And who could fail to see that thus in the schematization of the "satisfaction" theory the breath of the biblical idea of election remains clear, the idea that makes election, not a privilege of the elected, but the call to live for others? It is the call to that "for" in which man confidently lets himself fall, ceases to cling to himself, and ventures on the leap away from himself into the infinite, the leap through which alone he can come to himself. But even if all this is admitted, it cannot be denied, on the other hand, that the perfectly logical divine-*cum*-human legal system erected by Anselm distorts the perspectives and with its rigid logic can make the image of God appear in a sinister light. We shall have to go into this in detail when we come to talk about the meaning of the Cross. For the time being it will suffice to say that things immediately look different when, in place of the division of Jesus into work and person, it becomes clear that with Jesus Christ it is not a question of some work separate from himself, of a feat that God must demand because he himself is under an obligation to the concept of order; that with him it is not a question—to use Gabriel Marcel's terminology—of *having* humanity, but of *being* human. And how different things look farther on when one picks up the Pauline key, which teaches us to understand Christ as the "last man" (ἔσχατος Ἀδάμ: 1 Cor 15:45)—the final man, who takes man into his future, which consists of his being, not just man, but one with God.

3. CHRIST, "THE LAST MAN"

We have now reached the point at which we can try to summarize what we mean when we confess, "I believe in Jesus Christ, only begotten Son of God, our Lord". After all that has gone before we shall dare to say first: Christian faith believes in Jesus of Nazareth as the exemplary man (this is probably the best way to translate accurately the above-mentioned Pauline concept of the "last Adam"). But precisely because he is the exemplary, the authoritative man, he oversteps the bounds of humanity; only thus and only thereby is he the truly exemplary man. For man is the more himself the more he is with "the other". He only comes *to* himself by moving away *from* himself. Only through "the other" and through "being" with "the other" does he come to himself.

In the last analysis there is one final depth to this truth. If "the other" is just anyone, he can also cause man to lose himself. Man is finally intended for *the* other, the truly other, for God; he is all the more himself the more he is with the *entirely* Other, with God. Accordingly, he is completely himself when he has ceased to stand in himself, to shut himself off in himself, and to assert himself, when in fact he is pure openness to God. To put it again in different terms: man comes to himself by moving out beyond himself. Jesus Christ, though, is the one who has moved right out beyond himself and, *thus*, the man who has truly come to himself.

The Rubicon of becoming man, of "hominization", was first crossed by the step from animal to *logos*, from mere life to mind. Man came into existence out of the "clay" at the moment when a creature was no longer merely "there" but, over and above just being there and filling his needs, was aware of the whole. But this step, through which *logos*, understanding, mind, first came into this world, is only completed when the *Logos* itself, the whole creative meaning, and man merge into each other. Man's full "hominization" presupposes God's becoming man; only by this event is the Rubicon dividing the "animal" from the "logical" finally crossed for ever and the highest possible development accorded to the process that began when a creature of dust and earth looked out beyond itself and its environment and was able to address God as "You". It is openness to the whole, to the infinite, that makes man complete. Man is man by reaching out infinitely beyond himself, and he is consequently more of a man the less enclosed he is in himself, the less "limited" he is. For—let me repeat—that man is most fully man, indeed *the* true man, who is most unlimited, who not only has contact with the infinite—the Infinite Being!—but is one with him: Jesus Christ. In him "hominization" has truly reached its goal.[25]

---

[25] Cf. on this subject B. Welte, "*Homousios hemin*: Gedanken zum Verständnis und zur theologischen Problematik der Kategorien von Chalkedon", in A. Grillmeier and H. Bacht, *Das Konzil von Chalkedon*, vol. 3 (Würzburg, 1954), pp. 51–80; K. Rahner, "Zur Theologie der Menschwerdung", in *Schriften zur Theologie*, vol. 4 (Einsiedeln, 1960), pp. 137–55; Rahner, "Die Christologie innerhalb einer evolutiven Weltanschauung", in *Schriften*, vol. 5 (Einsiedeln, 1962), pp. 183–221.

But now there is a second point to be considered. We tried earlier, via the idea of the "exemplary man", to understand that first fundamental overstepping of one's own individuality which faith knows to be the decisive feature in the figure of Jesus; the feature that in him binds humanity and divinity into a unity. But in that concept there was already a hint of the abolition of yet another frontier. If Jesus is the exemplary man, in whom the true figure of man, God's intention for him, comes fully to light, then he cannot be destined to be merely an absolute exception, a curiosity, in which God demonstrates to us what sorts of things are possible. His existence concerns all mankind. The New Testament makes this perceptible by calling him an "Adam"; in the Bible this word expresses the unity of the whole creature "man", so that one can speak of the biblical idea of a "corporate personality".[26] So if Jesus is called "Adam", this implies that he is intended to gather the whole creature "Adam" in himself. But this means that the reality that Paul calls, in a way that is largely incomprehensible to us today, the "body of Christ" is an intrinsic postulate of this existence, which cannot remain an exception but must "draw to itself" the whole of mankind (cf. Jn 12:32).

It must be regarded as an important service of Teilhard de Chardin's that he rethought these ideas from the angle of the modern view of the world and, in spite of a not entirely unobjectionable tendency toward the biological approach, nevertheless on the whole grasped them correctly and in any case made them accessible once again. Let us listen to his own words: The human monad "can only be absolutely itself

[26] Cf. J. Pedersen, *Israel, Its Life and Culture*, 2 vols. (London, 1926 and 1940); H. W. Robinson, *The Hebrew Conception of Corporate Personality*, Beihefte zur Zeitschrift für die alttestamentliche Wissenschaft 66 (Berlin, 1936), pp. 49–62; J. de Fraine, *Adam und seine Nachkommen* (Cologne, 1962).

by ceasing to be alone".[27] In the background is the idea that in the cosmos, alongside the two orders or classes of the infinitely small and the infinitely big, there is a third order, which determines the real drift of evolution, namely, the order of the infinitely complex. It is the real goal of the ascending process of growth or becoming; it reaches a first peak in the genesis of living things and then continues to advance to those highly complex creations that give the cosmos a new center: "Imperceptible and accidental as the position they hold may be in the history of the heavenly bodies, in the last analysis the planets are nothing less than the vital points of the universe. It is through them that the axis now runs, on them is henceforth concentrated the main effort of an evolution aiming principally at the production of large molecules."[28] The examination of the world by the dynamic criterion of complexity thus signifies "a complete inversion of values. A reversal of the perspective."[29]

But let us return to man. He is so far the maximum in complexity. But even he as mere man-monad cannot represent an end; his growth itself demands a further advance in complexity: "At the same time as he represents an individual centered on himself (that is, a 'person'), does not Man also represent an *element* in relation to some new and higher synthesis?"[30] That is to say, man is indeed, on the one hand, already an end that can no longer be reversed, no longer be melted down again; yet in the juxtaposition of individual men he is not yet at the goal but shows himself to be an element, as it were, that longs

---

[27] Quoted by C. Tresmontant, *Introduction à la pensée de Teilhard de Chardin* (Paris, 1956), p. 68 (the quotation in fact comes from Teilhard's *La Vie Cosmique*, 1916—TRANS).

[28] Ibid., p. 38 (Teilhard, "Vie et Planètes", *Études*, May 1946, p. 157—TRANS.).

[29] Ibid., p. 37 (Teilhard, "Vie et Planètes", p. 155—TRANS.).

[30] Ibid., p. 68 (Teilhard, *La Place de l'Homme dans l'Univers*, 1942—TRANS.).

for a whole that will embrace it without destroying it. Let us look at a further text, in order to see in what direction such ideas lead: "Contrary to the appearances still accepted by Physics, the Great Stability is not below—in the infra-elemental—but above—in the ultra-synthetic." [31] So it must be discovered that, "If things hold and hold together, it is only by virtue of 'complexification', from the top." [32] I think we are confronted here with a crucial statement; at this point the dynamic view of the world destroys the positivistic conception, which seems so obvious to us, that stability is located only in the "mass", in hard material. That the world is in the last resort put together and held together "from above" here becomes evident in a way that is particularly striking because we are so little accustomed to it.

This leads to a further passage in Teilhard de Chardin that is worth quoting in order to give at least some indication here, by means of a few fragmentary excerpts, of his general outlook. "The Universal Energy must be a Thinking Energy if it is not to be less highly evolved than the ends animated by its action. And consequently ... the attributes of cosmic value with which it is surrounded in our modern eyes do not affect in the slightest the necessity obliging us to recognize in it a transcendent form of Personality." [33] From here it is possible to understand the final aim of the whole movement as Teilhard sees it: the cosmic drift moves "in the direction of an incredible 'mono-molecular' state, so to speak, in which ... each ego is destined to attain its climax in a sort of mysterious superego".[34] As an "I", man is indeed an end, but the whole tendency of his being and of his own

[31] Ibid., p. 72 (Teilhard, *Le Phénomène humain*, p. 301—Trans.).

[32] Ibid., p. 72 (Teilhard, *Le Phénomène humain*, p. 37—Trans.).

[33] Ibid., p. 78 (Teilhard, *L'Esprit de la Terre*—Trans.).

[34] Ibid., p. 69 (Teilhard, *Le Cœur de la Matière*, 1950—Trans.).

existence shows him also to be a creation belonging to a "super-I" that does not blot him out but encompasses him; only such an association can bring out the form of the future man, in which humanity will achieve complete fulfillment of itself.

One can safely say that here the tendency of Pauline Christology is in essentials correctly grasped from the modern angle and rendered comprehensible again, even if the vocabulary employed is certainly rather too biological. Faith sees in Jesus the man in whom—on the biological plane—the next evolutionary leap, as it were, has been accomplished; the man in whom the breakthrough out of the limited scope of humanity, out of its monadic enclosure, has occurred; the man in whom personalization and socialization no longer exclude each other but support each other; the man in whom perfect unity—"The body of Christ", says St. Paul, and even more pointedly "You are all one in Christ Jesus" (Gal 3:28)— and perfect individuality are one; the man in whom humanity comes into contact with its future and in the highest extent itself becomes its future, because through him it makes contact with God himself, shares in him, and thus realizes its most intrinsic potential. From here onward faith in Christ will see the beginning of a movement in which dismembered humanity is gathered together more and more into the being of one single Adam, one single "body"—the man to come. It will see in him the movement to that future of man in which he is completely "socialized", incorporated in one single being, but in such a way that the individual is not extinguished but brought completely to himself.

It would not be difficult to show that Johannine theology points in the same direction. One has only to recall the words briefly touched on earlier: "And I, when I am lifted up from the earth, will draw all men to myself" (Jn 12:32). This sentence is intended to explain the meaning of Jesus' death on the Cross; it thus expresses, since the Cross forms the center of Johannine theology, the direction in which the whole Gospel is intended to point. The event of the crucifixion appears there as a process of opening, in which the scattered man-monads are drawn into the embrace of Jesus Christ, into the wide span of his outstretched arms, in order to arrive, in this union, at their goal, the goal of humanity. But if this is so, then Christ as the man to come is not man for himself but essentially man for others; it is precisely his complete openness that makes him the man of the future. The man for himself, who wants to stand only in himself, is then the man of the past whom we must leave behind us in order to stride forward. In other words, this means that the future of man lies in "being for". This fundamentally confirms once again what we recognized as the meaning of the talk of sonship and, before that, as the meaning of the doctrine of three Persons in one God, namely, a reference to the dynamic, "actual" existence, which is essentially openness in the movement between "from" and "for". And once again it becomes clear that Christ is the completely open man, in whom the dividing walls of existence are torn down, who is entirely "transition" (Passover, "Pasch").

This brings us straight back again to the mystery of the Cross and Easter, a mystery that is, indeed, viewed by the Bible as a mystery of transition. John, who in particular reflects these ideas, concludes his portrait of the earthly Jesus with the image of an existence whose walls are torn down, which knows no more firm boundaries but is essentially openness. "One of the soldiers pierced his side with a spear, and at once there came out blood and water" (Jn 19:34). For John, the picture of the pierced side forms the climax not only of the crucifixion scene but of the whole story of Jesus. Now, after the piercing with a spear that ends his earthly life, his existence is completely open; now he is entirely "for"; now he is truly no longer a single individual but "Adam", from whose side Eve, a new mankind, is formed. That profound description in the Old Testament according to which the woman is taken from the side of the man (Gen 2:21ff.)—an inimitable expression of their perpetual dependence on each other and their unity in the one humanity—that story seems to be echoed here in the recurrence of the word "side" (πλευρά, usually translated—wrongly—by "rib"). The open side of the new Adam repeats the mystery of the "open side" of man at creation: it is the beginning of a new definitive community of men with one another, a community symbolized here by blood and water, in which John points to the basic Christian sacraments of baptism and Eucharist and, through them, to the Church as the sign of the new community of men.[35] The fully opened Christ, who completes the transformation of being into reception and transmission, is thus visible as what at the deepest level he always was: as "Son". So Jesus on the Cross has truly entered on *his* hour, as once again John says. This enigmatic mode of speech may now perhaps become to some extent comprehensible.

But the whole thing also shows what demands the talk of the man to come involves and how little it really has to do with the cheerful romanticism of progress. For to be the man for others, the man who is open and thereby opens up a new beginning, means being the man in the sacrifice, sacrificed man. The future of man hangs on the Cross—the redemption of man is the Cross. And he can only come to himself

---

[35] Cf. O. Cullmann, *Urchristentum und Gottesdienst* (Zürich, 1950), pp. 110ff.; J. Betz, *Die Eucharistie in der Zeit der griechischen Väter*, vol. 2, pt. 1: "Die Realpräsenz des Leibes und Blutes Jesu im Abendmahl nach dem NT" (Freiburg, 1961), pp. 189–200.

by letting the walls of his existence be broken down, by looking on him who has been pierced (Jn 19:37), and by following him who as the pierced and opened one has opened
the path into the future. This means in the end that Christianity, which as belief in the creation acknowledges the primacy of the *logos*, the creative meaning as beginning and
origin, also acknowledges it in a specific way as the end, the
future, the coming one. Indeed, in this gaze at him who is
coming lies the real historical dynamism of the Christian
approach, which in the Old and New Testaments perfects
faith into hope in the promise.

Christian faith is not just a look back at what has happened in the past, an anchorage in an origin that lies behind
us in time; thinking along those lines would finally end in
mere romanticism and reaction. Nor is it just an outlook on
the eternal; that would be Platonism and metaphysics. It is
also above all things a looking forward, a reaching-out of
hope. Not only that, certainly; hope would become uto-
pianism if its goal were only man's own product. It is true
hope precisely because it is situated in a three-dimensional
coordinate system: the past, that is, the breakthrough that
has already taken place; the present of the eternal, which
makes divided time like unity; and he who is to come, in
whom God and world will touch each other, and, thus, God
in world, world in God will truly be the Omega of history.

From the standpoint of Christian faith one may say that
for *history* God stands at the end, while for *being* he stands at
the beginning. This indicates Christianity's all-embracing
horizon, which distinguishes it both from mere metaphysics
and from the future-orientated ideology of Marxism. Since
Abraham and until the return of the Lord, faith advances to
meet him who is coming. But in Christ the countenance of
him who is to come is already revealed: it will be the man

who can embrace all men because he has lost himself and them to God. For this reason the emblem of him who is to come must be the Cross, and his face in this era of the world must be a bleeding, wounded countenance: the "last man", that is, the real, the future man, reveals himself in this age in *the* last men; whoever wishes to stand on *his* side must therefore stand on *their* side (cf. Mt 25:31–46).

EXCURSUS: CHRISTIAN STRUCTURES

Before we proceed to work through the separate christological statements in the Creed that follow the basic acknowledgment of Jesus as the Christ, it would be good to pause for a moment. The individual questions are only too apt to make us forget to look at the whole, and it is clear how essential such a general survey is today, especially when we are trying to talk to someone who does not believe. Sometimes one can get the impression from contemporary theology that it is so pleased with its progress—certainly very welcome—in the ecumenical field, and so glad that it is succeeding in removing old boundary stones (if only in most cases to erect them again at a different spot), that it does not pay sufficient attention to the immediate questions of the men of today, questions that often have little to do with the traditional points of conflict between the various denominations. For example, who can ever tell an inquirer comprehensibly and with reasonable brevity what "being a Christian" really means? Who can explain comprehensibly to someone else why he believes and what the plain direction, the nub, of the decision implicit in faith is?

When great numbers of people do begin, as they have done recently, to put such questions to themselves, quite often

they simultaneously slip into the habit of watering down
Christianity into sweet-sounding generalities, which certainly flatter the ears of their contemporaries (cf. 2 Tim 4:3)
but deny them the strong meat of the faith to which they are
entitled. Theology is not measuring up to its task when it
concentrates happily on itself and its own erudition; it is failing even more radically when it invents "doctrines to its own
taste" (2 Tim 4:3) and thus offers stones instead of bread, its
own talk instead of the Word of God. The task that thus
presents itself—between this Scylla and this Charybdis—is
immeasurably big. Nevertheless—or rather for this very
reason—let us try to rethink things along these lines and to
summarize the basic content of Christianity in a few easily
graspable statements. Even if the results remain somewhat
unsatisfactory, the enterprise may perhaps have the advantage of stimulating others to put further questions and thus
of helping things forward.[36]

1. The individual and the whole

For us men of today the basic stumbling block of Christianity lies first of all simply in the superficiality to which the
religious element seems to have settled down. It irritates us
that God should have to be mediated through outward forms:
through Church, sacrament, dogma, or even just through
the Gospel (kerygma), to which people like to withdraw to
reduce the irritation and which is nevertheless itself something external. All this provokes the question, Does God dwell

[36] What follows makes considerable use of ideas I first developed in my
little book *Vom Sinn des Christseins*, 2nd ed. (Munich, 1966). I have tried to
systematize what I said there and to incorporate it in the larger context of the
reflections contained in this present book.

in institutions, events, or words? As the eternal Being, does he not make contact with each of us from within? To this we must first of all simply say Yes and then go on to say that if there were only God and a collection of individuals, Christianity would be unnecessary. The salvation of the individual *as* individual can and could always be looked after directly and immediately by God, and this does happen again and again. He needs no intermediary channels by which to enter the soul of the individual, to which he is more present interiorly than he is to himself; nothing can reach more intimately and deeply into man than he, who touches this creature man in the very innermost depth of his being. For the salvation of the mere individual there would be no need of either a Church or a history of salvation, an Incarnation or a Passion of God in this world. But precisely at this point we must also add the further statement: Christian faith is not based on the atomized individual but comes from the knowledge that there is no such thing as the mere individual, that, on the contrary, man is himself only when he is fitted into the whole: into mankind, into history, into the cosmos, as is right and proper for a being who is "spirit in body".

The principle of "body" and "corporality" by which man is governed means two things: on the one hand, the body separates men from one another, makes them impenetrable to each other. As a space-filling and sharply defined shape, the body makes it impossible for one to be completely in the other; it erects a dividing line that signifies distances and limit; it keeps us at a distance from one another and is, to that extent, a dissociating principle. But at the same time existence in a corporal form necessarily also embraces history and community, for if pure spirit can be thought of as existing strictly for itself, corporality implies descent from one another: human beings depend in a very real and at the same time very complex sense on one another for their lives. For if this dependence is first of all a physical one (and even in this sphere it extends from parentage down to the manifold interactions of mutual daily care), it means, for him who is spirit only in a body and as body, that the spirit, too—in short, the one, whole man—is deeply marked by his belonging to the whole of mankind—the one "Adam".

It thus becomes clear that man is a being that can only "be" by virtue of others. Or, to put it in the words of the great Tübingen theologian Möhler: "Man, as a being set entirely in a context of relationship, cannot come to himself through himself, although he cannot do it without himself either." [37] This was expressed even more pointedly by Möhler's contemporary the Munich philosopher Franz von Baader, when he declared that it was just as absurd "to deduce the knowledge of God and the knowledge of all other intelligences and non-intelligences from self-knowledge (self-awareness) as to deduce all love from self-love". [38] Here we are confronted with a sharp rejection of the mode of thinking adopted by Descartes, whose grounding of philosophy in self-awareness ("Cogito, ergo sum": I think, therefore I am) has decisively influenced the fate of the modern mind right down to the present-day forms of transcendental philosophy. Just as self-love is not the primordial form of love but at the most a derivative of it, just as one has only arrived at the specific nature of love when one has grasped it as a relation, that is, something coming from another, so, too, human knowledge is only reality when it is *being* known, being

---

[37] This is how J. R. Geiselmann summarizes the ideas developed by Möhler in the *Theologische Quartalschrift*, 1830, pp. 582f.; J. R. Geiselmann, *Die Heilige Schrift und die Tradition* (Freiburg, 1962), p. 56.

[38] According to Geiselmann, *Heilige Schrift*, p. 56; F. von Baader, *Vorlesungen über spekulative Dogmatik* (1830), 7th lecture, in *Werke*, 8:231; cf. Möhler, *Theologische Quartalschrift*.

brought to knowledge, and thus again "from another". The real man does not come into it at all if I only plumb the loneliness of the "I", of self-knowledge, for then I exclude in advance the point of departure of his ability to come to himself and thus his most specific characteristic. That is why Baader, consciously and quite rightly, changed the Cartesian "Cogito, ergo sum" into "Cogitor, ergo sum": not "I think, therefore I am," but "I am thought, therefore I am". Only from man's being known can his knowledge and he himself be understood.

Let us go a step farther: being a man means being a fellow-man in every aspect, not just in the present moment, but in such a way that every man also contains the past and future of mankind, which really does prove, the closer one looks, to be one single "Adam". We cannot go into this in detail here; a few indications must suffice. One needs only to note that our mental life depends entirely on the medium of language and to add, then, that language was not invented today. It comes from a long way off; the whole of history has contributed to it and through it enters into us as the unavoidable premise of our present, indeed, as a constant part of it. And, vice versa, man is a being who lives for the future, who continually takes care to plan ahead beyond the passing moment and could no longer exist if he suddenly found himself without a future.[39] We must say, therefore, that such a thing as the mere individual, the man-monad of the Renaissance, the pure "Cogito ergo sum" being does not exist. Humanity belongs to man only in

[39] Cf. the observation by E. Mounier in *L'Esprit*, January 1947: a wireless announcer had succeeded only too well in creating the idea that the end of the world was at hand. Peak of absurdity: people took their own lives so as not to die. This quite obviously senseless reaction proves that we live far more on the future than on the present. A man who is violently robbed of the future is a man already robbed of life itself.—In "Sein des Daseins als Sorge", M. Heidegger, *Sein und Zeit*, 11th ed. (Tübingen, 1967), pp. 191–96.

the web of history that impinges on the individual through speech and social communication; and the individual for his part lives his life on the collective pattern in which he is already previously included and that forms the scene of his self-realization. It is simply not the case that every man plans himself anew from square one of his own freedom, as it seemed to the German idealist philosophers. He is not a being who keeps starting again from scratch; he can only work out his own new approach within the framework of the already existing whole of human life that stamps and molds him.

This brings us back to the question with which we started, and we can now say: The Church and being a Christian have to do with man so understood. They would have no function to fulfill if the only thing that existed was the man-monad, the being implied by "Cogito, ergo sum". They are related to the man who is a fellow being and only subsists in the collective entanglements that follow from the principle of corporality. Church and Christianity itself exist on account of history, because of the collective involvements that stamp man; they are to be understood on this plane. Their purpose is to save history as history and to break through or transform the collective grid that forms the site of human existence. According to the Epistle to the Ephesians, Christ's work of salvation consisted precisely in bringing to their knees the forces and powers seen by Origen in his commentary on this passage as the collective powers that encircle man: the power of the milieu, of national tradition; the conventional "they" or "one" that oppresses and destroys man.[40] Terms like original sin, resurrection of the body, Last Judgment,

---

[40] Cf. J. Ratzinger, "Menschheit und Staatenbau in der Sicht der frühen Kirche", in *Studium generale* 14 (1961): 664–82, especially 666–74; H. Schlier, *Mächte und Gewalten im Neuen Testament* (Freiburg, 1958), especially pp. 23f., 27, 29. On the "one": Heidegger, *Sein und Zeit*, pp. 126–30.

and so on, are only to be understood at all from this angle, for the seat of original sin is to be sought precisely in this collective net that precedes the individual existence as a sort of spiritual datum, not in any biological legacy passed on between otherwise utterly separated individuals. Talk of original sin means just this, that no man can start from scratch any more, in a *status integritatis* (completely unimpaired by history). No one starts off in an unimpaired condition in which he would only need to develop himself freely and make plans for his own happiness; everyone lives in a web that is a part of his very existence. Last Judgment, on the other hand, is the answer to these collective entanglements. Resurrection expresses the idea that the immortality of man can exist and be thought of only in the fellowship of men, in man as the creature of fellowship, as we shall see in more detail later on. Finally, even the concept of redemption, as we have already said, only has a meaning on this plane; it does not refer to the detached, monadic destiny of the individual. If, therefore, the plane of reality of Christianity is to be sought here, in a realm that can be summarily described, in the absence of a better term, as that of historicity, then we can now clarify further and say: Being a Christian is in its first aim not an individual but a social charisma. One is not a Christian because only Christians are saved; one is a Christian because for history Christian loving service has meaning and is a necessity.

At this point there occurs an absolutely decisive further step, which at first seems to represent a complete about-turn but in fact is the necessary corollary of our reflections up to now. If one is a Christian in order to share in a loving service for the whole, then this means at the same time that, precisely because of this relation to the whole, Christianity lives from the *individual* and for the individual, because only by

the action of the individual can the transformation of history, the destruction of the dictatorship of the milieu come
to pass. It seems to me that this is the reason for what to the
other world religions and to the man of today is always completely incomprehensible, namely, that in Christianity *everything* hangs in the last resort on one *individual*, on the man
Jesus of Nazareth, who was crucified by the milieu—public
opinion—and who on his Cross broke this very power of
the conventional "everyone", the power of anonymity, which
holds man captive. This power is now confronted by the name
of this individual, Jesus Christ, who calls on man to follow
him, that is, to take up the cross as he did, and, by being
crucified, to overcome the world and contribute to the
renewal of history. Precisely because Christianity wants history as a whole, its challenge is directed fundamentally at the
individual; precisely for this reason it depends on *the* single
individual in whom the bursting of the bondage to the forces
and powers took place. In other words, because Christianity
relates to the whole and can only be understood from the
idea of community and with reference to it, because it does
not mean the salvation of the isolated individual but being
enlisted in service to the whole, which he neither can nor
may escape, for this very reason it is committed to the principle of "the individual" in its most radical form. *Here* lies
the intrinsic necessity of the unheard-of scandal that a single
individual, Jesus Christ, is acknowledged as the salvation of
the world. The individual is the salvation of the whole, and
the whole receives its salvation only from the individual who
truly is salvation and who precisely for this reason ceases to
exist for himself alone.

I believe that this is also the key to understanding why
there is no comparable recourse to the individual in other
religions. In the last analysis Hinduism seeks, not the whole,

but the individual who saves himself, who escapes from the world, the wheel of Maja. Precisely because at bottom it does not want the whole but only to rescue the individual from wickedness, it can never recognize any *other* individual as finally significant and decisive for *my* salvation. Its devaluation of the whole thus becomes a devaluation of the individual as well, in that "for" disappears as a category.[41]

To summarize the conclusions of our reflections so far, we have established that Christianity proceeds from the principle of "corporeality" (historicity), that it is to be thought of on the plane of "the whole" and has meaning only on this plane, and that nevertheless for this very reason it sets up and must set up the "individual" as a principle, which is its scandal, the intrinsic necessity and rationality of which are nevertheless evident here.

2. The principle of "for"

Because Christian faith demands the individual but wants him for the whole and not for himself, the real basic law of Christian existence is expressed in the preposition "for": this is the final conclusion that necessarily emerges from what we have said so far. That is why in the chief Christian sacrament, which forms the center of Christian worship, the existence of Jesus Christ is explained[42] as existence "for the many", "for you", as an open existence that makes possible and creates the communication of all with one another through communication in him. That is why Christ's

[41] Cf. the instructive investigation by J. Neuner, "Religion und Riten: Die Opferlehre der Bhagavadgita", in *Zeitschrift für Katholische Theologie* 73 (1951): 170–213.

[42] In the canon of the Mass, for example, in accordance with the institution narratives, Mark 14:24, and parallel passages.

existence, as exemplary existence, is fulfilled and perfected, as we have seen, in his being opened on the Cross. That is why he can say, announcing and expounding his death: "I go away, and I will come to you" (Jn 14:28): By my going away the wall of my existence that now encloses me will be broken down, and thus this happening is my real coming, in which I make a reality of what I really am, the one who draws all into the unity of his new being, the one who is not boundary but unity.

This is how the Church Fathers interpreted the arms of the Lord outstretched on the Cross. They saw in them, first of all, the primordial form of the Christian position of prayer, the attitude of the *orantes* so movingly portrayed in the pictures in the catacombs. The arms of the crucified Christ thus show him to be the worshipper, but at the same time they also add a new dimension to worship, a dimension that forms the specifically Christian element in the glorification of God: these open arms are also the expression of worship precisely because they express complete devotion to men, because they are a gesture of embrace, of full and undivided brotherliness. On the Cross the theology of the Fathers found symbolically depicted in the Christian gesture of prayer the coincidence of worship and brotherliness, the indivisibility of service for man and the glorification of God.

Being a Christian means essentially changing over from being for oneself to being for one another. This also explains what is really meant by the often rather odd-seeming concept of election ("being chosen"). It means, not a preference that leaves the individual undisturbed in himself and divides him from the others, but embarking on the common task of which we spoke earlier. Accordingly, the basic Christian decision signifies the assent to being a Christian, the abandonment of self-centeredness and accession to Jesus

Christ's existence with its concentration on the whole. The same thing is meant by the phrase "the way of the cross", which does not indicate a private devotion at all but is in harmony with the basic idea that man, leaving behind the seclusion and tranquility of his "I", departs from himself in order by this frustration [*Durchkreuzung*] of his "I" to follow the crucified Christ and exist for others. All the great images of the history of salvation, which represent at the same time the great basic forms of Christian worship, are expressions of this principle of "for". Think, for example, of the image of the exodus ("departure"), which from Abraham onward and far beyond the classic Exodus of salvation history, the departure from Egypt, remains the basic idea governing the existence of the people of God and of him who belongs to it: he is called to the continual exodus of going beyond himself. There is an echo of the same thing in the image of the Pasch, in which the Christian faith has crystallized the connection between the mystery of Jesus' Cross and Resurrection and the exodus idea of the Old Covenant.

John expressed the whole thing in an image borrowed from nature. With this the horizon widens out beyond anthropology and salvation history to embrace the cosmic: what is here called the basic structure of Christian life already represents at bottom the stamp of the creation itself. "Truly, truly, I say to you, unless a grain of wheat falls into the earth and dies, it remains alone; but if it dies, it bears much fruit" (Jn 12:24). Even on the cosmic plane the law holds good that life comes only through death, through loss of self. What is thus hinted at in the creation is fulfilled in man and finally in *the* man par excellence, Jesus Christ: by embracing the fate of the grain of wheat, by going through the process of being sacrificed, by letting himself be broken down and by losing himself, he opens up access to true life. The findings of the history of religion, which precisely at this point approach very close to the testimony of the Bible, would also justify one in saying that the world lives on sacrifice. Those great myths that assert that the cosmos was built up out of an original sacrifice and that the cosmos only goes on existing through self-sacrifice, that it is dependent on sacrifice,[43] are here confirmed as true and valid. Through this mythological imagery, the Christian exodus principle becomes visible: "He who loves his life loses it, and he who hates his life in this world will keep it for eternal life" (Jn 12:25; cf. Mk 8:35 par.). In conclusion it must be stated that all man's own efforts to go beyond himself can never suffice. He who only wants to give and is not ready to receive, he who only wants to exist for others and is unwilling to recognize that he for his part, too, lives on the unexpected, unprovokable gift of others' "for", fails to recognize the basic mode of human existence and is thus bound to destroy the true meaning of living "for one another". To be fruitful, all self-sacrifices demand acceptance by others and, in the last analysis, by *the* other who is the truly "other" of all mankind and at the same time completely one with it: the God-man Jesus Christ.

3. The law of disguise

The fact that "for" is to be regarded as the decisive principle of human existence, and in coinciding with the principle of love becomes the real point at which the divine manifests itself in the world, brings a further consequence with it. It has the result that the "entirely-otherness" of God, which

---

[43] Cf. the Purusa myth of the Vedic religion; see on this P. Régamey, in F. König, *Christus und die Religionen der Erde: Handbuch der Religionsgeschichte* (Freiburg, 1951), 3:172f.; Régamey, in F. König, *Religionswissenschaftliches Wörterbuch* (Freiburg, 1956), pp. 470f.; J. Gonda, *Die Religionen Indiens*, vol. 1 (Stuttgart, 1960), pp. 186f. and passim. The chief text for this is the *Rigveda* 10, 90.

man can figure out for himself, becomes total dissimilarity, the complete unknowability of God. It means that the hidden quality of God, on which man counts, assumes the scandalous form of his palpability and visibility as the Crucified One. To put it in another way, the result is that God, the first principle, the Alpha of the world, appears as the Omega, the last letter in the alphabet of creation, as the lowliest creature in it. Luther speaks in this connection of God being hidden *sub contrario*, that is, in what seems to be the opposite of God. He thereby emphasizes the peculiarity of the Christian form of negative theology, the form determined by the Cross, as opposed to the negative theology of philosophical thinking. Even philosophy, man's own reflection on God, leads to the realization that God is the entirely Other, the absolutely hidden and incomparable. "As blind as the eyes of night birds", Aristotle had already said, "are our eyes before what is in itself the very brightest thing of all." [44] In fact, on the basis of faith in Jesus Christ, we shall reply: "God is the entirely other, invisible, unrecognizable. But when he really did appear upon the scene, so other, so invisible in regard to his divinity, so unrecognizable, it was not the kind of otherness and strangeness that we had foreseen and expected, and he thus remained in fact unrecognized. But should not that in itself prove him to be the *really* entirely Other, the one who casts overboard our notions of otherness and thereby shows himself to be the only one who genuinely is entirely other?"

All through the Bible one can find again and again the notion of God's double mode of appearing in the world. [45]

[44] Quoted by H. Meyer, *Geschichte der abendländischen Weltanschauung*, vol. 1 (Würzburg, 1947), p. 231 (= ed. Bekker 993 b 9ff.).

[45] Cf. P. Dessauer, "Geschöpfe von fremden Welten", *Wort und Wahrheit* 9 (1954): 569–83; J. Ratzinger, *Vom Sinn des Christseins*, 2nd ed. (Munich, 1966), pp. 32ff.

God affirms his presence, first of all, of course, in the cosmic power. Its greatness, the *logos* of the world that surpasses all our thinking and yet encompasses it, points to him whose thought this world is; to whom, before whom the peoples are like a "drop from a bucket", like "dust on the scales" (Is 40:15). There really is such a thing as the reference of the universe to its creator. However much we may rebel against proofs of the existence of God and whatever objections philosophical reflection may justifiably make to individual steps in the arguments, the fact remains that the radiance of the original creative idea and of its power to build does shimmer through the world and its intelligible structure.

But this is only one way in which God appears in the world. The other sign that he has adopted and that, by concealing him more, shows more truly his intrinsic nature, is the sign of the lowly, which, measured cosmically, quantitatively, is completely insignificant, actually a pure nothing. One could cite in this connection the series Earth–Israel–Nazareth–Cross–Church, in which God seems to keep disappearing more and more and, precisely in this way, becomes more and more manifest as himself. First there is the Earth, a mere nothing in the cosmos, which was to be the point of divine activity in the cosmos. Then comes Israel, a cipher among the powers, which was to be the point of his appearance in the world. Then comes Nazareth, again a cipher within Israel, which was to be the point of his definitive arrival. Then at the end there is the Cross, on which a man was to hang, a man whose life had been a failure; yet this was to be the point at which one can actually touch God. Finally there is the Church, the questionable shape of our history, which claims to be the abiding site of his revelation. We know today only too well how little, even in her, the hiddenness of the divine presence is abolished. Precisely when the Church believed, in all the glory of the Renaissance princedom, that she could cast off this hiddenness and be directly the "gate of heaven", the "house of God", she became once again, and almost more than before, God's disguise, with God scarcely to be found behind it. Thus what is small by a cosmic or even worldly scale represents the real sign of God wherein the entirely Other shows itself, which even in relation to our expectations is once again the completely unrecognizable. The cosmic Nothing is the true All, because "for" is the really divine thing.

4. The law of excess or superfluity

In the ethical statements of the New Testament, there is a tension that looks as if it cannot be resolved: the tension between grace and ethos, between total forgiveness and just as total a demand on man, between the complete endowment of man, who has everything showered upon him because he can achieve nothing, and the equally complete obligation to give himself, an obligation that culminates in the unheard-of demand, "You, therefore, must be perfect, as your heavenly Father is perfect" (Mt 5:48). When, confronted with this upsetting polarity, one looks for a connecting link, one comes across again and again, especially in Pauline theology, but also in the first three Gospels, the word "excess" (περίσσευμα), in which the talk of grace and that of demands meet and merge.

In order to take a good look at this principle, let us seize on that central passage in the Sermon on the Mount which acts as a sort of heading and label for the six great antitheses ("You have heard that it was said to the men of old. . . . But I say to you . . .") in which Jesus composes the new edition of the second Table of the Law. The text runs thus: "For I tell you, unless your righteousness exceeds that of the scribes and Pharisees, you will never enter the kingdom of heaven" (Mt 5:20). This statement means, first of all, that all human righteousness is dismissed as inadequate. Who could honestly boast of having really and unreservedly, in the depths of his soul, absorbed the full meaning of the individual demands and of having carried them out, completely fulfilled them in all their profundity, let alone fulfilled them to excess? True, there exists in the Church a "state of perfection", in which one undertakes to go beyond what is commanded, to go to excess. But those who belong to it would be the last to deny that for this very reason they are always finding themselves at the beginning again and full of deficiencies. The "state of perfection" is in reality the most dramatic depiction of the abiding imperfection of man.

Anyone not satisfied with this reference has only to read the next few verses of the Sermon on the Mount (Mt 5:21–48) to find himself exposed to a terrifying examination of conscience. In these paragraphs it becomes clear what it means when one takes really seriously the principles, at first sight apparently so simple, of the second table of the Decalogue, three of which are expounded here: "You shall not kill. You shall not commit adultery. You shall not bear false witness." At first glance it seems quite easy to feel righteous about these things. After all, one has not killed anyone; one has not broken one's marriage vows; one has not committed perjury. But as Jesus illuminates the depths of these demands, it becomes evident that man shares in these sins through anger, hatred, failure to forgive, envy, and covetousness. It becomes clear how very much man in his apparent righteousness is besmirched with what goes to make the unrighteousness of the world. If one takes the words of the Sermon on the Mount seriously, one realizes what happens to a man who moves over from party politics to reality. The beautiful black and white into which one is accustomed to divide men changes into the gray of a universal twilight. It becomes clear that with men there is no such thing as black and white and that, in spite of all the possible gradations, which do in fact span a wide range, nevertheless all men stand somewhere in the twilight. To change the metaphor, one could say that if the moral differences between men can be found to be total in the "macroscopic" realm, a microscopic, "micromoral" inspection discloses a different picture, in which the distinctions begin to look questionable. At any rate, there can be no further talk of an excess of righteousness.

Thus, if it depended on man, no one could enter heaven, that is, the realm of real, full righteousness. Heaven would have to remain an empty Utopia. And in fact it *does* have to remain an empty Utopia so long as it depends only on the goodwill of men. How often people say, "with a little bit of goodwill, everything in the world would be fine." This is true; a little bit of goodwill would really suffice; but it is the tragedy of mankind that it does not possess the strength for this very thing. Is Camus right, then, when he chooses as a symbol of humanity Sisyphus, who keeps trying to push the stone up the mountain and must continually see it slip down again? So far as human capacities are concerned, the Bible is as sober as Camus, but it does not stop at his scepticism. To the Bible, the limits of human righteousness, of human capabilities as a whole, become an indication of the way in which man is thrown back upon the unquestioning gift of love, a gift that unexpectedly opens itself to him and thereby opens up man himself, and without which man would remain shut up in all his "righteousness" and thus unrighteous. Only the man who accepts this gift can come to himself. Thus the proved speciousness of man's "righteousness" becomes at the same time a pointer to the righteousness of God, the excess of which is called Jesus Christ. He is the righteousness of God, which goes far beyond what need be, which does not calculate, which really overflows; the "notwithstanding" of his greater love, in which he infinitely surpasses the failing efforts of man.

Nevertheless, it would be a complete misunderstanding of the whole to deduce from this a devaluation of man and to feel inclined to say: "Then it is all the same anyway, and any attempt to attain righteousness or esteem in God's eyes is pointless." To this we must reply, "Not at all." In spite of everything and, indeed, just because of what we have just considered, the requirement to have an excess holds good, even if one can never attain full righteousness. But what is this supposed to mean? Is it not a contradiction? Well, it means, in short, that he who is always calculating how much he must do to be just adequate and to be able to regard himself, after a few casuistical flicks, as a man with a nice, white shirtfront, is still no Christian. And similarly, he who tries to reckon where duty ends and where he can gain a little extra merit by an *opus supererogatorium* (work of supererogation) is a Pharisee, not a Christian. Being a Christian does not mean duly making a certain obligatory contribution and perhaps, as an especially perfect person, even going a little farther than is required for the fulfillment of the obligation. On the contrary, a Christian is someone who knows that in any case he lives first and foremost as the beneficiary of a bounty and that, consequently, all righteousness can only consist in being himself a donor, like the beggar who is grateful for what he receives and generously passes part of it on to others. The calculatingly righteous man, who thinks he can keep his own shirtfront white and build himself up inside it, is the unrighteous man.

Human righteousness can only be attained by abandoning one's own claims and being generous to man and to God. It is the righteousness of "Forgive, as we have forgiven"— this request turns out to be the proper formula of human righteousness as understood in the Christian sense: it consists in continuing to forgive, since man himself lives essentially on the forgiveness he has received himself.[46]

But when it is studied in the New Testament, the theme of excess leads up another path where its meaning first becomes completely clear. We find the word occurring again in connection with the miracle of the loaves, where an "excess" of seven baskets is mentioned (Mk 8:8 par.). It forms an essential factor in the story of the multiplication of the loaves and is to be connected with the idea of the superfluous, of the more than necessary. One immediately recalls a related miracle preserved in the Johannine tradition: the changing of water into wine at the marriage feast at Cana (Jn 2:1–11). It is true that the *word* "excess" does not occur here, but the fact certainly does: according to the evidence of the Gospel, the new-made wine amounted to between 130 and 190 gallons, a somewhat unusual quantity for a private banquet! In the evangelists' view, both stories have to do with the central form of Christian worship, the Eucharist. They show it as the divine excess or abundance, which infinitely surpasses all needs and legitimate demands.

In this way both stories are concerned, through their reference to the Eucharist, with Christ himself and ultimately refer back to him: Christ is the infinite self-expenditure of God. And both point back, as we found with the principle of "for", to the structural law of creation, in which life

---

[46] This is probably the best angle from which to tackle the theme of law and Gospel; cf. G. Söhngen, *Gesetz und Evangelium* (Freiburg, 1957), pp. 11–22.

squanders a million seeds in order to save one living one; in which a whole universe is squandered in order to prepare at one point a place for spirit, for man. Excess is God's trademark in his creation; as the Fathers put it, "God does not reckon his gifts by the measure." At the same time excess is also the real foundation and form of salvation history, which in the last analysis is nothing other than the truly breathtaking fact that God, in an incredible outpouring of himself, expends not only a universe but his own self in order to lead man, a speck of dust, to salvation. So excess or superfluity—let us repeat—is the real definition or mark of the history of salvation. The purely calculating mind will always find it absurd that for man God himself should be expended. Only the lover can understand the folly of a love to which prodigality is a law and excess alone is sufficient. Yet if it is true that the creation lives from excess or superfluity, that man is a being for whom excess is necessity, how can we wonder that revelation is the superfluous and for that very reason the necessary, the divine, the love in which the meaning of the universe is fulfilled?

5. Finality and hope

Christian faith says that in Christ the salvation of man is accomplished, that in him the true future of mankind has irrevocably begun and thus, although remaining future, is yet also perfect, a part of our present. This assertion embraces a principle of finality that is of the highest importance for the form of Christian existence, that is to say, for the sort of existential decision that being a Christian entails. Let us try to work this out in more detail. We have just established that Christ is the beginning of the future, the already inaugurated finality of the being "man". This idea was expressed in the language of Scholastic theology by the statement that with Christ revelation is concluded. Naturally this cannot mean that a certain number of truths have now been imparted and God has decided to make no further communications. On the contrary, it means that God's dialogue with man, God's entry into mankind in Jesus, the man who is God, has achieved its goal. The point of this dialogue was not, and is not, to say *something*, many kinds of things, but to utter himself in the Word. Thus his purpose is fulfilled, not when the greatest possible sum of knowledge has been communicated, but when through the Word love becomes visible, when in the Word "You" and "You" make contact. Its meaning does not lie in a third thing, in some kind of factual knowledge, but in the partners themselves. It is called "union". In the man Jesus, God has once and for all uttered himself: he *is* his Word and, as his Word, himself. Revelation ends here, not because God deliberately puts an end to it, but because it has reached its goal; as Karl Rahner puts it, "Nothing fresh is said, not in spite of there being still much to say, but because everything is said, indeed, everything is given, in the Son of love in whom God and the world have become one." [47]

If one looks more carefully at this conclusion a further point emerges. The fact that in Christ the goal of revelation and, thereby, the goal of humanity is attained, because in him divine existence and human existence touch and unite, means at the same time that the goal attained is not a rigid boundary but an open space. For the union that has taken place at the one point "Jesus of Nazareth" must attain the whole of mankind, the whole one "Adam", and transform it into the "body of Christ". So long as this totality is not

[47] K. Rahner, *Schriften zur Theologie*, vol. 1 (Einsiedeln, 1954), p. 60, cf. J. Ratzinger, "Kommentar zur Offenbarungskonstitution", in LThK, supplementary 2:510.

achieved, so long as it remains confined to one point, what has happened in Christ remains simultaneously both end and beginning. Mankind can advance no farther or higher than it has, for God is the farthest and highest; any apparent progress beyond him is a plunge into the void. Humanity cannot go beyond him—to that extent Christ is the end; but it must enter into him—to that extent he is the real beginning.

We do not need to ponder here the interlacing of past and future that results from this for the Christian consciousness; or to reflect that while looking back at the historical Jesus the Christian faith is accordingly looking forward at the same time to the new Adam—to the future that comes to the world and to man from God. We have already considered all this earlier. Here we are concerned with something different. The fact that God's final decision for man has already been made means—according to the conviction of the Christian faith—that there is such a thing as finality in history, even if this finality is of such a kind that it does not exclude a future but inaugurates it. This has the further consequence that there is and must be such a thing as the final, the irrevocable in the life of man, too, especially where he encounters the divine finality of which we were just speaking. The confidence that the final already exists, and that precisely therein the future of man is kept open, is characteristic of the whole Christian attitude to reality: the Christian can find no validity in the circling movement of actualism, which adapts itself to each new "now" and never discovers finality. On the contrary, he is certain that history marches forward; but progress demands finality of direction—that is what distinguishes it from the circular movement that leads nowhere. The struggle for the irrevocability of Christianity was fought and won in the Middle Ages as a struggle against the idea of the "third Kingdom". According to this notion, Christianity so far represented the second Kingdom, that of the Son, which was better than that of the Old Testament, the "Kingdom of the Father", but had to be succeeded by the third Kingdom, the age of the Spirit.[48] Faith in the Incarnation of God in Jesus Christ can admit no "third Kingdom"; it believes in the finality of what has already occurred and knows that for this very reason it is open to the future.

We have already touched on the fact that this also brings with it decisive consequences for the life of the individual. It means that faith makes a definitive claim on man and cannot be succeeded one day, after the reign of the Father in childhood and that of the Son in youth, by an enlightened age of the Spirit that would obey only its own reason and insinuate that it was the Holy Spirit. To be sure, faith has its terms and stages, but it is precisely in this way that it constitutes the abiding ground of man's existence, a ground that is always one and the same. This is also how it comes about that faith can have final statements—dogma and Creed—in which its intrinsic finality is articulated. Again, this does not mean that these formulas cannot open further in the course of history and thus be understood in fresh ways, just as the individual must continually learn to understand the faith afresh as a result of his own experiences in life. But it does mean that in the course of this understanding and maturing the unity of what is understood neither can nor may be destroyed.

Lastly, it could be demonstrated that the finality of the alliance of two human beings, which Christian faith knows to be established by the Yes of love on which marriage is based, also has its roots here. Indissoluble marriage is in fact only comprehensible and feasible on the basis of faith in God's

[48] Cf. A. Dempf, *Sacrum Imperium* (1929; reprt., Darmstadt, 1954), pp. 269–398; E. Benz, *Ecclesia spiritualis* (Stuttgart, 1934); J. Ratzinger, *Die Geschichts-theologie des hl. Bonaventura* (Munich, 1959).

henceforward irrevocable decision, embodied in Christ, in favor of "marriage" with mankind (cf. Eph 5:22–33). It stands or falls with this faith; in the long run, it is just as impossible outside this faith as it is necessary within it. And once again it should be stated that it is precisely this apparent fixation on the decision of one moment in life that enables man to march forward, to consolidate himself stage by stage, while the continual annulment of such decisions keeps sending him back to the beginning again and condemns him to a circular motion that encloses itself in the fiction of eternal youth and thus refuses to accept the totality of human existence.

6. The primacy of acceptance and Christian positivity

Man is redeemed by the Cross; the crucified Christ, as the completely opened being, is the true redemption of man—this central tenet of Christian faith we have already striven in another context to make accessible to modern modes of thought. If we look at it now, not from the point of view of content, but from that of structure, we see that it expresses the primacy of acceptance over action, over one's own achievement, when it is a question of man's final end. Here lies possibly the deepest division between the Christian principle of hope and its Marxist modification. It is true that the Marxist principle, too, is based on the idea of passivity, inasmuch as according to Marxism the suffering proletariat is the redeemer of the world. But this suffering of the proletariat, which in the end is supposed to bring about the change to the classless society, has to be accomplished concretely in the active form of the class struggle. Only in this way can it become "redemptive" and lead to the downfall of the ruling class and the equality of all mankind. If the Cross of Christ is a suffering for, the passion of the proletariat, as the Marxist views it, takes the form of a struggle against, and if the Cross is essentially the work of one individual for the whole, this Marxist "passion" is essentially the activity of a mass organized as a party on behalf of itself. Thus, although they start very close together, the two paths lead off in opposite directions.

Accordingly, from the point of view of the Christian faith, man comes in the most profound sense to himself, not through what he does, but through what he accepts. He must wait for the gift of love, and love can only be received as a gift. It cannot be "made" on one's own, without anyone else; one must wait for it, let it be given to one. And one cannot become *wholly* man in any other way than by being loved, by letting oneself be loved. That love represents simultaneously both man's highest possibility and his deepest need and that this most necessary thing is at the same time the freest and the most unenforceable means precisely that for his "salvation" man is meant to rely on receiving. If he declines to let himself be presented with the gift, then he destroys himself. Activity that makes itself into an absolute, that aims at achieving humanity by its own efforts alone, is in contradiction with man's being. Louis Evely has expressed this perception splendidly:

> The whole history of mankind was led astray, suffered a break, because of Adam's false idea of God. He wanted to be like God. I hope that you never thought that Adam's sin lay in this.... Had God not invited him to nourish this desire? Adam only deluded himself about the model. He thought God was an independent, autonomous being sufficient to himself; and in order to become like him he rebelled and showed disobedience.

> But when God revealed himself, when God willed to show who he was, he appeared as love, tenderness, as outpouring of himself, infinite pleasure in another. Inclination, dependence. God showed himself obedient, obedient unto death.

In the belief that he was becoming like God, Adam turned
completely away from him. He withdrew into loneliness, and
yet God was fellowship.[49]

This whole thing indubitably signifies a relativization of
works, of doing; St. Paul's struggle against "justification by
works" is to be understood from this angle. But one must
add that this classification of human activity as only of penultimate importance gives it at the same time an inner liberation: man's activity can now be carried on in the tranquility,
detachment, and freedom appropriate to the penultimate. The
primacy of acceptance is not intended to condemn man to
passivity; it does not mean that man can now sit idle, as Marxism claims. On the contrary, it alone makes it possible to do
the things of this world in a spirit of responsibility, yet at the
same time in an uncramped, cheerful, free way, and to put
them at the service of redemptive love.

Yet another point emerges from this train of reasoning.
The primacy of acceptance includes Christian positivity and
shows its intrinsic necessity. We established that man does
not create his specific quality out of his own resources; it has
to come to him as something not made by himself; not as his
own product, but instead as a free exchange that gives itself
to him. But if this is so, then it also means that our relation
to God ultimately cannot rest on our own planning, on a
speculative knowledge, but demands the positivity of what
confronts us, what comes to us as something positive, something to be received. It seems to me that from here the squaring of the theological circle, so to speak, can be accomplished;
that the intrinsic necessity of the apparently historical con-
tingency of Christianity can be shown, the "must" of its—to

[49] L. Evely, *Manifest der Liebe: Das Vaterunser*, 3rd ed. (Freiburg, 1961), p. 26;
cf. Y. Congar, *Wege des lebendigen Gottes* (Freiburg, 1964), p. 93.

us—objectionable positivity as an event that comes from out-side. The antithesis, so heavily emphasized by Lessing, between *vérité de fait* (contingent factual truth) and *vérité de raison* (nec-essary intellectual truth) here becomes surmountable. The contingent, the external is what is necessary to man; only in the arrival of something from outside does he open up inwardly. God's disguise as man in history "must" be—with the necessity of freedom.

7. Summary: The "spirit of Christianity"

To summarize the whole, we are entitled to say that the six principles we have tried to sketch may be described as the blueprint, so to speak, of the Christian existence and at the same time the formula for the essence of Christianity, the "spirit of Christianity". These principles may also help to make clear what we call, in a phrase that can easily be mis-understood, the Christian claim to absoluteness. What is really meant by this comes to light above all in the principles "indi-vidual", "for", "finality", and "positivity". These basic asser-tions make clear the particular nature of the claim that the Christian faith raises in face of the history of religion and must raise if it is to remain true to itself.

But one other question is still left: If one keeps one's eyes on the six principles, as we have done, will one have the same experience as the physicists who looked for the pri-mary stuff of being and thought at first they had found it in the so-called elements? But the more they investigated, the more elements were discovered; today over a hundred are known. So they could not be the ultimate thing that it was thought had been discovered in the atoms. They, too, turned out to be composed of elementary particles, of which again so many are already known that one cannot stop at them but must launch out afresh in the hope of still meeting the primary matter. In the six principles we have identified the elementary particles, so to speak, of Christianity, but must there not exist behind these one single, simple center? Such a center does exist, and I think we can say, after all that we have said and without any danger of using a mere sentimental phrase, that the six principles finally coalesce into the one principle of love. Let us be blunt, even at the risk of being misunderstood: the true Christian is not the denominational party member but he who through being a Christian has become truly human; not he who slavishly observes a system of norms, thinking as he does so only of himself, but he who has become freed to simple human goodness. Of course, the principle of love, if it is to be genuine, includes faith. Only thus does it remain what it is. For without faith, which we have come to understand as a term expressing man's ultimate need to receive and the inadequacy of all personal achievement, love becomes an arbitrary deed. It cancels itself out and becomes self-righteousness: faith and love condition and demand each other reciprocally. Similarly, in the principle of love there is also present the principle of hope, which looks beyond the moment and its isolation and seeks the whole. Thus our reflections finally lead of their own accord to the words in which Paul named the main supporting pillars of Christianity: "So faith, hope, love abide, these three; but the greatest of these is love" (1 Cor 13:13).

Chapter II

THE DEVELOPMENT OF FAITH IN CHRIST
IN THE CHRISTOLOGICAL ARTICLES
OF THE CREED

I. "CONCEIVED BY THE POWER OF THE HOLY SPIRIT AND BORN OF THE VIRGIN MARY"

The origin of Jesus is shrouded in mystery. It is true that in St. John's Gospel the people of Jerusalem object to his Messianic claim on the grounds that "we know where this man comes from; and when the Christ appears, no one will know where he comes from" (Jn 7:27). But Jesus' immediately following words disclose how inadequate this alleged knowledge of his origin is: "I have not come of my own accord; he who sent me is true, and him you do not know" (7:28). Certainly Jesus comes from Nazareth. But what does one know of his true origin just by being able to name the geographical spot from which he comes? St. John's Gospel emphasizes again and again that the real origin of Jesus is "the Father", that he comes from him more totally than anyone sent by God before, and in a different way.

This descent of Jesus from the mystery of God, "which no one knows", is depicted in the so-called "infancy narratives" in the Gospels of St. Matthew and St. Luke, not with the object of eliminating that mystery, but precisely to confirm it. Both evangelists, but especially Luke, tell the beginning of the story of Jesus almost entirely in the words of the Old Testament, in order thus to demonstrate from within what happens here as the fulfillment of Israel's hope and to put it in the context of the whole story of God's covenant with men. The words with which in Luke the angel addresses the Virgin are closely akin to the greeting with which the prophet Zephaniah hails the saved Jerusalem of the last days (Zeph 3:14ff.), and they also echo the words of blessing with which the great women of Israel had been praised (Judg 5:24; Jud 13:18f.). Thus Mary is characterized as the holy remnant of Israel, as the true Zion on which hopes had centered in the wildernesses of history. With her begins, according to St. Luke's text, the new Israel; indeed, it does not just begin with her; she *is* it, the holy "daughter of Zion" in whom God sets the new beginning.[1]

No less full is the central promise: "The Holy Spirit will come upon you, and the power of the Most High will overshadow you; therefore the child to be born will be called holy, the Son of God" (Lk 1:35). Our gaze is led beyond the historical covenant with Israel to the creation: in the Old Testament the Spirit of God is the power of creation; he it was who hovered over the waters in the beginning and shaped chaos into cosmos (Gen 1:2); when he is sent, living beings are created (Ps 104 [103]:30). So what is to happen here to Mary is new creation: the God who called forth being out of nothing makes a new beginning amid humanity: his Word becomes flesh. The other image in this text—the "overshadowing by the power of the Most High"—points to the Temple of Israel and to the holy tent in the wilderness where God's presence was indicated in the cloud, which hides his

---

[1] Cf. R. Laurentin, *Struktur und Theologie der lukanischen Kindheitsgeschichte* (Stuttgart, 1967); L. Deiss, *Maria, Tochter Sion* (Mainz, 1961); A. Stöger, *Das Evangelium nach Lukas*, vol. 1 (Düsseldorf, 1964), pp. 38–42; G. Voss, *Die Christologie der lukanischen Schriften in Grundzügen*, Studia Neotestamentica, vol. 2 (Paris and Bruges, 1965).

glory as well as revealing it (Ex 40:34; 1 Kings 8:11). Just as Mary was depicted earlier as the new Israel, the true "daughter of Zion", so now she appears as the temple upon which descends the cloud in which God walks into the midst of history. Whoever puts himself at God's disposal disappears with him in the cloud, into oblivion and insignificance, and precisely in this way acquires a share in his glory.

The birth of Jesus from a virgin of whom things like these are reported in the Gospels has long been a thorn in the flesh of rationalizers of every kind. Distinguishing various sources is supposed to minimize the New Testament testimony; references to the unhistorical thinking of the ancients are supposed to remove the event to the realm of the symbolical; and insertion into the context of the history of religions is supposed to show that it is a variant of a myth. The myth of the miraculous birth of the child savior is, indeed, found all over the world. It expresses a longing on the part of humanity, the longing for the austere and pure embodied in the intact virgin; the longing for the truly maternal, protective, mature, and kind, and finally the hope that always rises again when a man is born—the hope and joy signified by a child. It may be regarded as probable that Israel, too, had myths of this sort; Isaiah 7:14 ("Behold, a young woman shall conceive . . .") could certainly be explained as the echo of an expectation of this sort, even though it is not absolutely clear from the text of this passage that a virgin in the strict sense of the term is meant.[2] If

---

[2] Cf. W. Eichrodt, *Theologie der AT*, vol. 1 (Leipzig, 1939), p. 257: "These features . . . taken together point to a savior image well known to the people, an image in which they find their ideal unity. This is corroborated by the discovery of a series of concordant statements about the savior-king in the whole Near Eastern world. These statements can actually be put together to form scenes from a sacred biography and show that Israel here shares widely in a common oriental heritage."

the passage were to be understood by reference to such sources, this would mean that via this detour the New Testament had taken up humanity's confused hopes in the virgin-mother. Such a primordial theme in human history is certainly not just meaningless.

But at the same time it is quite clear that the immediate antecedents of the New Testament accounts of Jesus' birth from the Virgin Mary lie, not in the realm of the history of religions, but in the Old Testament. Extrabiblical stories of this kind differ profoundly in vocabulary and imagery from the story of the birth of Jesus. The main contrast consists in the fact that in pagan texts the Godhead almost always appears as fertilizing, procreative power, thus under a more or less sexual aspect and, hence, in a physical sense as the "father" of the savior-child. As we have seen, nothing of this sort appears in the New Testament: the conception of Jesus is new creation, not begetting by God. God does not become the biological father of Jesus, and neither the New Testament nor the theology of the Church has fundamentally ever seen in this narrative or in the event recounted in it the ground for the real divinity of Jesus, his "Divine Sonship". For this does not mean that Jesus is half God, half man; it has always been a basic tenet of the Christian faith that Jesus is *completely* God and *completely* man. His Godhead does not imply a subtraction from his humanity; this was the path followed by Arius and Apollinaris, the great heretics of the ancient Church. In opposition to them the complete intactness of Jesus' humanity was defended with all possible emphasis, and the merging of the biblical account into the heathen myth of the god-begotten demi-god was thus frustrated. According to the faith of the Church, the Divine Sonship of Jesus does not rest on the fact that Jesus had no human father; the doctrine of Jesus' divinity would not be affected if Jesus had been the product of a normal human marriage. For the Divine Sonship of which faith speaks is not a biological but an onto-logical fact, an event not in time but in God's eternity; God is always Father, Son, and Spirit; the conception of Jesus means, not that a new God-the-Son comes into being, but that God as Son in the man Jesus draws the creature man to himself, so that he himself "is" man.

Nothing in all this is altered by two expressions that can, it is true, easily lead the uninformed astray. Is it not stated in Luke's account, in connection with the promise of the miraculous con-ception, that the child to be born "will be called holy, the Son of God" (Lk 1:35)? Are Divine Sonship and Virgin Birth not coupled here and the path of myth thus trodden? And so far as the theology of the Church is concerned, does it not speak con-tinually of the "physical" Divine Sonship of Jesus, and does it not thereby reveal its mythical background? Let us take the lat-ter point first. No doubt the formula about the "physical" Divine Sonship of Jesus is extremely unfortunate and wide open to misunderstanding; it shows that for almost two thou-sand years theology has not succeeded in freeing its concep-tual terminology from the shell of its Hellenistic origin. "Physical" is meant here in the sense of the ancient concept of *physis*, that is, nature, or, better, "innate character". It signifies that which belongs to being. "Physical Sonship" therefore means that Jesus is from God in his being, not just in his con-sciousness; the word consequently expresses opposition to the idea of the mere adoption of Jesus by God. Obviously the being-from-God indicated by the word "physical" is meant to be taken, not on the plane of biological generation, but on the plane of the divine being and its eternity. The word is assert-ing that in Jesus human nature was assumed by him who from eternity belongs "physically" (= really, by his being) to the tri-une relationship of the divine love.

But what is one to say when such a meritorious researcher as E. Schweizer expresses himself on our question in the following terms: "Since Luke is not interested in the biological question, he does not cross the frontier to a metaphysical understanding either." [3] Almost everything about this statement is false. The most staggering thing about it is the way in which biology and metaphysics are tacitly equated. To all appearances, the metaphysical (ontological) Divine Sonship is misinterpreted as biological descent, and its meaning thus turned completely upside down. It is in fact, as we saw, the express rejection of a biological interpretation of Jesus' divine origin. It is a little saddening to have to be the one to point out that the plane of metaphysics is not that of biology. The Church's teaching about the Divine Sonship of Jesus is based, not on the story of the Virgin Birth, but on the Abba-Son dialogue and on the relationship of Word and love that we found revealed in it. Its idea of being does not belong to the biological plane but to the "I am" of St. John's Gospel, which therein, as we have seen, had already developed the Son-idea in all of its radicality, which is far more comprehensive and wide-ranging than the biological God-man ideas of myth. We have already considered all this at some length; it has been mentioned again here only because one gets the distinct impression that the contemporary aversion to both the tidings of the Virgin Birth and the full acknowledgment of the Divine Sonship of Jesus rests on a fundamental misunderstanding of both and on the false connection between the two that seems to be widely assumed.

One question remains open: that of the concept of Son in the Lucan account of the Annunciation. The process of answering it leads us at the same time to the real question

---

[3] E. Schweizer, υἱός, in *Theologisches Wörterbuch zum NT*, 8:384.

that arises out of our previous reflections. If the conception of Jesus by the Virgin through God's creative power has nothing to do with his Divine Sonship, nothing directly at any rate, what kind of meaning does it possess? The question of what the phrase "Son of God" means in the passage about the Annunciation can be easily answered from our earlier investigations: In contrast to the simple expression "the Son", it belongs, as we heard, to the Old Testament theology of election and hope and designates Jesus as the true heir to the promises, as the king of Israel and of the world. The conceptual context in which the account is to be understood now becomes clearly visible: it is Israel's faith and hope, which, as we have said, did not remain completely unaffected by heathen hopes of miraculous births but gave them a completely new form and a totally changed meaning.

The Old Testament contains a whole series of miraculous births, always at decisive turning points in the history of salvation: Isaac's mother, Sarah (Gen 18), Samuel's mother (1 Sam 1–3), and the anonymous mother of Samson (Judg 13:2ff.) are all barren, and all human hope of their being blessed with children has been abandoned. With all three, the birth of the child who eventually contributes to Israel's salvation comes to pass as a manifestation of the gracious mercy of God, who makes the impossible possible (Gen 18:14; Lk 1:37), elevates the lowly (1 Sam 2:7; 1:11; Lk 1:52; 1:48), and puts down the mighty from their thrones (Lk 1:52). With Elizabeth, John the Baptist's mother, this process is continued (Lk 1:7–25, 36), and it reaches its climax and goal with Mary. The meaning of the occurrence is always the same: the salvation of the world does not come from man and from his own power; man must let it be bestowed upon him, and he can only receive it as a pure gift. The Virgin Birth is not a lesson in asceticism, nor does it belong directly to the doctrine of Jesus' Divine Sonship; it is first and last theology of grace, a proclamation of how salvation comes to *us*: in the simplicity of acceptance, as the voluntary gift of the love that redeems the world. This idea of salvation through God's power alone is formulated magnificently in the Book of Isaiah in the passage that runs: "Sing, O barren one, who did not bear; break forth into singing and cry aloud, you who have not been in travail! For the children of the desolate one will be more than the children of her that is married, says the LORD" (Is 54:1; cf. Gal 4:27; Rom 4:17–22). In Jesus, God has placed, in the midst of barren, hopeless mankind, a new beginning that is not a product of human history but a gift from above. Now every mere human being represents something unspeakably new, something more than the sum of the chromosomes and the product of a certain environment, in fact a unique creature of God; but Jesus is the truly new, coming, not from mankind's own resources, but from the spirit of God. For this reason he is Adam for the second time (1 Cor 15:47)—a new Incarnation begins with him. In contrast to all those chosen before him, he not only *receives* the spirit of God; in his earthly life he *exists* solely through the spirit, and, therefore, he is the fulfillment of all prophets: he is the true prophet.

It should not really be necessary to point out that all these statements have meaning only on the assumption that the happening whose meaning they seek to elucidate really took place. They are the interpretation of an event; if this event is removed, they become empty talk that would have to be described not only as frivolous but as downright dishonest. For the rest, such attempts, however well intentioned they may sometimes be, are colored by a contradictoriness that one feels half inclined to describe as tragic.

At a moment when we have investigated the corporality of the man with every fiber of our existence and can understand his spirit only as something incarnate, something that *is* body, not *has* body, people try to save the Christian faith by completely disembodying it, by taking refuge in a region of mere "mind", of pure self-satisfying interpretation, which seems to be immune from criticism only through its lack of contact with reality. But Christian faith really means precisely the acknowledgment that God is not the prisoner of his own eternity, not limited to the solely spiritual; that he is capable of operating here and now, in the midst of my world, and that he did operate in it through Jesus, the new Adam, who was born of the Virgin Mary through the creative power of God, whose spirit hovered over the waters at the very beginning, who created being out of nothing.[4]

---

[4] This should be compared with the speculations in which P. Schoonenberg seeks to justify the reserve of the Dutch Catechism on this matter in his contribution "De nieuwe Katechismus und die Dogmen", German translation in *Dokumentation des Holländischen Katechismus* (Freiburg, 1967), pp. XIV–XXXIX, especially XXXVII–XXXVIII.

What is particularly fatal about this attempt is the fundamental misunderstanding of the concept of dogma on which it rests; Schoonenberg understands "dogma" entirely from the narrow point of view of Jesuit dogmatic theology at the end of the nineteenth century and naturally looks in vain for a magisterial dogmatic pronouncement relating to the Virgin Birth analogous to the dogmatization of the "Immaculate Conception" (= freedom from original sin) and the physical Assumption of Mary into "heaven". He thus comes to the conclusion that in the matter of the birth of Jesus from the Virgin, as opposed to the other two statements, no firm teaching by the Church is extant. In reality such an assertion turns the history of dogma upside down and attributes absoluteness to a mode of exercising the teaching function only in regular use since Vatican I. This is unacceptable not only in view of the dialogue with the Eastern Churches but also from the very nature of the matter itself, and even Schoonenberg himself does not stick to it through thick and thin. In fact, dogma as a single tenet proclaimed by the pope *ex cathedra* is the latest and lowest way of forming dogma. The original form in which the Church states her faith in a binding fashion is the Creed or *symbolum*; the profession of faith in the birth of Jesus from the Virgin, a statement quite unequivocal in meaning, belongs firmly from the start to all *symbola* and is thus a constituent part

Another observation must be made. The meaning of the sign from God which is the Virgin Birth, if properly understood, indicates at the same time the proper theological place for a devotion to Mary that lets itself be guided by the faith of the New Testament. Devotion to Mary cannot be based on a Mariology that represents a sort of miniature second edition of Christology—such a duplication is neither right nor justifiable on the evidence. If one wanted to indicate a theological treatise to which Mariology belonged as its concrete illustration, it would probably be the doctrine of grace, which of course goes to form a whole with ecclesiology and anthropology. As the true "daughter of Zion", Mary is the image of the Church, the image of believing man, who can come to salvation and to himself only through the gift of love—through grace. The saying with which Bernanos ends his *Diary of a Country Priest*—"Everything is grace"—a saying in which a life that seemed to be only weakness and futility can see itself as full of riches and fulfillment—truly becomes in Mary, "full of grace" (Lk 1:28), a concrete reality. She does not contest or endanger the exclusiveness of salvation through Christ; she points to it. She represents mankind, which as a whole is expectation and which needs this image all the more when it is in danger of giving up waiting and putting its trust in doing, which—indispensable as it is—can never fill the void that threatens man when he does not find that absolute love which gives him meaning, salvation, all that is truly necessary in order to live.

---

of the original dogma of the Church. To question the binding nature of Lateran I or Paul V's bull of 1555, as Schoonenberg does, is thus a completely pointless proceeding; and the attempt to make even the *symbola* capable of merely "spiritual" interpretation would be enveloping the history of dogma in a smoke screen.

2. "SUFFERED UNDER PONTIUS PILATE, WAS CRUCIFIED, DIED, AND WAS BURIED"

a. *Righteousness and grace*

What position is really occupied by the Cross within faith in Jesus as the Christ? That is the question with which this article of the Creed confronts us once again. We have already assembled in our previous reflections the essential components of an answer and must now try to survey them as a whole. As we have already established, the universal Christian consciousness in this matter is extensively influenced by a much-coarsened version of St. Anselm's theology of atonement, the main lines of which we have considered in another context. To many, many Christians, and especially to those who only know the faith from a fair distance, it looks as if the Cross is to be understood as part of a mechanism of injured and restored right. It is the form, so it seems, in which the infinitely offended righteousness of God was propitiated again by means of an infinite expiation. It thus appears to people as the expression of an attitude that insists on a precise balance between debit and credit; at the same time one gets the feeling that this balance is based, nevertheless, on a fiction. One gives first secretly with the left hand what one takes back again ceremonially with the right. The "infinite expiation" on which God seems to insist thus moves into a doubly sinister light. Many devotional texts actually force one to think that Christian faith in the Cross imagines a God whose unrelenting righteousness demanded a human sacrifice, the sacrifice of his own Son, and one turns away in horror from a righteousness whose sinister wrath makes the message of love incredible.

This picture is as false as it is widespread. In the Bible the Cross does not appear as part of a mechanism of injured right; on the contrary, in the Bible the Cross is quite the reverse: it is the expression of the radical nature of the love that gives itself completely, of the process in which one is what one does and does what one is; it is the expression of a life that is completely being for others. To anyone who looks more closely, the scriptural theology of the Cross represents a real revolution as compared with the notions of expiation and redemption entertained by non-Christian religions, though it certainly cannot be denied that in the later Christian consciousness this revolution was largely neutralized and its whole scope seldom recognized. In other world religions, expiation usually means the restoration of the damaged relationship with God by means of expiatory actions on the part of men. Almost all religions center around the problem of expiation; they arise out of man's knowledge of his guilt before God and signify the attempt to remove this feeling of guilt, to surmount the guilt through conciliatory actions offered up to God. The expiatory activity by which men hope to conciliate the Divinity and to put him in a gracious mood stands at the heart of the history of religion.

In the New Testament the situation is almost completely reversed. It is not man who goes to God with a compensatory gift, but God who comes to man, in order to give to him. He restores disturbed right on the initiative of his own power to love, by making unjust man just again, the dead living again, through his own creative mercy. His righteousness is grace; it is active righteousness, which sets crooked man right, that is, bends him straight, makes him correct. Here we stand before the twist that Christianity put into the history of religion. The New Testament does not say that men conciliate God, as we really ought to expect, since, after all, it is they who have failed, not God. It says, on the contrary, that "God was in Christ reconciling the world to himself" (2 Cor 5:19). This is truly something new, something unheard of—the starting point of Christian existence and the center of New Testament theology of the Cross: God does not wait until the guilty come to be reconciled; he goes to meet them and reconciles them. Here we can see the true direction of the Incarnation, of the Cross.

Accordingly, in the New Testament the Cross appears primarily as a movement from above to below. It stands there, not as the work of expiation that mankind offers to the wrathful God, but as the expression of that foolish love of God's that gives itself away to the point of humiliation in order thus to save man; it is *his* approach to us, not the other way about. With this twist in the idea of expiation, and thus in the whole axis of religion, worship, too, man's whole existence, acquires in Christianity a new direction. Worship follows in Christianity *first of all* in thankful acceptance of the divine deed of salvation. The essential form of Christian worship is therefore rightly called *Eucharistia*, thanksgiving. In this form of worship human achievements are not placed before God; on the contrary, it consists in man's letting himself be endowed with gifts; we do not glorify God by supposedly giving to him out of our resources—as if they were not his already!—but by letting ourselves be endowed with his own gifts and thus recognizing him as the only Lord. We worship him by dropping the fiction of a realm in which we could face him as independent business partners, whereas in truth we can only exist at all in him and from him. Christian sacrifice does not consist in a giving of what God would not have without us but in our becoming totally receptive and letting ourselves be completely taken over by him. Letting God act on us—that is Christian sacrifice.

b. The Cross as worship and sacrifice

This is not the whole story, it is true. If one reads the New Testament from beginning to end one cannot suppress the question of whether it does not depict Jesus' deed of expiation as the offering of a sacrifice to the Father and the Cross as the sacrifice that Christ hands over obediently to the Father. In a whole series of texts it does appear as the upward movement of mankind to God, so that all that we have just rejected seems to rise to the surface again. In fact, the content of the New Testament cannot be harmonized with the descending line alone. How then are we to explain the relationship between the two lines? Must we perhaps exclude one in favor of the other? And if we wanted to do this, what criterion should we be justified in using? It is clear that we cannot proceed in this way: by doing so we should in the last analysis be elevating our own capricious opinion to the status of the criterion of faith.

In order to make any progress we must broaden our question and ask where the point of departure of the New Testament interpretation of the Cross lies. One must first realize that to the disciples the Cross of Jesus seemed at first like the end, the wreck of his enterprise. They had thought that they had found in him the king who could never more be overthrown and had unexpectedly become the companions of an executed criminal. The Resurrection, it is true, gave them the certainty that Jesus was nevertheless king, but the point of the Cross they had to learn slowly. The means of understanding was offered to them in Scripture, that is, the Old Testament, with whose images and concepts they strove to explain what had happened. So they adduced its liturgical texts and precepts, too, in the conviction that everything meant there was fulfilled in Jesus; indeed, that, vice versa, one could now understand properly for the first time from him what things in the Old Testament were really all about. In this way we find that in the New Testament the Cross is explained by, among other things, ideas taken from Old Testament cult theology.

The most consistent execution of this project is to be found in the Letter to the Hebrews, which connects the death of Jesus on the Cross with the ritual and theology of the Jewish feast of reconciliation and expounds it as the true cosmic reconciliation feast. The train of thought in the letter could be briefly summarized more or less as follows: All the sacrificial activity of mankind, all attempts to conciliate God by cult and ritual—and the world is full of them—were bound to remain useless human work, because God does not seek bulls and goats or whatever may be ritually offered to him. One can sacrifice whole hecatombs of animals to God all over the world; he does not need them, because they all belong to him anyway, and nothing is given to the Lord of All when such things are burned in his honor. "I will accept no bull from your house, nor he-goat from your folds. For every beast of the forest is mine, the cattle on a thousand hills. I know all the birds of the air, and all that moves in the field is mine. If I were hungry, I would not tell you; for the world and all that is in it is mine. Do I eat the flesh of bulls, or drink the blood of goats? Offer to God a sacrifice of thanksgiving...." So runs a saying of God in the Old Testament (Ps 50 [49]:9–14). The author of the Letter to the Hebrews places himself in the spiritual line of this and similar texts. With still more conclusive emphasis he stresses the fruitlessness of ritual effort. God does not seek bulls and goats but man; man's unqualified Yes to God could alone form true worship. Everything belongs to God, but to man is lent the freedom to say Yes or No, the freedom to love or to reject;

love's free Yes is the only thing for which God must wait—
the only worship or "sacrifice" that can have any meaning.
But the Yes to God, in which man gives himself back to
God, cannot be replaced or represented by the blood of bulls
and goats. "For what can a man give in return for his life",
it says at one point in the Gospel (Mk 8:37). The answer can
only be: There is nothing with which he could compensate
for himself.

But as all pre-Christian cults were based on the idea of
substitution, of representation, and tried to replace the
irreplaceable, this worship was bound to remain vain. In the
light of faith in Christ, the Letter to the Hebrews can dare to
draw up this devastating balance sheet of the history of religion, although to express this view in a world seething with
sacrifices must have seemed a tremendous outrage. It can
dare to make this unqualified assertion that religions have
run aground because it knows that in Christ the idea of the
substitute, of the proxy, has acquired a new meaning. Christ,
who in terms of the Law was a layman and held no office in
Israel's worship services, was—so the text says—the one true
priest in the world. His death, which from a purely historical angle represented a completely profane event—the execution of a man condemned to death as a political offender—was
in reality the one and only liturgy of the world, a cosmic
liturgy, in which Jesus stepped, not in the limited arena of
the liturgical performance, the Temple, but publicly, before
the eyes of the world, through the curtain of death into the
real temple, that is, before the face of God himself, in order
to offer, not things, the blood of animals, or anything like
that, but himself (Heb 9:11ff.).

Let us note the fundamental reversal involved in the central idea of this letter; what from the earthly point of view
was a secular happening is the true worship for mankind, for

he who performed it broke through the confines of the liturgical act and made truth: he gave himself. He took from man's
hands the sacrificial offerings and put in their place his sacrificed personality, his own "I". When our text says that Jesus
accomplished the expiation through his *blood* (9:12), this blood
is again not to be understood as a material gift, a quantitatively measurable means of expiation; it is simply the concrete expression of a love of which it is said that it extends
"to the end" (Jn 13:1). It is the expression of the totality of
his surrender and of his service; an embodiment of the fact
that he offers no more and no less than himself. The gesture
of the love that gives all—this, and this alone, according to
the Letter to the Hebrews, was the real means by which the
world was reconciled; therefore the hour of the Cross is the
cosmic day of reconciliation, the true and definitive feast of
reconciliation. There is no other kind of worship and no
other priest but he who accomplished it: Jesus Christ.

c. The nature of Christian worship

Accordingly, the nature of Christian worship does not consist in the surrender of things or in any kind of destruction,
an idea that has continually recurred since the sixteenth century in theories about the sacrifice of the Mass. According
to these theories God's sovereignty over all had to be recognized in this fashion. All these laborious efforts of thought
are simply overtaken by the event of Christ and its biblical
explanation. Christian worship consists in the absoluteness
of love, as it could only be poured out by the one in whom
God's own love had become human love; and it consists in
the new form of representation included in this love, namely,
that he stood for us and that we let ourselves be taken over
by him. So it means that we can put aside our own attempts

at justification, which at bottom are only excuses and range us against each other—just as Adam's attempt at justification was an excuse, a pushing of the guilt onto the other, indeed, in the last analysis, an attempt to accuse God himself: "The woman whom you gave to be with me, she gave me fruit of the tree" (Gen 3:12). It demands that, instead of indulging in the destructive rivalry of self-justification, we accept the gift of the love of Jesus Christ, who "stands in" for us, allow ourselves to be united in it, and thus become worshippers with him and in him. From this angle it should be possible to answer very briefly a few questions that still arise.

1. In view of the New Testament's message of love, there is more and more of a tendency today to resolve the Christian religion completely into brotherly love, "fellowship", and not to admit any direct love of God or adoration of God: only the horizontal is recognized; the vertical of immediate relationship to God is denied. It is not difficult to see, after what we have said, how this at first sight very attractive conception fails to grasp not only the substance of Christianity but also that of true humanity. Brotherly love that aimed at self-sufficiency would become for this very reason the extreme egoism of self-assertion. It refuses its last openness, tranquility, and selflessness if it does not also accept this love's need for redemption through him who alone loves sufficiently. And, for all its goodwill, in the last resort it does others and itself an injustice, for man cannot perfect himself in the reciprocity of human fellowship alone; he can do this only in the cooperation of that disinterested love which glorifies God himself. The disinterested character of simple adoration is man's highest possibility; it alone forms his true and final liberation.

2. Above all, the traditional Passiontide devotions again and again raise the question of the real connection between

sacrifice (and thus worship) and pain. According to the conclusions we reached above, the Christian sacrifice is nothing other than the exodus of the "for" that abandons itself,
a process perfected in the man who is all exodus, all self-
surpassing love. The fundamental principle of Christian worship is consequently this movement of exodus with its
two-in-one direction toward God and fellowman. By carrying humanity to God, Christ incorporates it in his salvation. The reason why the happening on the Cross is the
bread of life "for the many" (cf. Mt 26:28, Mk 14:24) is
that he who was crucified has smelted the body of humanity into the Yes of worship. It is completely "anthropocen-
tric", entirely related to man, because it was radical
theocentricity, delivery of the "I" and therefore of the creature man to God. Now to the extent that this exodus of
love is the ec-stasy of man outside himself, in which he is
stretched out infinitely beyond himself, torn apart, as it were,
far beyond his apparent capacity for being stretched, *to the
same extent* worship (sacrifice) is always at the same time
the Cross, the pain of being torn apart, the dying of the
grain of wheat that can come to fruition only in death. But
it is thus at the same time clear that this element of pain is
a secondary one, resulting only from a preceding primary
one, from which alone it draws its meaning. The fundamental principle of the sacrifice is not destruction but love.
And even this principle only belongs to the sacrifice to the
extent that love breaks down, opens up, crucifies, tears—as
the form that love takes in a world characterized by death
and self-seeking.

There is an important passage on this subject by Jean
Daniélou. It really forms part of a different inquiry but it
might well help to elucidate the idea we are striving to
understand:

Between the heathen world and the threefold God there is only one link, and that is the Cross of Christ. Yet when we move into this no-man's land and try afresh to twitch the threads that link the heathen world and the threefold God, should we still be surprised that we can only do it in the Cross of Christ? We must make ourselves resemble this Cross, bear it within ourselves, "always carrying in the body the death of Jesus", as St. Paul says of the preacher of the faith (2 Cor 4:10). This feeling of being torn asunder, which is a cross to us, this inability of our heart to carry within itself simultaneously love of the most holy Trinity and love of a world alienated from the Trinity, is precisely the death agony of the only begotten Son, an agony he calls on us to share. He who bore this division within himself in order to abolish it within himself, and who could only abolish it because he had previously borne it within himself—he reaches from one end to the other. Without leaving the bosom of the Trinity, he stretches out to the ultimate limit of human misery and fills the whole space in between. This stretching out of Christ, symbolized by the four directions of the Cross, is the mysterious expression of our own dismemberment and makes us like him.[5]

In the last analysis pain is the product and expression of Jesus Christ's being stretched out from being in God right down to the hell of "My God, why have you forsaken me?" Anyone who has stretched his existence so wide that he is simultaneously immersed in God and in the depths of the God-forsaken creature is bound to be torn asunder, as it were; such a one is truly "crucified". But this process of being torn apart is identical with love; it is its realization to the extreme (Jn 13:1) and the concrete expression of the breadth it creates.

[5] J. Daniélou, *Essai sur le mystère de l'histoire* (Paris, 1953).

From this standpoint it should be possible to bring out clearly the true basis of meaningful devotion to the Passion; it should also become evident how devotion to the Passion and apostolic spirituality overlap. It should become evident that the apostolic element—service to man and in the world—is permeated with the very essence of Christian mysticism and of Christian devotion to the Cross. The two do not impede each other; at the deepest level, each lives on the other. Thus it should now also be plain that with the Cross it is not a matter of an accumulation of physical pain, as if its redemptive value consisted in its involving the largest possible amount of physical torture. Why should God take pleasure in the suffering of his creature, indeed his own Son, or even see in it the currency with which reconciliation has to be purchased from him? The Bible and right Christian belief are far removed from such ideas. It is not pain as such that counts but the breadth of the love that spans existence so completely that it unites the distant and the near, bringing God-forsaken man into relation with God. It alone gives the pain an aim and a meaning. Were it otherwise, then the executioners around the Cross would have been the real priests; they, who had caused the pain, would have offered the sacrifice. But this was not the point; the point was that inner center that bears and fulfills the pain, and therefore the executioners were not the priests; the priest was Jesus, who reunited the two separated ends of the world in his love (Eph 2:13f.).

Basically this also answers the question with which we started, whether it is not an unworthy concept of God to imagine for oneself a God who demands the slaughter of his Son to pacify his wrath. To such a question one can only reply, indeed, God must not be thought of in this way. But in any case such a concept of God has nothing to do with the idea of God to be found in the New Testament. The New Testament is the story of the God who of his own accord wished to become, in Christ, the Omega—the last letter—in the alphabet of creation. It is the story of the God who is himself the act of love, the pure "for", and who therefore necessarily puts on the disguise of the smallest worm (Ps 22:6 [21:7]). It is the story of the God who identifies himself with his creature and in this *contineri a minimo*, in being grasped and overpowered by the least of his creatures, displays that "excess" that identifies him as God.

The Cross is revelation. It reveals, not any particular thing, but God and man. It reveals who God is and in what way man is. There is a curious presentiment of this situation in Greek philosophy: Plato's image of the crucified "just man". In the *Republic* the great philosopher asks what is likely to be the position of a completely just man in this world. He comes to the conclusion that a man's righteousness is only complete and guaranteed when he takes on the appearance of unrighteousness, for only then is it clear that he does not follow the opinion of men but pursues justice only for its own sake. So according to Plato the truly just man must be misunderstood and persecuted in this world; indeed, Plato goes so far as to write: "They will say that our just man will be scourged, racked, fettered, will have his eyes burned out, and at last, after all manner of suffering, will be cru- cified." [6] This passage, written four hundred years before Christ, is always bound to move a Christian deeply. Serious philosophical thinking here surmises that the completely just man in this world must be the crucified just man;

---

[6] *Republic*, bk. 2, 361e–362a, in A. D. Lindsay's translation. Cf. on this theme H. U. von Balthasar, *Herrlichkeit* III/1, Einsiedeln, 1965, pp. 156–161 [English translation: *The Glory of the Lord: A Theological Aesthetics*, vol. 4: *The Realm of Metaphysics in Antiquity*, trans. Brian McNeil et al. (San Francisco: Ignatius Press, 1989), pp. 170–75]; E. Benz, "Der gekreuzigte Gerechte bei Plato, im NT und in der alten Kirche", *Abhandlungen der Mainzer Akademie* 1950, no. 12.

something is sensed of that revelation of man which comes
to pass on the Cross.

The fact that when the perfectly just man appeared he was
crucified, delivered up by justice to death, tells us pitilessly who
man is: Thou art such, man, that thou canst not bear the just
man—that he who simply loves becomes a fool, a scourged
criminal, an outcast. Thou art such because, unjust thyself, thou
dost always need the injustice of the next man in order to feel
excused and thus canst not tolerate the just man who seems to
rob thee of this excuse. Such art thou. St. John summarized all
this in the *Ecce homo* ("Look, this is [the] man!") of Pilate, which
means quite fundamentally: This is how it is with man; this is
man. The truth of man is his complete lack of truth. The saying in the Psalms that every man is a liar (Ps 116 [115]:11 [*Douay-
Rheims*]) and lives in some way or other against the truth already
reveals how it really is with man. The truth about man is that
he is continually assailing truth; the just man crucified is thus
a mirror held up to man in which he sees himself unadorned.
But the Cross does not reveal only man; it also reveals God.
God is such that he identifies himself with man right down into
this abyss and that he judges him by saving him. In the abyss of
human failure is revealed the still more inexhaustible abyss of
divine love. The Cross is thus truly the center of revelation, a
revelation that does not reveal any previously unknown principles but reveals us to ourselves by revealing us before God and
God in our midst.

3. "DESCENDED INTO HELL"

Possibly no article of the Creed is so far from present-day attitudes of mind as this one. Together with the belief in the birth
of Jesus from the Virgin Mary and that in the Ascension of the

Lord, it seems to call most of all for "demythologization", a process that in this case looks devoid of danger and unlikely to provoke opposition. The few places where Scripture seems to say anything about this matter (1 Pet 3:19f.; 4:6; Eph 4:9; Rom 10:7; Mt 12:40; Acts 2:27, 31) are so difficult to understand that they can easily be expounded in many different ways. Thus if in the end one eliminates the statement altogether, one seems to have the advantage of getting rid of a curious idea, and one difficult to harmonize with our own modes of thought, without making oneself guilty of a particularly disloyal act. But is anything really gained by this? Or has one simply evaded the difficulty and obscurity of reality? One can try to deal with problems either by denying their existence or by facing up to them. The first method is the more comfortable one, but only the second leads anywhere. Instead of pushing the question aside, then, should we not learn to see that this article of faith, which liturgically is associated with Holy Saturday in the Church's year, is particularly close to our day and is to a particular degree the experience of our [twentieth] century? On Good Friday our gaze remains fixed on the crucified Christ, but Holy Saturday is the day of the "death of God", the day that expresses the unparalleled experience of our age, anticipating the fact that God is simply absent, that the grave hides him, that he no longer awakes, no longer speaks, so that one no longer needs to gainsay him but can simply overlook him. "God is dead and we have killed him." This saying of Nietzsche's belongs linguistically to the tradition of Christian Passiontide piety; it expresses the content of Holy Saturday, "descended into hell".[7]

---

[7] Cf. H. de Lubac, *The Drama of Atheist Humanism*, trans. Edith M. Riley, Anne Englund Nash, and Mark Sebanc (San Francisco: Ignatius Press, 1995), pp. 42–58.

This article of the Creed always reminds me of two scenes in the Bible. The first is that cruel story in the Old Testament in which Elijah challenges the priests of Baal to implore their God to give them fire for their sacrifice. They do so, and naturally nothing happens. He ridicules them, just as the "enlightened rationalist" ridicules the pious person and finds him laughable when nothing happens in response to his prayers. Elijah calls out to the priests that perhaps they had not prayed loud enough: "Cry aloud, for he [Baal] is a god; either he is musing, or has gone aside, or he is on a journey, or perhaps he is asleep and must be awakened" (1 Kings 18:27). When one reads today this mockery of the devotees of Baal, one can begin to feel uncomfortable; one can get the feeling that *we* have now arrived in that situation and that the mockery must now fall on us. No calling seems to be able to awaken God. The rationalist seems entitled to say to us, "Pray louder, perhaps your God will then wake up." "Descended into hell"; how true this is of our time, the descent of God into muteness, into the dark silence of the absent.

But alongside the story of Elijah and its New Testament analogue, the story of the Lord sleeping in the midst of the storm on the lake (Mk 4:35–41, par.), we must put the Emmaus story (Lk 24:13–35). The disturbed disciples are talking of the death of their hope. To them, something like the death of God has happened: the point at which God finally seemed to have spoken has disappeared. The One sent by God is dead, and so there is a complete void. Nothing replies any more. But while they are there speaking of the death of their hope and can no longer see God, they do not notice that this very hope stands alive in their midst; that "God", or rather the image they had formed of his promise, had to die so that he could live on a larger scale. The image they had

formed of God, and into which they sought to compress
him, had to be destroyed, so that over the ruins of the demol-
ished house, as it were, they could see the sky again and him
who remains the infinitely greater. The German Romantic
poet Eichendorff formulated the idea—in the comfortable,
to us almost too harmless fashion of his age—like this:

> *Du bist's, der, was wir bauen,*
> *Mild über uns zerbricht,*
> *Dass wir den Himmel schauen—*
> *Darum so klag ich nicht.*[8]

Thus the article about the Lord's descent into hell reminds
us that not only God's speech but also his silence is part of
the Christian revelation. God is not only the comprehensible word that comes to us; he is also the silent, inaccessible,
uncomprehended, and incomprehensible ground that eludes
us. To be sure, in Christianity there is a primacy of the *logos*,
of the word, over silence; God *has* spoken. God *is* word. But
this does not entitle us to forget the truth of God's abiding
concealment. Only when we have experienced him as silence
may we hope to hear his speech, too, which proceeds in
silence.[9] Christology reaches out beyond the Cross, the
moment when the divine love is tangible, into the death, the

---

[8] "Thou art he who gently breaks about our heads what we build, so that
we can see the sky—therefore I have no complaint."–Trans.

[9] Cf. the significance of silence in the writings of Ignatius of Antioch: *Epistola ad Ephesios*, 19, 1: "And to the prince of this world the virginity of Mary
and her confinement remained hidden, likewise also the death of the Lord—
three loudly calling secrets that were accomplished in God's peace." Quoted
by J. A. Fischer, *Die Apostolischen Väter* (Darmstadt, 1956), p. 157; cf. *Epistola ad
Magnesios* 8, 2, which speaks of the λόγος ἀπὸ σιγῆς προελθών (the word
that comes from silence), and the meditation on speech and silence in the
Epistola ad Ephesios 15, 1. On the historical background, H. Schlier, *Religions-
geschichtliche Untersuchungen zu den Ignatiusbriefen* (Berlin, 1929).

silence and the eclipse of God. Can we wonder that the
Church and the life of the individual are led again and again
into this hour of silence, into the forgotten and almost discarded article, "Descended into hell"?

When one ponders this, the question of the "scriptural
evidence" solves itself; at any rate in Jesus' death cry, "My
God, my God, why have you forsaken me?" (Mk 15:34), the
mystery of Jesus' descent into hell is illuminated as if in a
glaring flash of lightning on a dark night. We must not forget that these words of the crucified Christ are the opening
line of one of Israel's prayers (Ps 22:1 [21:2]), which summarizes in a shattering way the needs and hopes of this people chosen by God and apparently at the moment so utterly
abandoned by him. This prayer that rises from the sheer misery of God's seeming eclipse ends in praises of God's greatness. This element, too, is present in Jesus' death cry, which
has been recently described by Ernst Käsemann as a prayer
sent up from hell, as the raising of a standard, the first commandment, in the wilderness of God's apparent absence: "The
Son still holds on to faith when faith seems to have become
meaningless and the earthly reality proclaims absent the God
of whom the first thief and the mocking crowd speak—not
for nothing. His cry is not for life and survival, not for himself, but for the Father. His cry stands against the reality of
the whole world." After this, do we still need to ask what
worship must be in our hour of darkness? Can it be anything
else but the cry from the depths in company with the Lord
who "has descended into hell" and who has established the
nearness of God in the midst of abandonment by God?

Let us try to investigate another aspect of this complex mystery, which cannot be elucidated from one side alone. Let us
first take account of one of the findings of exegesis. We are told
that in this article of the Creed the word "hell" is only a wrong

translation of *sheol* (in Greek, Hades), which denoted in Hebrew the state after death, which was very vaguely imagined as a kind of shadow existence, more nonbeing than being. Accordingly, the statement meant originally, say the scholars, only that Jesus entered *sheol*, that is, that he died. This may be perfectly correct, but the question remains whether it makes the matter any simpler or less mysterious. In my view it is only at this point that we come face to face with the problem of what death really is, what happens when someone dies, that is, enters into the fate of death. Confronted with this question, we all have to admit our embarrassment. No one really knows the answer because we all live on this side of death and are unfamiliar with the experience of death. But perhaps we can try to begin formulating an answer by starting again from Jesus' cry on the Cross, which we found to contain the heart of what Jesus' descent into hell, his sharing of man's mortal fate, really means. In this last prayer of Jesus, as in the scene on the Mount of Olives, what appears as the innermost heart of his Passion is not any physical pain but radical loneliness, complete abandonment. But in the last analysis what comes to light here is simply the abyss of loneliness of man in general, of man who is alone in his innermost being. This loneliness, which is usually thickly overlaid but is nevertheless the true situation of man, is at the same time in fundamental contradiction with the nature of man, who cannot exist alone; he needs company. That is why loneliness is the region of fear, which is rooted in the exposure of a being that must exist but is pushed out into a situation with which it is impossible for him to deal.

A concrete example may help to make this clearer. When a child has to walk through the woods in the dark, he feels frightened, however convincingly he has been shown that there is no reason at all to be frightened. As soon as he is alone in the darkness, and thus has the experience of utter loneliness, fear arises, the fear peculiar to man, which is not fear of anything in particular but simply fear in itself. Fear of a particular thing is basically harmless; it can be removed by taking away the thing concerned. For example, if someone is afraid of a vicious dog, the matter can be swiftly settled by putting the dog on a chain. Here we come up against something much deeper, namely, the fact that where man falls into extreme loneliness he is not afraid of anything definite that could be explained away; on the contrary, he experiences the fear of loneliness, the uneasiness and vulnerability of his own nature, something that cannot be overcome by rational means. Let us take another example. If someone has to keep watch alone in a room with a dead person, he will always feel his position to be somehow or other eerie, even if he is unwilling to admit it to himself and is capable of explaining to himself rationally the groundlessness of his fear. He knows perfectly well in his own mind that the corpse can do him no harm and that his position might be more dangerous if the person concerned were still alive. What arises here is a completely different kind of fear, not fear of anything in particular, but, in being alone with death, the eeriness of loneliness in itself, the exposed nature of existence.

How then, we must ask, can such fear be overcome if proof of its groundlessness has no effect? Well, the child will lose his fear the moment there is a hand there to take him and lead him and a voice to talk to him; at the moment therefore at which he experiences the fellowship of a loving human being. Similarly, he who is alone with the corpse will feel the bout of fear recede when there is a human being with him, when he experiences the nearness of a "You". This conquest of fear reveals at the same time once again the nature of the fear: that it is the fear of loneliness, the anxiety of a being that can only live with a fellow being. The fear peculiar to man cannot be overcome by reason but only by the presence of someone who loves him.

We must examine our question still further. If there were such a thing as a loneliness that could no longer be penetrated and transformed by the word of another; if a state of abandonment were to arise that was so deep that no "You" could reach into it any more, then we should have real, total loneliness and dreadfulness, what theology calls "hell". We can now define exactly what this word means: it denotes a loneliness that the word love can no longer penetrate and that therefore indicates the exposed nature of existence in itself. In this connection who can fail to remember that writers and philosophers of our time take the view that basically all encounters between human beings remain superficial, that no man has access to the real depths of another? According to this view, no one can really penetrate into the innermost being of someone else; every encounter, beautiful as it may seem, basically only dulls the incurable wound of loneliness. Thus hell, despair, would dwell at the very bottom of our existence, in the shape of that loneliness which is as inescapable as it is dreadful. As is well known, Sartre based his anthropology on this idea. But even such an apparently conciliatory and tranquilly cheerful poet as Hermann Hesse allows the same thought to appear in his work:

> *Seltsam, im Nebel zu wandern!*
> *Leben ist Einsamsein.*
> *Kein Mensch kennt den andern,*
> *Jeder ist allein!*[10]

[10] Curious, to walk in a mist
Life is loneliness.
No man knows his neighbor,
Everyone is alone

In truth—one thing is certain: there exists a night into whose solitude no voice reaches; there is a door through which we can only walk alone—the door of death. In the last analysis all the fear in the world is fear of this loneliness. From this point of view, it is possible to understand why the Old Testament has only one word for hell *and* death, the word *sheol*; it regards them as ultimately identical. Death is absolute loneliness. But the loneliness into which love can no longer advance is—hell.

This brings us back to our starting point, the article of the Creed that speaks of the descent into hell. This article thus asserts that Christ strode through the gate of our final loneliness, that in his Passion he went down into the abyss of our abandonment. Where no voice can reach us any longer, there is he. Hell is thereby overcome, or, to be more accurate, death, which was previously hell, is hell no longer. Neither is the same any longer because there is life in the midst of death, because love dwells in it. Now only deliberate self-enclosure is hell or, as the Bible calls it, the second death (Rev 20:14, for example). But death is no longer the path into icy solitude; the gates of *sheol* have been opened. From this angle, I think, one can understand the images—which at first sight look so mythological—of the Fathers, who speak of fetching up the dead, of the opening of the gates. The apparently mythical passage in St. Matthew's Gospel becomes comprehensible, too, the passage that says that at the death of Jesus tombs opened and the bodies of the saints were raised (Mt 27:52). The door of death stands open since life—love—has dwelt in death.

4. "ROSE AGAIN [FROM THE DEAD]"

To the Christian, faith in the Resurrection of Jesus Christ is an expression of certainty that the saying that seems to be only a beautiful dream is in fact true: "Love is strong as death" (Song 8:6). In the Old Testament this sentence comes in the middle of praises of the power of *eros*. But this by no means signifies that we can simply push it aside as a lyrical exaggeration. The boundless demands of *eros*, its apparent exaggerations and extravagance, do in reality give expression to a basic problem, indeed *the* basic problem of human existence, insofar as they reflect the nature and intrinsic paradox of love: love demands infinity, indestructibility; indeed, it *is*, so to speak, a call for infinity. But it is also a fact that this cry of love's cannot be satisfied, that it demands infinity but cannot grant it; that it claims eternity but in fact is included in the world of death, in its loneliness and its power of destruction. Only from this angle can one understand what "resurrection" means. It *is* the greater strength of love in face of death.

At the same time it is proof of what only immortality can create: being in the other who still stands when I have fallen apart. Man is a being who himself does not live forever but is necessarily delivered up to death. For him, since he has no continuance in himself, survival, from a purely human point of view, can only become possible through his continuing to exist in another. The statements of Scripture about the connection between sin and death are to be understood from this angle. For it now becomes clear that man's attempt "to be like God", his striving for autonomy, through which he wishes to stand on his own feet alone, means his death, for he just cannot stand on his own. If man—and this is the real nature of sin—nevertheless refuses to recognize his own limits and tries to be completely self-sufficient, then precisely by adopting this attitude he delivers himself up to death.

Of course man does understand that his life alone does not endure and that he must therefore strive to exist in others, so as to remain through them and in them in the land of the living. Two ways in particular have been tried. First, living on in one's own children: that is why in primitive peoples failure to marry and childlessness are regarded as the most terrible curse; they mean hopeless destruction, final death. Conversely, the largest possible number of children offers at the same time the greatest possible chance of survival, hope of immortality, and thus the most genuine blessing that man can expect. Another way discloses itself when man discovers that in his children he only continues to exist in a very unreal way; he wants more of himself to remain. So he takes refuge in the idea of fame, which should make him really immortal if he lives on through all ages in the memory of others. But this second attempt of man's to obtain immortality for himself by existing in others fails just as badly as the first: what remains is not the self but only its echo, a mere shadow. So self-made immortality is really only a Hades, a *sheol*: more nonbeing than being. The inadequacy of both ways lies partly in the fact that the other person who holds my being after my death cannot carry this being itself but only its echo; and even more in the fact that even the other person to whom I have, so to speak, entrusted my continuance will not last—he, too, will perish.

This leads us to the next step. We have seen so far that man has no permanence in himself and consequently can only continue to exist in another but that his existence in another is only shadowy and once again not final, because this other must perish, too. If this is so, then only *one* could truly give lasting stability: he who *is*, who does not come into existence and pass away again but abides in the midst of transience: the God of the living, who does not hold just the shadow and echo of my being, whose ideas are not just copies of reality. I myself am his thought, which establishes me more securely, so to speak, than I am in myself; his thought is not the posthumous shadow but the original source and strength of my being. In him I can stand as more than a shadow; in him I am truly closer to myself than I should be if I just tried to stay by myself.

Before we return from here to the Resurrection, let us try to see the same thing once again from a somewhat different side. We can start again from the dictum about love and death and say: Only where someone values love more highly than life, that is, only where someone is ready to put life second to love, for the sake of love, can love be stronger and more than death. If it is to be more than death, it must first be more than mere life. But if it could be this, not just in intention but in reality, then that would mean at the same time that the power of love had risen superior to the power of the merely biological and taken it into its service. To use Teilhard de Chardin's terminology, where that took place, the decisive complexity or "complexification" would have occurred; *bios*, too, would be encompassed by and incorporated in the power of love. It would cross the boundary— death—and create unity where death divides. If the power of love for another were so strong somewhere that it could keep alive not just his memory, the shadow of his "I", but that person himself, then a new stage in life would have been reached. This would mean that the realm of biological evolutions and mutations had been left behind and the leap made to a quite different plane, on which love was no longer subject to *bios* but made use of it. Such a final stage of "mutation" and "evolution" would itself no longer be a biological stage; it would signify the end of the sovereignty of *bios*, which is at the same time the sovereignty of death; it would open up the realm that the Greek Bible calls *zoe*, that is, definitive life, which has left behind the rule of death. The last stage of evolution needed by the world to reach its goal would then no longer be achieved within the realm of biology but by the spirit, by freedom, by love. It would no longer be evolution but decision and gift in one.

But what has all this to do, it may be asked, with faith in the Resurrection of Jesus? Well, we previously considered the question of the possible immortality of man from two sides, which now turn out to be aspects of one and the same state of affairs. We said that, as man has no permanence in himself, his survival could only be brought about by his living on in another. And we said, from the point of view of this "other", that only the love that takes up the beloved in itself, into its own being, could make possible this existence in the other. These two complementary aspects are mirrored again, so it seems to me, in the two New Testament ways of describing the Resurrection of the Lord: "Jesus has risen" and "God (the Father) has awakened Jesus." The two formulas meet in the fact that Jesus' total love for men, which leads him to the Cross, is perfected in totally passing beyond to the Father and therein becomes stronger than death, because in this it is at the same time total "being held" by him.

From this a further step results. We can now say that love always establishes some kind of immortality; even in its prehuman stage, it points, in the form of preservation of the species, in this direction. Indeed, this founding of immortality is not something incidental to love, not one thing that it does among others, but what really gives it its specific character. This principle can be reversed; it then signifies that immortality *always* proceeds from love, never out of the autarchy of that which is sufficient to itself. We may even be bold enough to assert that this principle, properly understood, also applies even to God as he is seen by the Christian faith. God, too, is absolute permanence, as opposed to everything transitory, for the reason that he is the relation of three

Persons to one another, their incorporation in the "for one another" of love, act-substance of the love that is absolute and therefore completely "relative", living only "in relation to". As we said earlier, it is not autarchy, which knows no one but itself, that is divine; what is revolutionary about the Christian view of the world and of God, we found, as opposed to those of antiquity, is that it learns to understand the "absolute" as absolute "relatedness", as *relatio subsistens*.

To return to our argument, love is the foundation of immortality, and immortality proceeds from love alone. This statement to which we have now worked our way also means that he who has love for all has established immortality for all. That is precisely the meaning of the biblical statement that *his* Resurrection is *our* life. The—to us—curious reasoning of St. Paul in his First Letter to the Corinthians now becomes comprehensible: if he has risen, then we have, too, for then love is stronger than death; if he has not risen, then we have not either, for then the situation is still that death has the last word, nothing else (cf. 1 Cor 15:16f.). Since this is a statement of central importance, let us spell it out once again in a different way: Either love is stronger than death, or it is not. If it has become so in him, then it became so precisely as love for others. This also means, it is true, that our own love, left to itself, is not sufficient to overcome death; taken in itself it would have to remain an unanswered cry. It means that only his love, coinciding with God's own power of life and love, can be the foundation of our immortality. Nevertheless, it still remains true that the *mode* of our immortality will depend on our mode of loving. We shall have to return to this in the section on the Last Judgment.

A further point emerges from this discussion. Given the foregoing considerations, it goes without saying that the life of him who has risen from the dead is not once again *bios*, the bio-logical form of our mortal life within history; it is *zoe*, new, different, definitive life; life that has stepped beyond the mortal realm of *bios* and history, a realm that has here been surpassed by a greater power. And in fact the Resurrection narratives of the New Testament allow us to see clearly that the life of the Risen One lies, not within the historical *bios*, but beyond and above it. It is also true, of course, that this new life begot itself *in* history and had to do so, because after all it is there *for* history, and the Christian message is basically nothing else than the transmission of the testimony that love has managed to break through death here and thus has transformed fundamentally the situation of all of us. Once we have realized this, it is no longer difficult to find the right kind of hermeneutics for the difficult business of expounding the biblical Resurrection narratives, that is, to acquire a clear understanding of the sense in which they must properly be understood. Obviously we cannot attempt here a detailed discussion of the questions involved, which today present themselves in a more difficult form than ever before; especially as historical and—for the most part inadequately pondered—philosophical statements are becoming more and more inextricably intertwined, and exegesis itself quite often produces its own philosophy, which is intended to appear to the layman as a supremely refined distillation of the biblical evidence. Many points of detail will here always remain open to discussion, but it is possible to recognize a fundamental dividing line between explanation that remains explanation and arbitrary adaptations [to contemporary ways of thinking].

First of all, it is quite clear that after his Resurrection Christ did not go back to his previous earthly life, as we are told the young man of Nain and Lazarus did. He rose again to definitive life, which is no longer governed by chemical and biological laws and therefore stands outside the possibility of death, in the eternity conferred by love. That is why the encounters with him are "appearances"; that is why he with whom people had sat at table two days earlier is not recognized by his best friends and, even when recognized, remains foreign: only where *he* grants vision *is* he seen; only when he opens men's eyes and makes their hearts open up can the countenance of the eternal love that conquers death become recognizable in our mortal world, and, in that love, the new, different world, the world of him who is to come. That is also why it is so difficult, indeed absolutely impossible, for the Gospels to describe the encounter with the risen Christ; that is why they can only stammer when they speak of these meetings and seem to provide contradictory descriptions of them. In reality they are surprisingly unanimous in the dialectic of their statements, in the simultaneity of touching and not touching, or recognizing and not recognizing, of complete identity between the crucified and the risen Christ and complete transformation. People recognize the Lord and yet do not recognize him again; people touch him, and yet he is untouchable; he is the same and yet quite different. As we have said, the dialectic is always the same; it is only the stylistic means by which it is expressed that changes.

For example, let us examine a little more closely from this point of view the Emmaus story, which we have already touched upon briefly. At first sight it looks as if we are confronted here with a completely earthly and material notion of resurrection; as if nothing remains of the mysterious and indescribable elements to be found in the Pauline accounts. It looks as if the tendency to detailed depiction, to the concreteness of legend, supported by the apologist's desire for something tangible, had completely won the upper hand and fetched the risen Lord right back into earthly history. But this impression is soon contradicted by his mysterious appearance and his no less mysterious disappearance. The notion is contradicted even more by the fact that here, too, he remains unrecognizable to the accustomed eye. He cannot be firmly grasped as he could be in the time of his earthly life; he is discovered only in the realm of faith; he sets the hearts of the two travelers aflame by his interpretation of the Scriptures and by breaking bread he opens their eyes. This is a reference to the two basic elements in early Christian worship, which consisted of the liturgy of the word (the reading and expounding of Scripture) and the eucharistic breaking of bread. In this way the evangelist makes it clear that the encounter with the risen Christ lies on a quite new plane; he tries to describe the indescribable in terms of the liturgical facts. He thereby provides both a theology of the Resurrection and a theology of the liturgy: one encounters the risen Christ in the word and in the sacrament; worship is the way in which he becomes touchable to us and recognizable as the living Christ. And conversely, the liturgy is based on the mystery of Easter; it is to be understood as the Lord's approach to us. In it he becomes our traveling companion, sets our dull hearts aflame, and opens our sealed eyes. He still walks with us, still finds us worried and downhearted, and still has the power to make us see.

Of course, all this is only half the story; to stop at this alone would mean falsifying the evidence of the New Testament. Experience of the risen Christ is something other than a meeting with a man from within our history, and it must certainly not be traced back to conversations at table and recollections that would have finally crystallized in the idea that he still lived and went about his business. Such an interpretation reduces what happened to the purely human level and robs it of its specific quality. The Resurrection narratives are something other and more than disguised liturgical scenes:

they make visible the founding event on which all Christian liturgy rests. They testify to an approach that did not rise from the hearts of the disciples but came to them from outside, convinced them *despite* their doubts and made them certain that the Lord had truly risen. He who lay in the grave is no longer there; he—really he himself—lives. He who had been transposed into the other world of God showed himself powerful enough to make it palpably clear that he himself stood in their presence again, that in him the power of love had really proved itself stronger than the power of death.

Only by taking this just as seriously as what we said first does one remain faithful to the witness borne by the New Testament; only thus, too, is its seriousness in world history preserved. The comfortable attempt to spare oneself the belief in the mystery of God's mighty actions in this world and yet at the same time to have the satisfaction of remaining on the foundation of the biblical message leads nowhere; it measures up neither to the honesty of reason nor to the claims of faith. One cannot have both the Christian faith and "religion within the bounds of pure reason"; a choice is unavoidable. He who believes will see more and more clearly, it is true, how rational it is to have faith in the love that has conquered death.

5. "HE ASCENDED INTO HEAVEN AND IS SEATED AT THE RIGHT HAND OF THE FATHER"

To our generation, whose critical faculty has been awakened by Bultmann, talk of the Ascension, together with that of the descent into hell, conjures up that picture of a three-story world that we call mythical and regard as finished with once and for all. "Above" and "below", the world is everywhere just world, governed everywhere by the same physical laws, in principle susceptible everywhere of the same kind of investigation. It has no stories, and the concepts "above" and "below" are relative, depending on the standpoint of the observer. Indeed, since there is no absolute point of reference (and the earth certainly does not represent one), basically one can no longer speak at all of "above" and "below"—or even of "left" and "right"; the cosmos no longer exhibits any fixed directions.

No one today will seriously contest these discoveries. There is no longer such a thing as a world arranged literally in three stories. But was such a conception ever really intended in the articles of faith about the Lord's descent into hell and Ascension to heaven? It certainly provided the imagery for them, but it was just as certainly not the decisive factual element in them. On the contrary, the two tenets, together with faith in the historical Jesus, express the total range of human existence, which certainly spans three metaphysical dimensions if not three cosmic stories. To that extent it is only logical that the attitude that at the moment is considered "modern" should dispense not only with the Ascension and the descent into hell but also with the historical Jesus, that is, with all three dimensions of human existence; what is left *can* only be a variously draped ghost, on which—understandably—no one any longer wishes to build anything serious.

But what do our three dimensions really imply? We have already come to see that the descent into hell does not really refer to any outer depths of the cosmos; these are quite unnecessary to it. In the basic text, the prayer of the crucified Christ to the God who has abandoned him, there is no trace of any cosmic reference. On the contrary, this article of the Creed turns our gaze to the depths of human existence, which reach down into the valley of death, into the zone of untouchable loneliness and rejected love, and thus embrace the dimension of hell, carrying it within themselves as one of their own possibilities. Hell, existence in the definitive rejection of "being for", is not a cosmographical destination but a dimension of human nature, the abyss into which it reaches down at its lower end. We know today better than ever before that everyone's existence touches these depths; and since in the last analysis mankind is "*one* man", these depths affect not only the individual but also the one body of the whole human race, which must therefore bear the burden of them as a corporate whole. From this angle it can be understood once again how Christ, the "new Adam", undertook to bear the burden of these depths with us and did not wish to remain sublimely unaffected by them; conversely, of course, total rejection in all its unfathomability has only now become possible.

On the other hand, the Ascension of Christ points to the opposite end of human existence, which stretches out an infinite distance above and below itself. This existence embraces, as the opposite pole to utter solitude, to the untouchability of rejected love, the possibility of contact with all other men through the medium of contact with the divine love itself, so that human existence can find its geometrical place, so to speak, inside God's own being. The two possibilities of man thus brought to mind by the words heaven and hell are, it is true, completely different in nature and can be quite clearly distinguished from each other. The depths we call hell man can only give to himself. Indeed, we must put it more pointedly: Hell consists in man's being unwilling to receive anything, in his desire to be self-sufficient. It is the expression of enclosure in one's own being alone. These depths accordingly consist by nature of just this: that man will not accept, will not take anything, but wants to stand entirely on his own feet, to be sufficient unto himself. If this becomes utterly radical, then man has become the untouchable, the solitary, the reject. Hell is wanting only to be oneself; what happens when man barricades himself up in himself. Conversely, it is the nature of that upper end of the scale which we have called heaven that it can only be received, just as one can only give hell to oneself. "Heaven" is by nature what one has not made oneself and cannot make oneself; in Scholastic language it was said to be, as grace, a *donum indebitum et superadditum naturae* (an unowed gift added over and above nature). As fulfilled love, heaven can always only be granted to man; but hell is the loneliness of the man who will not accept it, who declines the status of beggar and withdraws into himself.

Only from this standpoint does it become clear now what is really meant in the Christian view by heaven. It is not to be understood as an everlasting place above the world or simply as an eternal metaphysical region. On the contrary, "heaven" and "the Ascension of Christ" are indivisibly connected; it is only this connection that makes clear the christological, personal, history-centered meaning of the Christian tidings of heaven. Let us look at it from another angle: heaven is not a place that, before Christ's Ascension, was barred off by a positive, punitive decree of God's, to be opened up one day in just as positive a way. On the contrary, the reality of heaven only comes into existence through the confluence of God and man. Heaven is to be defined as the contact of the being "man" with the being "God"; this confluence of God and man took place once and for all in Christ when he went beyond *bios* through death to new life. Heaven is accordingly that future of man and of mankind which the latter cannot give to itself, which is therefore closed to it so long as it waits for itself, and which was first and fundamentally opened up in the man whose field of existence was God and through whom God entered into the creature "man".

Therefore heaven is always more than a private, individual destiny; it is necessarily connected with the "last Adam", with the definitive man, and, accordingly, with the future of man as a whole. I think that from this point it should be possible to gain several more important hermeneutic insights, which in this context can only be hinted at. One of the most striking facts in the biblical evidence, a fact by which exegesis and theology have been profoundly exercised for the last fifty years or so, is formed by the so-called "eschatology of imminence". By this is meant that in the preaching of Jesus and the apostles it looks as if the end of the world is being announced as imminent. Indeed, one can even gain the impression that news of the approaching end is the real heart of the preaching of Jesus and the early Church. The figure of Jesus, his death, and his Resurrection are brought into connection with this idea in a way that is as strange as it is incomprehensible. Obviously we cannot here deal in detail with the many questions involved. But have not our last reflections indicated the direction in which the answer can be sought? We described Resurrection and Ascension as the final confluence of the being "man" with the being "God", a process that offers man the possibility of everlasting existence. We have tried to understand the two happenings as love's being stronger than death and thus as the decisive "mutation" of man and cosmos, in which the frontier of *bios* is broken down and a new field of existence created. If this is all correct, then it means the beginning of "eschatology", of the end of the world. With the crossing of the frontier of death, the future dimension of mankind is opened up and its future has in fact already begun. It thus also becomes evident how the individual's hope of immortality and the possibility of immortality for mankind as a whole intertwine and meet in Christ, who may just as well be called the "center" as, properly understood, the "end" of history.

Another idea must be weighed in connection with the article of the Creed that speaks of the Lord's Ascension. The statement about the Ascension that, as we have now seen, is decisive for the understanding of man's existence beyond the grave is just as decisive for an understanding of his life here and now or, alternatively, for the question of how this world and the beyond can approach each other and, therefore, for the question of the possibility and meaning of human relations with God. In our consideration of the first article of the Creed, we replied affirmatively to the question of whether the infinite can hear the finite, the eternal the temporal, and demonstrated that the true God's greatness is to be seen precisely in the fact that to him the smallest thing is not too small and the biggest not too big; we tried to understand that, as the *Logos*, he is the reason that not only speaks to all but also hears all and from which nothing remains excluded because of its insignificance. We replied to the worried questioning of our age: "Yes, God can hear." But one question still remains open. If anyone, following our train of thought, says, "Good, he can hear", must he not go on to ask, "But can he also answer our prayers?" Or is not the prayer of petition, the call of the creature up to God, in the last analysis a pious trick to elevate man psychologically and to comfort him, because he is seldom capable of higher forms of prayer? Surely the whole thing serves solely to set man in motion somehow or other toward transcendence, although in reality nothing can happen or be changed as a result of his prayers; for what is eternal is eternal, and what is temporal is temporal—no path seems to lead from one to the other.

This, too, we cannot consider in detail here, because a very searching critical analysis of the concepts of time and eternity would be required. One would have to investigate their foundations in ancient thought and the synthesis of this thought with the biblical faith, a synthesis whose imperfection lies at the root of modern questioning. One would have to reflect once again on the relationship of scientific and technical thinking to the thinking of faith. These are tasks that go far beyond the scope of this book. So here again, instead of detailed answers, we must settle for an indication of the general direction in which the answer is to be sought.

Modern thinking usually lets itself be guided by the idea that eternity is imprisoned, so to speak, in its unchangeableness; God appears as the prisoner of his eternal plan conceived "before all ages". "Being" and "becoming" do not mingle. Eternity is thus understood in a purely negative sense as timelessness, as the opposite to time, as something that cannot make its influence felt in time for the simple reason that it would thereby cease to be unchangeable and itself become temporal. Fundamentally these ideas remain the products of a pre-Christian mentality that takes no account of a concept of God that finds utterance in a belief in creation and incarnation. At bottom they take for granted the dualism of antiquity—something that we cannot go into here—and are signs of an intellectual naïveté that looks at God in human terms. For if one thinks that God cannot alter retrospectively what he planned "before" eternity, then unwittingly one is again conceiving eternity in terms of time, with its distinction between "before" and "after".

But eternity is not the very ancient, which existed before time began, but the entirely other, which is related to every passing age as its today and is really contemporary with it; it is not itself barred off into a "before" and "after"; it is much rather the power of the present in all time. Eternity does not stand by the side of time, quite unrelated to it; it is the creatively supporting power of all time, which encompasses passing time in its own present and thus gives it the ability to be. It is not timelessness but dominion over time. As the Today that is contemporary with all ages, it can also make its influence felt in any age.

The Incarnation of God in Jesus Christ, by virtue of which the eternal God and temporal man combine in one single person, is nothing else than the last concrete manifestation of God's dominion over time. At this point of Jesus' human existence, God took hold of time and drew it into himself. His power over time stands embodied before us, as it were, in Christ. Christ is really, as St. John's Gospel says, the "door" between God and man (Jn 10:9), the "mediator" (1 Tim 2:5), in whom the Eternal One has time. In Jesus we temporal beings can speak to the temporal one, our contemporary; but in him, who with us is time, we simultaneously make contact with the Eternal One, because with us Jesus is time, and with God he is eternity.

Hans Urs von Balthasar—speaking, it is true, in a somewhat different context—has cast a searching light on the spiritual significance of these insights. He first recalls that in his earthly life Jesus did not stand above time and space but lived from the midst of his time and in his time. The humanity of Jesus, which placed him in the midst of that age, is presented to us in every line of the Gospels; and we have, in many respects, a clearer and more living picture of him than was vouchsafed to earlier periods. But this "standing in time" is not just an outward cultural and historical framework, behind which could be found somewhere or other, untouched by it, the supratemporal essence of his real being; it is much rather an anthropological state of affairs, which profoundly affects the form of human existence itself. Jesus has time and does not anticipate in sinful impatience the will of the Father. "Hence the Son, who has time, in the world, for God, is the point at which God has time for the world. Apart from the Son, God has no time for the world, but in him he has *all* time."[11] God is not the prisoner of his eternity: in Jesus he has time—for us, and Jesus is thus in actual fact "the throne of grace" to which at any time we can "with confidence draw near" (Heb 4:16).

6. "HE WILL COME AGAIN TO JUDGE THE LIVING AND THE DEAD"

Rudolf Bultmann reckons that the belief in an "end of the world" signaled by the return of the Lord in judgment is one of those ideas, like the Lord's descent into hell and Ascension into heaven, which for modern man are "disposed of". Every reasonable person, he declares, is convinced that the world will go on as it has done now for nearly two thousand years since the eschatological proclamation of the New Testament. It seems all the more important to clarify our thinking on this point since the biblical treatment of it unquestionably contains marked cosmological elements and therefore reaches into the domain that we view as the field of natural science. Of course, in the phrase about the end of the world, the word "world" does not mean primarily the physical structure of the cosmos but the world of man, human history; thus in the first

---

[11] H. U. von Balthasar, *Theology of History* (San Francisco, 1994), 40–41. cf. G. Hasenhüttl, *Der Glaubensvollzug* (Essen, 1963), p. 327.

instance this manner of speaking means that *this* kind of world—the human world—will come to an end that is dictated and achieved by God. But it cannot be denied that the Bible presents this essentially anthropological event in cosmological (and also partly in political) imagery. How far it is a question *only* of imagery and how close the imagery is to the reality is difficult to determine.

Certainly one can only base one's observations on this subject on the larger context of the Bible's whole view of the world. And for the Bible the cosmos and man are not two clearly separable quantities, with the cosmos forming the fortuitous scene of human existence, which in itself could be parted from the cosmos and allowed to accomplish itself without a world. On the contrary, world and human existence belong necessarily to one another, so that neither a worldless man nor even a world without man seems thinkable. The first of these two concepts can be accepted again today without argument; and after what we have learned from Teilhard, the second should no longer be entirely incomprehensible, either. Going on from there, one might be tempted to say that the biblical message about the end of the world and the return of the Lord is not simply anthropology in cosmic imagery; that it does not even merely present a cosmological aspect alongside an anthropological one but depicts with the inner logic of the total biblical view the coincidence of anthropology and cosmology in definitive Christology and, precisely *therein*, portrays the end of the "world", which in its two-in-one construction out of cosmos and man has always pointed to this unity as its final goal. Cosmos and man, which already belong to each other even though they so often stand opposed to one another, become one through their "complexification" in the larger entity of the love that, as we said earlier, goes beyond and encompasses *bios*. Thus it becomes evident here once again how very much end-eschatology and the breakthrough represented by Jesus' Resurrection are in reality one and the same thing; it becomes clear once again that the New Testament rightly depicts this Resurrection as *the* eschatological happening.

In order to make any further progress we must elaborate this thought a little more clearly. We said just now that the cosmos was not just an outward framework of human history, not a static mold—a kind of container holding all kinds of living creatures that could just as well be poured into a different container. This means, stated positively, that the cosmos is movement; that it is not just a case of history *existing in* it, that the cosmos itself *is* history. It does not merely form the scene of human history; before human history began and later with it, cosmos is itself "history". Finally, there is only one single all-embracing world history, which for all the ups and downs, all the advances and setbacks that it exhibits, nevertheless has a general direction and goes "forward". Of course, to him who only sees a section of it, this piece, even though it may be relatively big, looks like a circling in the same spot. No direction is perceptible. It is only observed by him who begins to see the whole. But in this cosmic movement, as we have already seen, spirit is not just some chance by-product of development, of no importance to the whole; on the contrary, we were able to establish that, in this movement or process, matter and its evolution form the prehistory of spirit or mind.

From this perspective the belief in the second coming of Jesus Christ and in the consummation of the world in that event could be explained as the conviction that our history is advancing to an "omega" point, at which it will become finally and unmistakably clear that the element of stability that seems to us to be the supporting ground of reality, so to speak, is not mere unconscious matter; that, on the contrary, the real, firm ground is mind. Mind holds being together, gives it reality, indeed *is* reality: it is not from below but from above that being receives its capacity to subsist. That there is such a thing as this process of "complexification" of material being through spirit, and from the latter its concentration into a new kind of unity, can already be seen today in a certain sense in the remodeling of the world through technology. In reality's susceptibility to manipulation, the boundaries between nature and technology are already beginning to disappear; we can no longer clearly distinguish one from the other. To be sure, this analogy must be regarded as questionable in more than one respect. Yet such processes hint at a kind of world in which spirit and nature do not simply stand alongside each other but in which spirit, in a new "complexification", draws what apparently is merely natural into itself, thereby creating a new world that at the same time necessarily means the end of the old one. Now the "end of the world" in which the Christian believes is certainly something quite different from the total victory of technology. But the welding together of nature and spirit that occurs in it enables us to grasp in a new way how the reality of belief in the return of Christ is to be conceived: as faith in the final unification of reality by spirit or mind.

This opens the way to a further step. We said before that nature and mind form one single history, which advances in such a way that mind emerges more and more clearly as the all-embracing element and thus anthropology and cosmology finally in actual fact coalesce. But this assertion of the increasing "complexification" of the world through mind necessarily implies its unification around a personal center, for mind is not just an undefined something or other; where it exists in its own specific nature, it subsists as individuality, as person. It is true that there is such a thing as "objective mind", mind invested in machines, in works of the most varied kind; but in all these cases mind does not exist in its original, specific form; "objective mind" is always derived from subjective mind; it points back to person, mind's only real mode of existence. Thus the assertion that the world is moving toward a "complexification" through mind also implies that the cosmos is moving toward a unification in the personal.

This confirms once again the infinite precedence of the individual over the universal. This principle, which we developed earlier, appears again here in all its importance. The world is in motion toward unity in the person. The whole draws its meaning from the individual, not the other way about. To appreciate this is also to justify once again Christology's apparent positivism, the conviction—a scandal to men of all periods—that makes one individual the center of history and of the whole. The intrinsic necessity of this "positivism" is thus demonstrated anew: if it is true that at the end stands the triumph of spirit, that is, the triumph of truth, freedom, and love, then it is not just some force or other that finally ends up victorious; what stands at the end is a countenance. The omega of the world is a "you", a person, an individual. The all-encompassing "complexification", the unification infinitely embracing all, is at the same time the final denial of all collectivism, the denial of the fanaticism of the mere idea, even the so-called "idea of Christianity". Man, the person, always takes precedence over the mere idea.

This implies a further and very important consequence. If the breakthrough to the ultra-complexity of the final phase is based on spirit and freedom, then it is by no means a neutral, cosmic drift; it includes responsibility. It does not happen of its own accord, like physical process, but is based on decisions. That is why the second coming of the Lord is not only salvation, not only the omega that sets everything right, but also judgment. Indeed at this stage we can actually define the meaning of the talk of judgment. It means precisely this, that the final stage of the world is not the result of a natural current but the result of responsibility that is grounded in freedom. This must also be regarded as the key to understanding why the New Testament clings fast, in spite of its message of grace, to the assertion that at the end men are judged "by their works" and that no one can escape giving account of the way he has lived his life. There is a freedom that is not cancelled out even by grace and, indeed, is brought by it face to face with itself: man's final fate is not forced upon him regardless of the decisions he has made in his life. This assertion is in any case also necessary in order to draw the line between faith and false dogmatism or a false Christian self-confidence. This line alone confirms the equality of men by confirming the identity of their responsibility. Since the days of the early Church Fathers, it has always been an essential task of Christian preaching to make people aware of this identity of responsibility and to contrast it with the false confidence engendered by merely saying, "Lord, Lord!"

It might be useful in this context to recall certain things said by the great Jewish theologian Leo Baeck. The Christian will not entirely agree with them, but he cannot disregard their seriousness. Baeck points to the fact that Israel's "life apart" turned into an awareness of serving the future of mankind. "The *special character of the call* is asserted, but *no exclusiveness of salvation* is proclaimed. Judaism was preserved from falling into the religious narrowness of the concept of a Church that alone confers salvation. Where it is not faith but the deed that leads to God, where the community offers to its children as a sign of spiritual membership the ideal and the task, a place in the covenant of faith cannot of itself guarantee the salvation of the soul." Baeck then shows how this universalism of the salvation founded on the deed crystallizes more and more firmly in the Jewish tradition and finally emerges quite clearly in the "classical" saying: "Even the pious who are not Israelites share in the eternal bliss." No one will be able to read without dismay when Baeck then goes on to say that one need only "compare with this principle Dante's picture of the place of damnation, the destination of even the best pagans, with all its cruel images corresponding to the notions entertained by the Church in the centuries before and after, to feel the sharpness of the contrast." [12]

Of course, much in this passage is inaccurate and provokes a counterassertion; nevertheless, it contains a serious statement. It can make clear in its fashion wherein the indispensability of the article about the universal judgment of all men "according to their works" lies. It is not part of our task to consider in detail how this assertion can coexist with the full weight of the doctrine of grace. Perhaps in the last analysis it is impossible to escape a paradox whose logic is completely disclosed only to the experience of a life based on faith. Anyone who entrusts himself to faith becomes aware that both exist: the radical character of the grace that frees helpless man and, no less, the abiding seriousness of the responsibility that summons man day after day. Both together mean that the Christian enjoys, on the one hand, the liberating, detached tranquility of him who lives on that excess of divine justice known as Jesus Christ. There is a tranquility that knows: in the last analysis, I cannot destroy

[12] L. Baeck, *Das Wesen des Judentums*, 6th ed. (Cologne, 1960), p. 69.

what *he* has built up. For in himself man lives with the dreadful knowledge that his power to destroy is infinitely greater than his power to build up. But this same man knows that in Christ the power to build up has proved infinitely stronger. This is the source of a profound freedom, a knowledge of God's unrepentant love; he sees through all our errors and remains well disposed to us. It becomes possible to do one's own work fearlessly; it has shed its sinister aspect because it has lost its power to destroy: the issue of the world does not depend on us but is in God's hands. At the same time the Christian knows, however, that he is not free to do whatever he pleases, that his activity is not a game that God allows him and does not take seriously. He knows that he must answer for his actions, that he owes an account as a steward of what has been entrusted to him. There can only be responsibility where there is someone to be responsible to, someone to put the questions. Faith in the Last Judgment holds this questioning of our life over our heads so that we cannot forget it for a moment. Nothing and no one empowers us to trivialize the tremendous seriousness involved in such knowledge; it shows our life to be a serious business and precisely by doing so gives it its dignity.

"To judge the living and the dead"—this also means that no one but *he* has the right to judge in the end. This implies that the unrighteousness of the world does not have the last word, not even by being wiped out indiscriminately in a universal act of grace; on the contrary, there is a last court of appeal that preserves justice in order thus to be able to perfect love. A love that overthrew justice would create injustice and thus cease to be anything but a caricature of love. True love is excess of justice, excess that goes farther than justice, but never destruction of justice, which must be and must remain the basic form of love.

Of course, one must guard against the opposite extreme. It cannot be denied that belief in the Last Judgment has at times assumed in the Christian consciousness a form in which, in practice, it was bound to lead to the destruction of the full faith in the redemption and the promise of mercy. The example always adduced is the profound contrast between *Maran atha* and *Dies irae*. The early Christians, with their cry "Our Lord, come" (*Maran atha*), interpreted the second coming of Jesus as an event full of hope and joy, stretching their arms out longingly toward it as the moment of the great fulfillment. To the Christians of the Middle Ages, on the other hand, that moment appeared as the terrifying "day of wrath" (*Dies irae*), which makes man feel like dying of woe and terror, and to which he looks forward with fear and dread. The return of Christ is then only judgment, the day of the great reckoning that threatens everyone. Such a view forgets a decisive aspect of Christianity, which is thus reduced for all practical purposes to moralism and robbed of that hope and joy which are the very breath of its life.

Perhaps it will have to be admitted that the tendency to such a false development, which only sees the dangers of responsibility and no longer the freedom of love, is already present in the Creed, in which the idea of Christ's second coming is reduced, at any rate verbally, to the idea of judgment: "He will come again to judge the living and the dead." Of course, in the circles that formed the spiritual home of the Creed, the original Christian tradition was still very much alive; the phrase about the Last Judgment was taken in self-evident conjunction with the message of mercy. The statement that it is *Jesus* who judges immediately tinged the judgment with hope. I should just like to quote a passage from the so-called *Second Epistle of Clement* in which this becomes quite clear: "Brothers, we must think of Jesus as

God, as he who judges the living and the dead. We must not think little of our salvation, for by thinking little of him we also think little of our hope." [13]

Here the real emphasis of this article of the Creed becomes evident: it is not simply—as one might expect—God, the Infinite, the Unknown, the Eternal, who judges. On the contrary, he has handed the judgment over to one who, as man, is our brother. It is not a stranger who judges us but he whom we know in faith. The judge will not advance to meet us as the entirely Other, but as one of us, who knows human existence from inside and has suffered.

Thus over the judgment glows the dawn of hope; it is not only the day of wrath but also the second coming of our Lord. One is reminded of the mighty vision of Christ with which the Book of Revelation begins (1:9–19): the seer sinks down as though dead before this being full of unearthly power. But the Lord lays his hand on him and says to him as once in the days when they were crossing the Lake of Gennesaret in wind and storm: "Fear not, it is I" (cf. 1:17). The Lord of all power is that Jesus whose comrade the visionary had once become in faith. The article in the Creed about the judgment transfers this very idea to our meeting with the judge of the world. On that day of fear the Christian will be allowed to see in happy wonder that he to whom "all authority in heaven and on earth has been given" (Mt 28:18) was the companion in faith of his days on earth, and it is as if through the words of the Creed Jesus were already laying his hands on him and saying: Be without fear, it is I. Perhaps the problem of the intertwining of justice and mercy can be answered in no more beautiful way than it is in the idea that stands in the background of our Creed.

[13] 2 Clem. 1, 1f.; cf. Kattenbusch 2:660.

PART THREE

THE SPIRIT AND THE CHURCH

Chapter I

THE INTRINSIC UNITY OF THE LAST
STATEMENTS IN THE CREED

In the original Greek text the central statement in the third section of the Creed runs simply: "I believe in Holy Spirit." The definite article to which we are accustomed in our translation is thus missing. This is very important for the interpretation of the original meaning, for it means that this article was at first really understood in terms of salvation history, not of the Trinity. In other words, the third section of the Creed refers in the first place, not to the Holy Spirit as the third Person in the Godhead, but to the Holy Spirit as God's gift to history in the community of those who believe in Christ.

Of course, the trinitarian interpretation, the reference to the triune God, is not thereby excluded. After all, we saw in our introductory reflections that the whole Creed grew up out of the triple baptismal question about faith in the Father, Son, and Spirit, a question that for its part rests on the baptismal formula recorded in Matthew (Mt 28:19). To that extent the oldest form of the Creed with its tripartite arrangement is indeed one of the main roots of the trinitarian image of God. It was only the gradual expansion of the baptismal questions into a detailed creed that somewhat obscured the trinitarian structure. The whole story of Jesus from conception to second coming was now incorporated to form the central section, as we have seen. As a result, the first section, too, was now taken in a more historical sense; it was referred essentially to the story of creation and the pre-Christian age. This made a historical view of the whole text inevitable: the third section was bound to be understood as a prolongation of the story of Christ in the gift of the Spirit and, therefore, as a reference to the "last days" between the coming of Christ and his return. Of course, this development did not simply cancel out the trinitarian view, just as conversely the baptismal questions were not concerned with an other-worldly God outside history but with the God who has turned his face to us. To this extent the interplay of "salvation history" and trinitarian viewpoints is characteristic of the oldest stages of Christian thought. Later on this interaction was more and more forgotten, with unfortunate results, so that a division resulted between theological metaphysics, on the one side, and theology of history, on the other. Henceforth both coexist alongside each other as two completely different things; people indulge either in ontological speculation or anti-philosophical theology of salvation history, thus losing in a really tragic way the original unity of Christian thought. At the start Christian thinking is neither merely "soteriological" nor merely "metaphysical" but molded by the unity of history and being. Here lies an important task for modern theological work, which is torn once again by this dilemma.[1]

But let us leave these general considerations and ask what in fact our text, as it stands now, really means. It speaks, as we have already seen, not of God's inner life, but of "God facing outward", of the Holy Spirit as the power through which the risen Lord remains present in the history of the

[1] Cf. J. Ratzinger, "Heilsgeschichte und Eschatologie", in *Theologie im Wandel*, Tübinger Festschrift (Munich, 1967), pp. 68–89.

world as the principle of a new history and a new world. This tendency produced of its own accord a further consequence. The fact that it is a question here, not of the Spirit as a person within God, but as the power of God in the history that opens with the Resurrection of Jesus produced the effect that, in the consciousness of those praying, faith in the "Spirit" and faith in the Church interfered with each other. This is, after all, only a practical application of the interaction between Trinity and salvation history discussed above. Once again one must regard it as unlucky for later developments that this interaction ceased to operate; as a result, both the teaching about the Church and the teaching about the Holy Spirit suffered. The Church was no longer understood charismatically from the angle of pneumatology but was seen exclusively from the standpoint of the Incarnation as something all too earthbound and finally explained entirely on the basis of the power categories of worldly thinking. In this fashion the teaching about the Holy Spirit also became homeless; insofar as it did not drag out a miserable existence in the realm of mere edification, it was absorbed into the general speculation about the Trinity and thus for all practical purposes had no function for the Christian consciousness. Here the text of the Creed poses a completely concrete problem: teaching about the Church must take its departure from teaching about the Holy Spirit and his gifts. But its goal lies in a doctrine of the history of God with men or, alternatively, of the function of the story of Christ for mankind as a whole. This indicates at the same time in what direction Christology must evolve. It is not to be developed as a doctrine of God's taking root in the world, a doctrine that, starting from Jesus' humanity, interprets the Church in an all too worldly fashion. Christ remains present through the Holy Spirit with all his openness and breadth and freedom, which by no means exclude the institutional form but limit its claims and do not allow it simply to make itself the same as worldly institutions.

The remaining statements in the third section of the Creed are intended to be nothing more than developments of its basic profession, "I believe in Holy Spirit." These developments proceed in two directions. First comes the phrase about the communion of saints, which did not figure in the original text of the creed formulated in the city of Rome itself but nevertheless represents an ancient tradition of the Church. Then comes the phrase about the forgiveness of sins. Both statements are to be understood as concretizations of the words about the Holy Spirit, as descriptions of the way in which this Spirit works in history. Both have a directly sacramental meaning of which we are hardly aware today. The saying about the communion of saints refers, first of all, to the eucharistic community, which through the Body of the Lord binds the Churches scattered all over the earth into *one* Church. Thus originally the word *sanctorum* (of the holy ones) does not refer to persons but means the holy gifts, the holy *thing*, granted to the Church in her eucharistic feast by God as the real bond of unity. Thus the Church is not defined as a matter of offices and organization but on the basis of her worship of God: as a community at one table around the risen Christ, who gathers and unites them everywhere. Of course, very soon people began to include in this idea the persons who themselves are united with one another and sanctified by God's one, holy gift. The Church began to be seen, not just as the unity of the eucharistic table, but also as the community of those who through this table are united among themselves. Then from this point a cosmic breadth very soon entered into the concept of Church: the communion of saints spoken of here extends beyond the frontier of death; it binds together all those who have received the one Spirit and his one, life-giving power.

The phrase about the forgiveness of sins, on the other hand, refers to the other fundamental sacrament of the Church, namely, baptism; and from there it very soon came to include the sacrament of penance. At first, of course, baptism was the great sacrament of forgiveness, the moment when a visible transformation took place. Only gradually, through painful experience, did people come to see that even the baptized Christian needs forgiveness, with the result that the renewed remission of sins granted by the sacrament of penance advanced more and more into the foreground, especially since baptism moved to the beginning of life and thus ceased to be an expression of active conversion. Nevertheless, the fact remains even now that one cannot become a Christian by birth but only by rebirth: Christianity only ever comes into being by man's turning his life around, turning away from the self-satisfaction of mere existence and being "converted". In this sense baptism remains, as the start of a lifelong conversion, the fundamental pattern of the Christian existence, as the phrase about the "remission of sins" is intended to remind us. But if Christianity is regarded, not as a chance grouping of men, but as the about-turn into real humanity, then this profession of faith goes beyond the circle of the baptized and means that man does not come to himself if he simply abandons himself to his natural inclination. To become truly a man, he must oppose this inclination; he must turn around: even the waters of his nature do not climb upward of their own accord.

To summarize all this, we can now say that in our Creed the Church is understood in terms of the Holy Spirit, as the center of the Spirit's activity in the world. Concretely, she is seen from the two angles of baptism (penance) and the Eucharist. This sacramental approach produces a completely theocentric understanding of the Church: the foreground is occupied, not by the group of men composing her, but by the gift of God that turns man around toward a new being that he cannot give to himself, to a communion he can only receive as a gift. Yet precisely this theocentric image of the Church is entirely human, entirely real; by centering around conversion and unification, and understanding both as a process that cannot be brought to completion within history, it reveals the meaningful human connection between sacrament and Church. Thus the "objective" view (from the angle of the gift of God) brings the personal element into play of its own accord: the new being of forgiveness leads us into fellowship with those who live from forgiveness; forgiveness establishes communion; and communion with the Lord in the Eucharist leads necessarily to the communion of the converted, who all eat one and the same bread, to become in it "one body" (1 Cor 10:17) and, indeed, "one single new man" (cf. Eph 2:15).

The concluding words of the Creed, too, the profession of faith in the "resurrection of the body" and "life everlasting", are to be understood as the unfolding of faith in the Holy Spirit and his transforming power, whose final effect they depict. For the prospect of resurrection, on which the whole section here converges, follows necessarily from faith in the transformation of history that started with the Resurrection of Jesus. With this event, as we have seen, the frontier of *bios*, in other words, death, was crossed and a new continuum was opened up: the biological has been overtaken by the spirit, by love, which is stronger than death. Thus the barrier of death has been broken through in principle, and a definitive future has been opened up for man and world. This conviction, in which faith in Christ and acknowledgment of the power of the Holy Spirit meet, is expressly applied in the last words of the Creed to the future of all of us. The sight of the Omega of world history, in which everything will be fulfilled, results by an inner necessity from faith in the God who himself wished to be, in the Cross, the Omega of the world, its last letter. Precisely by this he has made the Omega into *his* point, so that one day love is definitively stronger than death, and out of the "complexification" of *bios* by love the final complex emerges, the finality of the person and the finality of unity that comes from love. Because God himself became a mere worm, the last letter in the alphabet of creation, the last letter has become his letter and thereby turned history toward the final victory of love: the Cross really is the salvation of the world.

Chapter II

TWO MAJOR QUESTIONS POSED BY
THE ARTICLES ON THE SPIRIT
AND THE CHURCH

In the foregoing reflections we tried to bring out the wealth
and scope of the last few articles of the Creed. The Christian
notion of man, the problem of sin and redemption, are echoed
in them once again, but their chief function is to affirm the sacramental idea that for its part forms the heart of the concept of
the Church: Church and sacrament stand or fall together; a
Church without sacraments would be an empty organization,
and sacraments without a Church would be rites without meaning or inner cohesion. So one of the important questions thrown
up by the last article of the Creed is that of the nature of the
Church; the other big problem that it poses is contained in the
saying about the resurrection of the body, an idea that is no less
of a stumbling block to the modern mind, albeit for different
reasons, than it was to the "spiritualism" of the Greek world.
To conclude our survey of the Creed, we shall now try to explore
a little further the implications of these two questions.

1. "THE HOLY, CATHOLIC CHURCH"

Obviously it cannot be our aim here to develop a complete doctrine of the Church; leaving aside the individual, specialized

theological questions, we shall simply make a brief attempt to discern the real nature of the stumbling block we encounter in pronouncing the formula about the "holy, catholic Church" and strive to understand the answer implied in the text of the Creed itself. What we have to say presupposes our earlier reflections about the spiritual location and inner coherence of these words, which, on the one hand, refer to the powerful operation of the Holy Spirit in history and, on the other, are explained in the phrases about the forgiveness of sins and the communion of saints, phrases in which baptism, penance, and Eucharist are declared to be the framework of the Church, her real content and her true mode of existence.

Perhaps much of what disturbs us about the profession of faith in the Church is removed by the mere consideration of this double context. Nevertheless, let us speak out and say plainly what worries us today at this point in the Creed. We are tempted to say, if we are honest with ourselves, that the Church is neither holy nor catholic: the Second Vatican Council itself ventured to the point of speaking no longer merely of the holy Church but of the sinful Church, and the only reproach it incurred was that of still being far too timorous; so deeply aware are we all of the sinfulness of the Church. This may well be partly due to the Lutheran theology of sin and also to an assumption arising out of dogmatic prejudgments. But what makes this "dogmatic theology" so reasonable is its harmony with our own experience. The centuries of the Church's history are so filled with all sorts of human failure that we can quite understand Dante's ghastly vision of the Babylonian whore sitting in the Church's chariot; and the dreadful words of William of Auvergne, Bishop of Paris in the thirteenth century, seem perfectly comprehensible. William said that the barbarism of the Church had to make everyone who saw it go rigid with horror: "We are no longer

dealing with a bride but with a monster of terrible defor-
mity and ferocity." [1]

The catholicity of the Church seems just as questionable
as her holiness. The one garment of the Lord is torn between
the disputing parties, the one Church is divided up into many
Churches, every one of which claims more or less insistently
to be alone in the right. And so for many people today the
Church has become the main obstacle to belief. They can
no longer see in her anything but the human struggle for
power, the petty spectacle of those who, with their claim to
administer official Christianity, seem to stand most in the
way of the true spirit of Christianity.

There is no theory in existence that could compellingly refute
such ideas by mere reason, just as, conversely, these ideas themselves do not proceed from mere reason but from the bitterness of a heart that may perhaps have been disappointed in its
high hopes and now, in the pain of wronged love, can see only
the destruction of its hopes. How, then, are we to reply? Ultimately one can only acknowledge why one can still love this
Church in faith, why one still dares to recognize in the dis-
torted features the countenance of the holy Church. Nevertheless, let us start from the objective elements. As we have
already seen, in all these statements of faith the word "holy"
does not apply in the first place to the holiness of human persons but refers to the divine gift that bestows holiness in the
midst of human unholiness. The Church is not called "holy"
in the Creed because her members, collectively and individ-
ually, are holy, sinless men—this dream, which appears afresh

[1] Cf. the great contribution by H. U. von Balthasar, "Casta Meretrix", in
his *Explorations in Theology*, vol. 2: *Spouse of the Word* (San Francisco: Ignatius
Press, 1991), pp. 193–288; the passages referred to occur on pp. 194–97; see
also H. Riedlinger, *Die Makellosigkeit der Kirche in den lateinischen Hoheliedkom-
mentaren des Mittelalters* (Münster, 1958).

in every century, has no place in the waking world of our text, however movingly it may express a human longing that man will never abandon until a new heaven and a new earth really grant him what this age will never give him. Even at this point we can say that the sharpest critics of the Church in our time secretly live on this dream and, when they find it disappointed, bang the door of the house shut again and denounce it as a deceit. But to return to our argument: The holiness of the Church consists in that power of sanctification which God exerts in her in spite of human sinfulness. We come up here against the real mark of the "New Covenant": in Christ, God has bound himself to men, has let himself be bound by them. The New Covenant no longer rests on the reciprocal keeping of the agreement; it is granted by God as grace that abides even in the face of man's faithlessness. It is the expression of God's love, which will not let itself be defeated by man's incapacity but always remains well disposed toward him, welcomes him again and again precisely because he is sinful, turns to him, sanctifies him, and loves him.

Because of the Lord's devotion, never more to be revoked, the Church is the institution sanctified by him forever, an institution in which the holiness of the *Lord* becomes present among men. But it is really and truly the holiness of the *Lord* that becomes present in her and that chooses again and again as the vessel of its presence—with a paradoxical love—the dirty hands of men. It is holiness that radiates as the holiness of Christ from the midst of the Church's sin. So the paradoxical figure of the Church, in which the divine so often presents itself in such unworthy hands, in which the divine is only ever present in the form of a "nevertheless", is to the faithful the sign of the "nevertheless" of the ever greater love shown by God. The thrilling interplay of God's loyalty and man's disloyalty that characterizes the structure of the Church is the dramatic form of grace, so to speak, through which the reality of grace as the pardoning of those who are in themselves unworthy continually becomes visibly present in history. One could actually say that precisely in her paradoxical combination of holiness and unholiness the Church is in fact the shape taken by grace in this world.

Let us go a step farther. In the human dream of a perfect world, holiness is always visualized as untouchability by sin and evil, as something unmixed with the latter; there always remains in some form or other a tendency to think in terms of black and white, a tendency to cut out and reject mercilessly the current form of the negative (which can be conceived in widely varying terms). In contemporary criticism of society and in the actions in which it vents itself, this relentless side always present in human ideals is once again only too evident. That is why the aspect of Christ's holiness that upset his contemporaries was the complete absence of this condemnatory note—fire did not fall on the unworthy, nor were the zealous allowed to pull up the weeds they saw growing luxuriantly on all sides. On the contrary, this holiness expressed itself precisely as mingling with the sinners whom Jesus drew into his vicinity; as mingling to the point where he himself was made "to be sin" and bore the curse of the law in execution as a criminal—complete community of fate with the lost (cf. 2 Cor 5:21; Gal 3:13). He has drawn sin to himself, made it his lot, and so revealed what true "holiness" is: not separation, but union; not judgment, but redeeming love. Is the Church not simply the continuation of God's deliberate plunge into human wretchedness; is she not simply the continuation of Jesus' habit of sitting at table with sinners, of his mingling with the misery of sin to the point where he actually seems to sink under its weight? Is there not revealed in the unholy holiness of the Church, as opposed to man's expectation of purity, God's true holiness, which is love,

love that does not keep its distance in a sort of aristocratic, untouchable purity but mixes with the dirt of the world, in order thus to overcome it? Can, therefore, the holiness of the Church be anything else but the bearing with one another that comes, of course, from the fact that all of us are borne up by Christ?

I must admit that to me this unholy holiness of the Church has in itself something infinitely comforting about it. Would one not be bound to despair in face of a holiness that was spotless and could only operate on us by judging us and consuming us by fire? Who would dare to assert of himself that he did not need to be tolerated by others, indeed borne up by them? And how can someone who lives on the forbearance of others himself renounce forbearing? Is it not the only gift he can offer in return, the only comfort remaining to him, that he endures just as he, too, is endured? Holiness in the Church begins with forbearance and leads to bearing up; where there is no more forbearing, there is no more bearing up either, and existence, lacking support, can only sink into the void. People may well say that such words express a sickly existence—but it is part of being a Christian to accept the impossibility of autonomy and the weakness of one's own resources. At bottom there is always hidden pride at work when criticism of the Church adopts that tone of rancorous bitterness which today is already beginning to become a fashionable habit. Unfortunately it is accompanied only too often by a spiritual emptiness in which the specific nature of the Church as a whole is no longer seen, in which she is only regarded as a political instrument whose organization is felt to be pitiable or brutal, as if the real function of the Church did not lie beyond organization, in the comfort of the Word and of the sacraments that she provides in good and bad days alike. Those who really believe do not attribute too much importance to the struggle for the reform of ecclesiastical structures. They live on what the Church always is; and if one wants to know what the Church really is one must go to them. For the Church is most present, not where organizing, reforming, and governing are going on, but in those who simply believe and receive from her the gift of faith that is life to them. Only someone who has experienced how, regardless of changes in her ministers and forms, the Church raises men up, gives them a home and a hope, a home that is hope—the path to eternal life—only someone who has experienced this knows what the Church is, both in days gone by and now.

This does not mean that everything must be left undisturbed and endured as it is. Endurance can also be a highly active process, a struggle to make the Church herself more and more that which supports and endures. After all, the Church does not live otherwise than in us; she lives from the struggle of the unholy to attain holiness, just as of course this struggle lives from the gift of God, without which it could not exist. But this effort only becomes fruitful and constructive if it is inspired by the spirit of forbearance, by real love. And here we have arrived at the criterion by which that critical struggle for better holiness must always be judged, a criterion that is not only not in contradiction with forbearance but is demanded by it. This criterion is constructiveness. A bitterness that only destroys stands self-condemned. A slammed door can, it is true, become a sign that shakes up those inside. But the idea that one can do more constructive work in isolation than in fellowship with others is just as much of an illusion as the notion of a Church of "holy people" instead of a "holy Church" that is holy because the Lord bestows holiness on her as a quite unmerited gift.[2]

---

[2] Cf. H. de Lubac, *Die Kirche*, trans. from the 3rd French ed., 1954 (Einsiedeln, 1968), pp. 251–82 [English trans.: *The Splendor of the Church*, trans. M. Mason (San Francisco: Ignatius Press, 1999)].

This brings us to the other word applied to the Church by the Creed: it calls her "catholic". The shades of meaning acquired by this word during the course of time are numerous, but one main idea can be shown to be decisive from the start. This word refers in a double way to the unity of the Church. It refers, first, to local unity—only the community united with the bishop is the "Catholic Church", not the sectional groups that have broken away from her, for whatever reasons. Second, the term describes the unity formed by the combination of the many local Churches, which are not entitled to encapsulate themselves in isolation; they can only remain the Church by being open to one another, by forming one Church in their common testimony to the Word and in the communion of the eucharistic table, which is open to everyone everywhere. In the old commentaries on the Creed, the "Catholic" Church is contrasted with those "Churches" that only exist "from time to time in their provinces" [3] and thereby contradict the true nature of the Church.

Thus the word "catholic" expresses the episcopal structure of the Church and the necessity for the unity of all the bishops with one another; there is no allusion in the Creed to the crystallization of this unity in the bishopric of Rome. It would indubitably be a mistake to conclude from this that such a focal point was only a secondary development. In Rome, where our Creed arose, this idea was taken for granted from the start. But it is true enough that it is not to be counted as one of the primary elements in the concept of "Church" and certainly cannot be regarded as the point around which the concept was constructed. Rather, the basic elements of

---

[3] Kattenbusch 2:919. See also pp. 917–27 on the history of the reception of the word "catholic" in the Apostles' Creed and on the history of the word in general; cf. also W. Beinert, *Um das dritte Kirchenattribut*, 2 vols. (Essen, 1964).

the Church appear as forgiveness, conversion, penance, eucharistic communion, and hence plurality and unity: plurality of the local Churches that yet remain "the Church" only through incorporation in the unity of the one Church. This unity is first and foremost the unity of Word and sacrament: the Church is one through the one Word and the one bread. The episcopal organization appears in the background as a *means* to this unity. It is not there for its own sake but belongs to the category of means; its position is summed up by the phrase "in order to": it serves to turn the unity of the local Churches in themselves and among themselves into a reality. The function of the Bishop of Rome would thus be to form the next stage in the category of means.

One thing is clear: the Church is not to be deduced from her organization; the organization is to be understood from the Church. But at the same time it is clear that for the visible Church visible unity is more than "organization". The concrete unity of the common faith testifying to itself in the Word and of the common table of Jesus Christ is an essential part of the sign that the Church is to erect in the world. Only if she is "catholic", that is, visibly one in spite of all her variety, does she correspond to the demand of the Creed.[4] In a world torn apart, she is to be the sign and means of unity; she is to bridge nations, races, and classes and unite them. How often she has failed in this, we know: even in antiquity it was infinitely difficult for her to be simultaneously the Church of the barbarians and that of the Romans; in modern times she was unable to prevent strife between the Christian nations; and today she is still not succeeding in

---

[4] I have given my view on "Church and Churches", the problem that arises in connection with this, in J. Ratzinger, *Das Konzil auf dem Weg* (Cologne, 1964), pp. 48–71.

so uniting rich and poor that the excess of the former becomes the satisfaction of the latter—the ideal of sitting at a common table remains largely unfulfilled. Yet even so one must not forget all the imperatives that have issued from the claim of catholicity; above all, instead of reckoning up the past, we should face the challenge of the present and try in it not only to profess catholicity in the Creed but to make it a reality in the life of our torn world.

2. "THE RESURRECTION OF THE BODY"

a. The content of the New Testament hope of resurrection[5]

The article about the resurrection of the body puts us in a curious dilemma. We have discovered anew the indivisibility of man; we live our corporality with a new intensity and experience it as the indispensable way of realizing the one being of man. From this angle we can understand afresh the biblical message, which promises immortality, not to a separated soul, but to the whole man. Such feelings have in this century made Lutheran theology in particular turn emphatically against the Greek doctrine of the immortality of the soul, which is wrongly regarded as a Christian idea, too. In reality, so it is said, this idea expresses a thoroughly un-Christian dualism; the Christian faith knows only of the waking of the dead by God's power. But doubts arise at once here: The Greek doctrine of immortality may well be problematical, but is not the biblical testimony still more incapable of fulfillment for us? The unity of man, fine, but who

[5] The following arguments are closely linked to those in my article "Auferstehung" in *Sacramentum Mundi*, vol. 1, ed. Rahner and Darlap (Freiburg, 1967), pp. 397–402, where there is also a bibliography.

can imagine, on the basis of our present-day image of the world, a resurrection of the body? This resurrection would also imply—or so it seems, at any rate—a new heaven and a new earth; it would require immortal bodies needing no sustenance and a completely different condition of matter. But is this not all completely absurd, quite contrary to our understanding of matter and its modes of behavior, and therefore hopelessly mythological?

Well, I think that in fact one can only arrive at an answer if one inquires carefully into the real intentions of the biblical testimony and at the same time considers anew the relation between the biblical and the Greek ideas. For their encounter with each other has modified both conceptions and thus overlaid the original intentions of both approaches with a new combined view that we must first remove if we want to find our way back to the beginning. First of all, the hope for the resurrection of the dead simply represents the basic form of the biblical hope for immortality; it appears in the New Testament not really as a supplement to a preceding and independent immortality of the soul but as the fundamental statement on the fate of man. There were, it is true, in late Jewish teachings hints of immortality on the Greek pattern, and this was probably one of the reasons why very soon the all-embracing scope of the idea of resurrection in the Graeco-Roman world was no longer grasped. Instead, the Greek notion of the immortality of the soul and the biblical message of the resurrection of the dead were each understood as half the answer to the question of the fate of man, and the two were added together. It was thought that, to the already existing Greek foreknowledge about the immortality of the soul, the Bible added the revelation that at the end of the world bodies would be awakened, too, to share henceforth forever the fate of the soul—damnation or bliss.

As opposed to this, we must grasp the fact that originally it was not a question of two complementary ideas; on the contrary, we are confronted with two different outlooks, which cannot simply be added together: the image of man, of God, and of the future is in each case quite different, and thus at bottom each of the two views can only be understood as an attempt at a total answer to the question of human fate. The Greek conception is based on the idea that man is composed of two mutually foreign substances, one of which (the body) perishes, while the other (the soul) is in itself imperishable and therefore goes on existing in its own right independent of any other beings. Indeed, it was only in the separation from the body, which is essentially foreign to it, so they thought, that the soul came fully into its own. The biblical train of thought, on the other hand, presupposes the undivided unity of man; for example, Scripture contains no word denoting only the body (separated and distinguished from the soul), while conversely in the vast majority of cases the word soul, too, means the whole corporeally existing man; the few places where a different view can be discerned hover to a certain extent between Greek and Hebrew thinking and in any case by no means abandon the old view. The awakening of the dead (not of bodies!) of which Scripture speaks is thus concerned with the salvation of the *one*, undivided man, not just with the fate of one (perhaps secondary) half of man. It now also becomes clear that the real heart of the faith in resurrection does not consist at all in the idea of the restoration of bodies, to which we have reduced it in our thinking; such is the case even though this is the pictorial image used throughout the Bible. What, then, is the real content of the hope symbolically proclaimed in the Bible in the shape of the resurrection of the dead? I think that this can best be worked out by means of a comparison with the dualistic conception of ancient philosophy.

1. The idea of immortality denoted in the Bible by the word "resurrection" is an immortality of the "person", of the *one* creation "man". Whereas in Greek thought the typical man is a perishable creature, which as such does not live on but goes two different ways in accordance with its heterogeneous formation out of body and soul, according to the biblical belief it is precisely this being, man, that as such goes on existing, even if transformed.

2. It is a question of a "dialogic" immortality (= awakening!); that is, immortality results not simply from the self-evident inability of the indivisible to die but from the saving deed of the lover who has the necessary power: man can no longer totally perish because he is known and loved by God. All love wants eternity, and God's love not only wants it but effects it and is it. In fact the biblical idea of awakening grew directly out of this dialogical theme: he who prays knows in faith that God will restore the right (Job 19:25ff.; Ps 73:23ff.); faith is convinced that those who have suffered in the interests of God will also receive a share in the redemption of the promise (2 Macc 7:9ff.). Immortality as conceived by the Bible proceeds, not from the intrinsic power of what is in itself indestructible, but from being drawn into the dialogue with the Creator; *that is why* it must be called awakening. Because the Creator intends, not just the soul, but the man physically existing in the midst of history and gives *him* immortality, it must be called "awakening of the dead" = "of men". It should be noted here that even in the formula of the Creed, which speaks of the "resurrection of the body", the word "body" means in effect "the world of man" (in the sense of biblical expressions like "all flesh will see God's salvation", and so on); even here the

word is not meant in the sense of a corporality isolated from the soul.

3. That the awakening is expected on the "Last Day", at the end of history, and in the company of all mankind indicates the communal character of human immortality, which is related to the whole of mankind, from which, toward which, and with which the individual has lived and hence finds salvation or loses it. At bottom this association results automatically from the collective character of the biblical idea of immortality. To the soul as conceived by the Greeks, the body, and so history, too, is completely exterior; the soul goes on existing apart from them and needs no other being in order to do so. For man understood as a unity, on the other hand, fellowship with his fellowmen is constitutive; if *he* is to live on, then this dimension cannot be excluded. Thus, on the biblical premise, the much-discussed question of whether after death there can be any fellowship between men seems to be solved; at bottom it could only arise at all through a preponderance of the Greek element in the intellectual premises: where the "communion of saints" is an article of faith, the idea of the *anima separata* (the "separated soul" of Scholastic theology) has in the last analysis become obsolete.

The full elaboration of these ideas became possible only after the New Testament had given concrete shape to the biblical hope—the Old Testament by itself ultimately leaves the question about the future of man in the air. Only with Christ, the man who is "one with the Father", the man through whom the being "man" has entered into God's eternity, does the future of man definitely appear open. Only in him, the "second Adam", is the question of man's identity finally answered. Christ is man, completely; to that extent the question of who we men are is present in him. But he is at the same time God speaking to us, the "Word of God". In him the conversation between God and man that has been going on since the beginning of history has entered a new phase: in him the Word of God became "flesh" and really gained admission into our existence. But if the dialogue of God with man means life, if it is true that God's partner in the dialogue himself has life precisely through being addressed by him who lives forever, then this means that Christ, as God's Word to us, is himself "the resurrection and the life" (Jn 11:25). It also means that the entry into Christ known as faith becomes in a qualified sense an entry into that being known and loved by God which is immortality: "Whoever believes in the Son *has* eternal life" (see Jn 3:15; 3:36; 5:24). Only from this angle is it possible to understand the train of thought of the fourth evangelist, who in his account of the Lazarus episode wants to make the reader understand that resurrection is not just a distant happening at the end of the world but happens now through faith. Whoever believes is in the conversation with God that is life and that outlasts death. At this point, too, the "dialogic" strand in the biblical concept of immortality, the one related directly to God, and the "human fellowship" strand meet and join. For in Christ, the man, we meet God; but in him we also meet the community of those others whose path to God runs through him and so toward one another. The orientation toward God is in him at the same time toward the community of mankind, and only the acceptance of this community is movement toward God, who does not exist apart from Christ and thus not apart either from the context of the whole history of humanity and its common task.

This also clarifies the question, much discussed in the patristic period and again since Luther, of the "intermediate state" between death and resurrection: the existence with Christ

inaugurated by faith is the start of resurrected life and therefore outlasts death (see Phil 1:23; 2 Cor 5:8; 1 Thess 5:10).
The dialogue of faith is itself already life, which can no longer be shattered by death. The idea of the sleep of death that
has been continually discussed by Lutheran theologians and
recently also brought into play by the Dutch Catechism is
therefore untenable on the evidence of the New Testament
and not even justifiable by the frequent occurrence in the
New Testament of the word "sleep": the whole train of
thought of every book in the New Testament is completely
at variance with such an interpretation, which could hardly
be inferred even from late Jewish thinking about the life after
death.

b. The essential immortality of man

The foregoing reflections may have clarified to some extent
what is involved in the biblical pronouncements about the resurrection: their essential content is not the conception of a
restoration of bodies to souls after a long interval; their aim is
to tell men that they, they themselves, live on; not by virtue of
their own power, but because they are known and loved by God
in such a way that they can no longer perish. In contrast to the
dualistic conception of immortality expressed in the Greek
body-soul schema, the biblical formula of immortality through
awakening means to convey a collective and dialogic conception of immortality: the essential part of man, the person,
remains; that which has ripened in the course of this earthly
existence of corporeal spirituality and spiritualized corporeality goes on existing in a different fashion. It goes on existing
because it lives in God's memory. And because it is the man
himself who will live, not an isolated soul, the element of
human fellowship is also part of the future; for this reason the

future of the individual man will only then be full when the future of humanity is fulfilled.

A whole series of questions arises at this point. The first is this: Does this view not make immortality into a pure grace, although in reality it must fall to man's lot by virtue of his nature as man? In other words, does one not finish up here with an immortality only for the pious and, thus, in a division of human fate that is unacceptable? To put it in theological terms, are we not here confusing the natural immortality of the being "man" with the supernatural gift of eternal love that makes man happy? Must we not hold fast, precisely for the sake of the humanity of the Christian faith, to natural immortality, for the reason that a continued existence conceived in purely christological terms would necessarily slide into the miraculous and mythological? This last question can indubitably be answered only in the affirmative. But this is by no means at variance with our original premise. It, too, entitled us to say decisively: The immortality that, precisely because of its dialogic character, we have called "awakening" falls to the lot of man, *every* man, as man, and is not some secondary "supernatural" addition. But we must then go on to ask: What really makes man into man? What is the definitive distinguishing mark of man? To that we shall have to answer: The distinguishing mark of man, seen from above, is his being addressed by God, the fact that he is God's partner in a dialogue, the being called by God. Seen from below, this means that man is the being that can think of God, the being opened onto transcendence. The point here is not whether he really does think of God, really does open himself to him, but that he is in principle the being who is in himself capable of doing so, even if in fact, for whatever reasons, he is perhaps never able to utilize this capacity.

Now one could say: Is it not, then, much simpler to see the distinguishing mark of man in the fact that he has a spiritual, immortal soul? This definition is perfectly sound; but we are in fact at this moment engaged in the process of trying to elucidate its concrete meaning. The two definitions are not in the least contradictory; they simply express the same thing in different modes of thought. For "having a spiritual soul" means precisely being willed, known, and loved by God in a special way; it means being a creature called by God to an eternal dialogue and therefore capable for its own part of knowing God and of replying to him. What we call in substantialist language "having a soul" we will describe in a more historical, actual language as "being God's partner in a dialogue". This does not mean that talk of the soul is false (as is sometimes asserted today by a one-sided and uncritical biblical approach); in one respect it is, indeed, even necessary in order to describe the whole of what is involved here. But, on the other hand, it also needs to be complemented if we are not to fall back into a dualistic conception that cannot do justice to the dialogic and personalistic view of the Bible.

So when we say that man's immortality is based on his dialogic relationship with and reliance upon God, whose love alone bestows eternity, we are not claiming a special destiny for the pious but emphasizing the essential immortality of man as man. After the foregoing reflections, it is also perfectly possible to develop the idea out of the body-soul schema, whose importance, perhaps even indispensability, lies in the fact that it emphasizes this essential character of human immortality. But it must also be continually put back in the biblical perspective and corrected by it in order to remain serviceable to the view of man's future opened up by faith. For the rest, it becomes evident once again at this point that in the last analysis one cannot make a neat distinction between "natural" and "supernatural": the basic dialogue that first makes man into man makes a smooth transition into the dialogue of grace known as Jesus Christ. How could it be otherwise if Christ actually is the "second Adam", the real fulfillment of that infinite longing that arises from the first Adam—from man in general?

c. The question of the resurrected body

We have still not reached the end of our questions. If this is the position, is there really such a thing as a resurrected body, or can the whole thing be reduced to a mere symbol for the immortality of the person? This is the problem that still awaits us. It is no new problem; even Paul was bombarded with questions of this sort by the Corinthians, as we can see from the fifteenth chapter of the First Letter to the Corinthians, where the Apostle tries to provide an answer, so far as such a thing is at all possible on this point, which lies beyond the limits of our imagination and those of the world accessible to us. Many of the images employed by Paul have become alien to us: but his answer as a whole is still the noblest, boldest, and most convincing one ever formulated to this question.

Let us start from verse 50, which seems to me to be a sort of key to the whole: "I tell you this, brethren: flesh and blood cannot inherit the kingdom of God, nor does the perishable inherit the imperishable." It seems to me that the sentence occupies much the same position in this text as verse 63 occupies in the eucharistic chapter 6 of St. John's Gospel: for these two seemingly widely separated texts are much more closely related than is apparent at first sight. There, in St. John, it says, just after the real presence of the flesh and blood of Jesus in the Eucharist has been sharply emphasized: "It is the spirit that gives life, the flesh is of no avail." In both the Johannine and the Pauline texts, it is a question of developing the Christian realism of "the flesh". In John the realism of the sacraments, that is, the realism of Jesus' Resurrection and of his "flesh" that comes to us from it, is emphasized; in Paul it is a question of the realism of the resurrection of the "flesh", of the resurrection of Christians and of the salvation achieved for us in it. But both passages also contain a sharp counterpoint that emphasizes Christian realism as realism beyond the physical world, realism of the Holy Spirit, as opposed to a purely worldly, quasi-physical realism.

Here English cannot fully convey the enigmatic character of the biblical Greek. In Greek the word *soma* means something like "body", but at the same time it also means "the self". And this *soma* can be *sarx*, that is, "body" in the earthly, historical, and thus chemical, physical, sense; but it can also be "breath"—according to the dictionary, it would then have to be translated "spirit"; in reality this means that the self, which now appears in a body that can be conceived in chemico-physical terms, can, again, appear definitively in the guise of a transphysical reality. In Paul's language "body" and "spirit" are not opposites; the opposites are called "physical body" and "spiritual body". We do not need to try here to pursue the complicated historical and philosophical problems posed by this. One thing at any rate may be fairly clear: both John (6:63) and Paul (1 Cor 15:50) state with all possible emphasis that the "resurrection of the flesh", the "resurrection of the body", is not a "resurrection of physical bodies". Thus, from the point of view of modern thought, the Pauline sketch is far less naïve than later theological erudition with its subtle ways of construing how there can be eternal physical bodies. To recapitulate, Paul teaches, not the resurrection of physical bodies, but the resurrection of persons, and this not in the return of the "fleshly body", that is, the biological structure, an idea he expressly describes as impossible ("the perishable cannot become imperishable"), but in the different form of the life of the resurrection, as shown in the risen Lord.

Has, then, the resurrection no relation at all to matter? And does this make the "Last Day" completely pointless in comparison with the life that always comes from the call of the Lord? Basically we have already answered this last question in our reflections on the second coming of Christ. If the cosmos is history and if matter represents a moment in the history of spirit, then there is no such thing as an eternal, neutral combination of matter and spirit; rather, there is a final "complexity" in which the world finds its omega and unity. In that case there is a final connection between matter and spirit in which the destiny of man and of the world is consummated, even if it is impossible for us today to define the nature of this connection. In that case there is such a thing as a "Last Day", on which the destiny of the individual man becomes full because the destiny of mankind is fulfilled.

The goal of the Christian is not private bliss but the whole. He believes in Christ, and for that reason he believes in the future of the world, not just in his own future. He knows that this future is more than he himself can create. He knows that there is a meaning he is quite incapable of destroying. Is he therefore to sit quietly with his hands in his lap? On the contrary; because he knows there is such a thing as meaning, he can and must cheerfully and intrepidly do the work of history, even though from his little segment of it he will have the feeling that it is a labor of Sisyphus and that the stone of human destiny is rolled anew, generation after generation, up the hill only to roll down again once more and nullify all previous efforts. Whoever believes knows that things move

"forward", not in a circle. Whoever believes knows that history is not like Penelope's tapestry, which was always being
woven anew only to be undone again. Even the Christian
may be assailed by the nightmares, induced by the fear of
fruitlessness, out of which the pre-Christian world created
these moving images of the anxiety that all human activity is
vain. But his nightmare is pierced by the saving, transforming voice of reality: "Be of good cheer, I have overcome the
world" (Jn 16:33). The new world, with the description of
which, in the image of the final Jerusalem, the Bible ends, is
no Utopia but certainty, which we advance to meet in faith.
A salvation of the world does exist—that is the confidence
that supports the Christian and that still makes it rewarding
even today to be a Christian.

GENERAL INDEX

SCRIPTURE INDEX

OLD TESTAMENT